FRAUD 101

Techniques and Strategies for Detection

Howard R. Davia

JOHN WILEY & SONS, INC.

New York • Chichester • Weinheim • Brisbane • Singapore • Toronto

Library of Congress Cataloging-in-Publication Data:

Davia, Howard R., 1947–
    Fraud 101: techniques and strategies for detection / Howard R. Davia.
      p. cm.
    Includes index.
    ISBN 0-471-37309-5 (cloth : alk. paper)
    1. Commercial crimes—United States—Prevention. 2. Fraud investigation—United States. I. Title: Fraud one hundred one. II. Title: fraud one hundred and one. III. Title.

HV6769.D38 2000
363.25'963—dc21   00-038206

Printed in the United States of America.
10 9 8 7 6 5 4 3 2 1

PREFACE

This book has been written to serve as a primer in proactive fraud-specific auditing. Society currently is in desperate need of the services of proactive fraud-specific auditing and proactive fraud-specific auditors. The book has been written primarily to provide basic instruction to college students and auditors with no training or experience in this craft, through the intermediate level of fraud auditor. Beyond that point the best instruction is interactive training between experienced instructors and auditors with at least intermediate skills.

The need for this book was eloquently expressed in a complementary reference text published in 1995:

> A maxim in the auditing profession is, "Most frauds are discovered by accident, not by audit or accounting system design." This has been repeated so many times by so many accountants and auditors that the general public accepts it as an axiom or self-evident truth. Yet many authors have written books about fraud auditing and most of them have found willing buyers and readers.
>
> Most fraud audit books address the problem from an after-the-fact perspective. The fraud was discovered (usually by accident), and the author confirmed and corroborated it by certain methods. Discovery, not detection, is the main theme of the books. The authors of these books attribute their discoveries of fraud to chance, luck, or happenstance, never to statistics, probabilities, or scientific method. Neither inductive or inductive logic nor the rigors of science had anything to do with their success.
>
> If fraud auditing has no scientific basis and most frauds are discovered by accident, what value can be assigned to the books that are written? Are they simply the memoirs and war stories of old men who stumbled or muddled through audits and got lucky? . . . So the search for a generally accepted methodology goes on. To our knowledge, there is none to date.[1]

The book has been written to provide the necessary background information needed for any reader—especially management readers—to fully appreciate the pernicious and largely uncontrolled nature of the fraud that threatens all entities today. It provides the history of the withdrawal of independent auditors (certified public accountants) from auditing to discover fraud in their annual audits—including why they cannot now provide this service to their clients without generally accepted prerequisite auditing standards.

It also urges independent auditors to take the necessary steps to once again begin to proactively perform auditing to discover fraud and provides the fundamental skills and methodology needed for all auditors to begin to perform fraud auditing proactively. Finally, it attempts to cultivate an appropriate questioning attitude in the minds of prospective fraud auditors.

As with all texts, this one will greatly benefit from the comments and recommendations of its readers. Accordingly, comments and recommendations are invited and will be carefully considered for inclusion in subsequent editions. Those individuals furnishing constructive comments and recommendations will be recognized for their contributions.

NOTES

1. G. Jack Bologna and Robert J. Lindquist, *Fraud Auditing and Forensic Accounting* (New York: John Wiley & Sons, 1995), p. 39.

CONTENTS

INTRODUCTION

Fraud was a very serious, underrated, and somewhat ignored threat to private and public entities for most of the 19th century. As a consequence, it has undoubtedly prospered relatively undeterred and has cost many entities enormous sums of money. By the end of that century, however, there appeared to be a growing appreciation of the need to combat fraud more aggressively. But effective combat was to be—and will continue to be for some time—elusive. A near 75-year hiatus from auditing to detect fraud has left society with a major shortage of skilled proactive fraud combatants and a diminished educational capability for training new ones. Society has come to be in the precarious position of being in urgent need of aggressive proactive fraud auditing, while experiencing a severe shortage of trained proactive fraud auditors to respond to it.

The emergence of fraud as a serious threat began in the early years of the 19th century, when the emphasis of ordinary audit examinations—customarily performed by independent auditors—shifted from auditing to detect fraud to audits incidental to the issuance of opinions on financial statements. Among auditors, an evolving attitude of minimal concern for the detection of fraud evolved. Further, independent auditors advised entities that they did not need to be overly concerned with fraud. In lieu of costly audits to detect it, the auditors stated that clients could rely instead on adequate systems of accounting records with appropriate internal control.

Entity complacency was further nurtured by unwavering assurances from independent accountants—in an apparent reversal of their earlier stance—that they *did* accept responsibility for detecting any material fraud in the course of their periodic audits. However, although the assurances were comforting to entities at risk, they were irresponsibly misleading. The fraud they referred to—and this determination requires extensive reading of material normally available only to independent accountants—was not all inclusive but included "only deliberate misstatements of financial statements." The fraud not included in their assurances was the theft by fraud of an entity's assets that did not misstate financial statements.

By the turn of the 20th century, the long hiatus in proactive fraud-specific auditing had cost society much of its capability to combat fraud. Whatever fraud auditing skills people possessed early in the 19th century had largely dissipated as a result of nonuse, and begining any practice of proactive fraud-specific auditing was extremely difficult. Audit procedures for conducting proactive fraud-specific auditing are very different from those used to practice reactive fraud-specific auditing. In proactive auditing, the auditor has few if any clues that fraud has occurred. His or her job can literally be compared to hunting for needles in haystacks. In reactive fraud-specific auditing, or investigating, the auditor begins with evidence that fraud has occurred, or has a good idea that it exists, knows what to look for, and perhaps where it may be found. His or her job is only to fully confirm and document it. Many auditors and/or investigators are skilled in reactive auditing. Very few are skilled in proactive fraud auditing.

This text was written to provide fundamental training to undergraduate college students and practicing auditors up through the intermediate auditor level. More advanced training is best suited to interactive settings—where more involved and realistic case studies can be discussed and studied—led by individuals experienced in fraud auditing.

What makes this text unique is the fact that it was written by an author who has had considerable actual experience as a proactive fraud-specific auditor and upon whose personal experience much of this text is based. Of course, most perpetrators rarely discuss details of their crimes. Of the 20 percent of all fraud that has been revealed and has been prosecuted, most has been discovered accidentally, and there are few if any proactive audit lessons to be learned in studying it. Accordingly, proactive fraud auditors are among the relatively few who are best qualified to instruct on proactive fraud auditing procedures.

This text provides fundamental instruction to anyone interested in engaging in proactive fraud-specific auditing. It provides entry- to intermediate-level instruction for auditors in need of knowing what to search for, how to search for it, when they are finished, when the case in progress is ready for reactive case development, and when to quit. To assure complete understanding, it is enriched with illustrations and case studies selected to illuminate topics under discussion. All illustrations are either actual events or hypothetical examples structured from actual events from the author's personal experience.

1

WORLD OF FRAUD

THREE TYPES OF FRAUD

The world of fraud may be defined as a vast aggregation of all the fraud that has occurred in any given time frame. It undoubtedly includes millions of cases of fraud, fraud villains, and fraud victims. It is so vast and so hidden that it defeats any attempt at empirical study. No one can ever know the true nature of fraud with any degree of specificity. Nevertheless, it is possible, by using reasonable conjectures, to estimate its probable makeup. To do so we can begin with the reasonable certainty that all the fraud in the world can be classified as falling into one of only three primary groups.

1. Group 1: Fraud that has been exposed and is in the public domain.
2. Group 2: Fraud that has been discovered by entities, but details have not been made public.
3. Group 3: Fraud that has not been detected.

Group 1 Fraud: Exposed and in the Public Domain

Group 1 fraud is the only fraud that we can know with reasonable certainty by virtue of empirical studies. With very few exceptions, this type of fraud has four points in common:

1. Victims have discovered it.
2. It was discovered mostly by accident.
3. Sufficient evidence was gathered to prosecute the perpetrators successfully.
4. The fraud has been submitted to and accepted by prosecutors for prosecution.

Group 1 fraud can be known by anyone who has a serious interest in studying it, due to the fact that normally, during the process of prosecution, details of the fraud cases that prosecutors and defendants chose to release become a part of the public record.

Group 2 Fraud: Known by a Few but Not Made Public

Group 2 fraud is that fraud which has been discovered by victims—in many cases they have little more than suspicions that they may have discovered fraud—and which, with few if any exceptions, is kept confidential by victims. Confidentiality is maintained because any frivolous release of case details that risks identifying a suspected perpetrator or perpetrators also risks defaming them and may be just cause for litigation by injured parties. Generally speaking, the release of case details for purposes other than prosecution could be considered frivolous. In fact, the release of perpetrator-identifying details for purposes of prosecution, where the prosecution results in a finding of not guilty, could be found to be frivolous. Accordingly, often victims are counseled not to seek prosecution where conviction is not reasonably certain.

The second reason why Group 2 fraud is kept confidential is that the cases vary in the degree of evidence that the victim possesses, from faint indications that fraud may have occurred, to an abundance of evidence that leaves little doubt that fraud has occurred. For those cases where there is any question as to the sufficiency of evidence or the suspected perpetrator's involvement, it would be unwise to release publicly any information of the suspected crime. For those cases at the upper end of the spectrum of evidence possessed, and where there are no or few doubts as to the crime or the suspect's guilt, it also would be unwise to publicize case details without good reason, in those instances where busy prosecutors have declined or delayed prosecution. Although some details of a relatively few group 2 fraud cases are accidentally or unwisely revealed from time to time, there is no possible way for anyone to determine the true nature of cases in this group.

Group 3 Fraud: Undetected

Group 3 fraud includes those fraud cases that are known only to the perpetrator(s). Victims do not know or suspect the fraud. Such cases include everything that does not fall into groups 1 and 2. Group 3 fraud cases, by definition, can never be known by anyone other than the perpetrator(s). Accordingly, there is no possible way for anyone to determine the true nature of group 3 fraud cases.

NATURE OF FRAUD

Regardless of the fact that only fraud in group 1 can be studied, a generally accepted view of all fraud—including groups 2 and 3 fraud—has arisen as a result of observations of group 1 fraud. There are four reasons why we can be certain that researchers have accurately determined the true nature of group 1 fraud.

1. The cases in group 1 are available for empirical study.
2. They have been studied many times by different researchers.
3. Experienced fraud auditors and investigators tend to concur with the conclusions.
4. All observations tend to ratify each other.

The findings basically conclude that fraud perpetrators, for the most part, are generally inept and greedy and that most of their crimes are discovered by accident (i.e., no one sets out to discover fraud perpetrators). These latter points also are corroborated. Accordingly, there is no question that the true nature of group 1 fraud is well known. However, group 1 fraud is only one sector of the fraud world. What do we know about groups 2 and 3?

Society has come to accept that the nature of group 1 fraud is typical of all fraud. In other words, it is generally believed that all fraud—with some exceptions, of course—is largely committed by inept and greedy perpetrators, whose ineptness and greed tends to eventually result in their accidental discovery. The problem is very much akin to that made by the six blind men of Indostan and detailed in Exhibit 1.1. The significant difference is that the only part of the fraud world that researchers have to examine is the leg of the elephant, and the entire elephant is being judged by it.

This is a very serious error, a fallacious supposition at the root of two critical decisions made by independent auditors over the years:

1. It is not necessary to audit for the purpose of discovering fraud.
2. Good accounting records and internal control are sufficient to control fraud.

Exhibit 1.1   The Blind Man and the Elephant

A Version of the Famous Indian Legend
By John Godfrey Saxe
(1816–1887)

It was six men of Indostan
To learning much inclined,
Who went to see the elephant
(Though all of them were blind),
That each by observation
Might satisfy his mind.

The First approached the Elephant,
And happening to fall
Against his broad and sturdy side,
At once began to bawl:
"Bless me! But the Elephant
Is very like a wall! "

The Second, feeling of the tusk,
Cried, "Ho what have we here,
So round and smooth and sharp?
To me 'tis mighty clear
The wonder of an Elephant
Is very like a spear!"

The Third approached the animal,
And happening to take
This squirming trunk within his hands,
Thus boldly up and spake:
"I see," quoth he, "the Elephant
Is very like a snake!"

The Fourth reached out his eager hand,
And felt about the knee.
"What most this wondrous beast is like
Is mighty plain," quoth he;
'Tis clear enough the Elephants
Is very like a tree!"

The Fifth, who chanced to touch the ear,
Said, "E'en the blindest man
Can tell what this resembles most;
Deny the fact who can,
This marvel of an Elephant
Is very like a fan!"

The Sixth no sooner had begun
About the beast to grope,
Than, seizing on his swinging tail
That fell within his scope,
"I see," quoth he, "the Elephant
Is very like a rope!"

And so these men of Indostan
Disputed loud and long,
Each in his own opinion
Exceeding stiff and strong,
Though each was partly in the right,
And all were in the wrong!

This text describes fraud of a different nature. It accepts the current view of fraud for cases in group 1 but submits that fraud in groups 2 and 3 is perpetrated by cunning and conservative perpetrators who do not make the mistakes that lead to self-disclosure. This point illustrates how a given finding of fact can be interpreted differently.

In the past, users of data developed by fraud researchers—who determined that the fraud they examined was committed largely by inept and greedy perpetrators whose mistakes often led to self-disclosure—concluded that the unseen portion of the fraud world contained fraud of the same nature. Accordingly, they tended to assume that fraud was not an invidious threat. They believed that doing nothing would allow those inept and careless perpetrators to make the mistakes leading to their discovery.

Contrary to this generally accepted view, this text takes the position that it is unreasonable to conclude that perpetrators of fraud who have not been discovered will be similarly inept and greedy. Hence, it is unreasonable to conclude that their acts will also be self-revealing. Rather, they are the hardcore remainder left after the inept and greedy have been discovered. It is this remainder that comprises group 2 and group 3 fraud, and which will require proactive detection practices to disclose it. Were the latter conclusion generally adopted, rather than the first, society would have been motivated to take much more aggressive measures to combat fraud than it did. And, had the latter conclusion been reached, businesses would very likely not have the serious fraud problem that exists today and would not have lost huge amounts of money that most surely has been lost to fraud.

PROBABLE CONFIGURATION OF THE FRAUD WORLD

It is difficult to know how much group 2 and group 3 fraud exists. However, it is possible to approximate the fraud that we cannot see or otherwise know with certainty. It has been estimated that the fraud world can be broken down into the following percentages:

Makeup of the Fraud World

Group 1 fraud: 20 percent
Group 2 fraud: 40 percent
Group 3 fraud: 40 percent

The significance of these percentages, if only reasonably accurate, is that society's appraisal of the total fraud threat is based on only 20 percent of all fraud. Further, this text's assertion that the group 1 fraud is atypical of the remaining 80 percent strongly suggests the frightening notion that the tail is wagging the dog and is resulting in significant harm in the process.

PERCENTAGE OF GROUP 1 FRAUD

The process of estimating the relative percentages of the groups of fraud must necessarily begin with the only group of fraud on which we have reliable knowledge—group 1. From that knowledge it is estimated that group 1 fraud is about 20 percent of the fraud world. Before reviewing how that percentage is arrived at, let it be recognized that 20 percent is not considered an absolute figure. It could easily vary 5 percent either way. Regardless, the point is that whether group 1 fraud makes up 15 percent or 25 percent of total fraud, it comprises only a minority share of the fraud world.

There are five reasons why group 1 fraud is considered to be only about 20 percent of the fraud world:

1. Most of the fraud in group 1 has been discovered by accident.
2. Independent auditors do not proactively audit to detect fraud.
3. Entities without internal audit staffs can not audit to detect fraud proactively.
4. Most internal auditors do not have adequate training or experience to detect fraud proactively.
5. Most internal controls are inadequate to prevent fraud.

Accepting for the moment that these points are factual (they will be discussed more comprehensively in the text which immediately follows), what percentage of all fraud is group 1 fraud likely to be? In other words, consider the low probability of group 1 fraud being greater than 20 percent of all fraud when 80 percent of it has been discovered by accident, in an environment where no one is competently searching for it, and where internal controls are generally not fraud-specific. Consider the likely probability that only the greedy and incompetent perpetrators are being discovered.

Largely Discovered by Accident

A maxim in the auditing profession is "Most frauds are discovered by accident, not by audit or accounting system design."[1]

In a recent article, Joseph T. Wells said that "Most fraud cases are discovered by accident."[2] He also quoted a study by W. Stephen Albrecht, an accounting professor at Brigham Young University, and then president of the National Association of Certified Fraud Examiners (NACFE), who reported that one-half of all frauds were discovered by accident, one-third come from coworker complaints—which could also be classified as accidental discoveries—with about one-fifth coming from audit discoveries. It is unknown how many of the auditors' discoveries were accidental.

Also, in that article, items 2, 3, and 4, listed as generally accepted facts, are consistent with and explain why it is that 80 percent or more of all fraud cases are discovered by accident. The old axiom that you do not discover what you do not look for was never more applicable. Case Study 1.1 shows the typical fraud that makes up group 1.

CASE 1.1 $3.28 Million Embezzled
Over 9 Years—Discovered When Savings Bank Alerted
Victim of Suspicious Transactions

A Maryland woman, on a salary of $36,000 a year, embezzled $3.28 million from a union general fund over a period of nine years before union officials became suspicious in 1995 when a credit union notified union officials that large sums of money were moving in and out of union accounts. She had been responsible for transferring employee automatic payroll deductions to a credit union. She was required to issue one check to the credit union each pay period to cover all the employee deductions, to be credited to each employee's credit union account. Her scheme involved writing a larger check than was necessary and keeping the excess. The inflated amounts were as high as $50,000 in excess. She was able to cover the fraud by falsifying financial records and was also responsible for assuring that the accounts were in balance.[3]

Lack of Proactive Fraud Auditing

The fact that independent auditors do not audit proactively to detect fraud will not be discussed at length here but will be in Chapter 2. However, the following excerpts taken from AICPA literature leave little doubt as to the factual nature of this statement: "The ordinary examination incident to the issuance of an opinion respecting financial statements is not designed and cannot be relied upon to disclose defalcations and other similar irregularities. . . . If an auditor were to discover defalcations and other similar irregularities he would have to extend his work to a point where its cost would be prohibitive.[4]

"8. Normally, an audit performed in accordance with generally accepted auditing standards does not include audit procedures specifically designed to detect illegal acts."[5]

Most internal auditors do not have adequate training or experience to proactively detect fraud. While many are intensely interested in proactive fraud-specific auditing, it is difficult for them to become proficient in the art. The independent auditing community provides no leadership or guidance. And, since many internal auditors come from the independent auditor ranks, they bring no fraud auditing expertise with them. Few training sources are capable of providing proactive training. And without an active practice of proactive fraud-specific auditing, there is little opportunity for learning on the job. Due to the general complacency of entities at risk, often insufficient resources are made available to internal auditors for proactive fraud-specific examinations. And, last but not least, given the limited resources that may be available to internal auditors for proactive fraud-specific examinations, any failure to disclose fraud often is regarded as evidence of the nonexistence of fraud rather than the failure to allocate sufficient trained resources. It is frustrating for internal auditors to see their employers not think twice in spending money on fire insurance, and hope there is never a fire, yet question the value of fraud-specific auditing when no fraud is disclosed.

Inadequate Internal Controls

Internal controls tend to be designed primarily to ensure that accounting records are accurate—to ensure, for example, that all accounting documents applicable to an accounting period have been processed, and processed correctly. Although many internal controls deny access to accounting systems by unauthorized users, without fraud-auditing reinforcement, existing internal controls usually are not a deterrent to dedicated fraud perpetrators. In fact, few internal controls are effective in preventing fraud when two or more perpetrators conspire to evade them. For a more extensive discussion on internal controls—including fraud-specific controls and the more fraud-effective passive controls—please see the second edition of *Accountant's Guide to Fraud Detection and Control.*[6]

At this point, each reader is asked to reconsider what percentage of all the fraud that is in the fraud world is likely to be in group 1. Consider the serious consequences that a fraud perpetrator faces should his or her fraudulent act be discovered and how many perpetrators are apt to be so inept that they leave evidence trails that not only cause them to be discovered *by accident*—by people not looking for their crimes—but evidence in such abundance that prosecution is possible. Consider the precautions you would take were you to seriously consider committing a fraudulent act. Would you say the percentage is 10 percent of all perpetrators are so reckless that they do not carefully plot out their crimes? 20 percent? 30 percent? or higher? How many perpetrators would you think are so inept that they make the sort of mistakes illustrated in Case 1.2?

CASE 1.2 The Arrogant Kickback Solicitor

The case began one day when a building security system contractor, a Mr. Johnson, walked into the office of the director of auditing of a major government agency, opened a small suitcase he was carrying, and set a number of cans of health foods on the desk. He then told how he came to have those articles.

He explained that he had gone to New York to submit his bid to install a new security system in a federal building. The first night in New York, while in his hotel room, there was a knock at the door. He opened it to find an elderly woman carrying two full shopping bags. She introduced herself as a Mrs. Smith, emphasizing that she was the mother-in-law of Mr. Jones, the man he would have to deal with to get his security system contract the next day. She emphasized that things would go better for him the next day if he were to buy her health foods. He bought the entire contents of both bags with all the cash he carried (several hundred dollars).

Mr. Johnson went on to describe what happened when he met with her son-in-law, Mr. Jones, the next day. Despite the fact that the contract was outwardly competitive, Mr. Jones said Mr. Johnson could count on getting the contract if he gave him, Mr. Jones, 10 percent of the total contract value. The total price bid by Mr. Johnson was $50,000. Mr. Johnson told him that the 10 percent kickback would be a problem. He said that to gain entry into government contracting, he had reduced his price offer to the very minimum and anticipated making no profit as it was. A $5,000 kickback would certainly be a total loss for him.

Mr. Jones was unsympathetic with his explanation. He replied that this contract could be the start of a very prosperous relationship. Mr. Johnson, he replied, should keep in mind that in future contracts, he would be allowed to build the 10 percent kickback amount into the total price he offered, and be assured that he would win many awards.

Mr. Johnson said that he would think about it and returned to his home in a Washington, DC, suburb. Shortly after returning home Mr. Jones called him and said that he and his family were planning to visit Washington, DC, and would like Mr. Johnson to arrange for his transportation, hotel accommodations, meals, and other miscellaneous needs. Mr. Johnson complied, picking up the cost of the Jones family's entire trip.

When Mr. Jones made other similar requests for gratuities, Mr. Johnson decided he had had enough and visited the director of audits to tell this tale.

The auditor referred Mr. Johnson's disclosures to the agency's criminal investigative office, which compiled the evidence needed to prosecute Mr. Jones. The evidence package included a tape recording of Mr. Jones's proposition to Mr. Johnson.

What percentage of similarly inept fraud perpetrators did you come up with?

This author estimates that 20 percent of all fraud is in group 1. Estimates 5 percent either way do not materially affect the argument that there is a significant body of fraud in groups 2 and 3 that is not available to public scrutiny. If you estimated that group 1 fraud is greater than 25 percent, the author would like to hear from you, together with your reasons. The author may be contacted by writing to: Howard R. Davia, CPA, 347 Warren Court, Warrenton, VA 20186.

PERCENTAGE OF FRAUD IN GROUPS 2 AND 3

Once a percentage is decided on as reasonably representing group 1 fraud, obviously the combined percentage of groups 2 and 3 fraud makes up the balance. If 20 percent is accepted as the probable relative size of group 1, then it follows that groups 2 and 3 must be 80 percent. Next, having established the combined relative size of groups 2 and 3, it is reasonably logical to divide the amount into two equal groups. If the combined size is 80 percent, then the size of group 2 is 40 percent and group 3 is 40 percent.

If the millions of fraud cases that comprise fraud groups 2 and 3 were arranged according to the amount of evidence which exists and could be detected—note that this does not mean that the evidence that has been detected—it is logical to assume that they would form an evenly progressive array of fraud cases ranging from the 0 evidence cases at the bottom of group 3 to the 100 percent evidence cases at the top of group 2. (See Exhibit 1.2.) Accordingly, the question arises: At what point in that array of cases does the first detection of indicia occur that raise a suspicion of fraud? Of course, no one will ever know for sure. But it seems reasonable—at least for our purposes—to assume that recognition occurs at the halfway point. Once again, indicia recognition could occur at a point 10 percent either way. But, in the absence of more defining data, an even split

Exhibit 1.2   The Fraud World

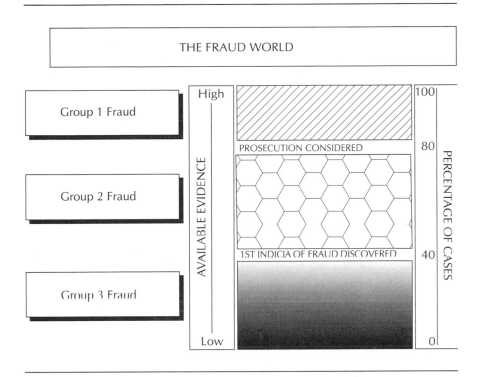

of groups 2 and 3 fraud suffices. However, it is tempting to make the distribution skewed more to favor group 3 fraud. Consider, for example, how many fraud cases there are which go undetected without a clue for many years, such as in Case 1.3.

CASE 1.3 The Protracted Payroll Fraud

Accidentally discovered in Maryland in 1997, the case involved a woman who was employed by the University of Maryland for 20 years. She embezzled $158,000 from the university over a period of seven years and no one at the university seemed to notice, despite the fact that during the seven years she was active, some of her thefts involved $149,190 in payroll checks written to ghost employees. The auditors certainly did not suspect her, and it is likely that they were never engaged in fraud-specific audits. She was a highly respected employee of the university and in 1996 was given the President's Award as the university's most valued employee.

Her luck changed in 1997, however, when postal service inspectors suspected her husband as being involved in a stolen check ring. While searching her residence for evidence of her husband's suspected crime, they found University of Maryland payroll stubs under different names that she had saved. Their suspicions led to detection of her fraud. In a replay of the old story where the farmer locked the door to the barn after his horse was stolen, the university tightened payroll procedures.

If all of the cases in the fraud world could be represented by a simple statistical chart in terms of the discoverable evidence of each crime, they would form a chart such as that depicted by Exhibit 1.2. Note that as evidence increases, so does the discovery rate.

Bear in mind that the divisions between the fraud groups represent decision or recognition points. That is, the area between groups 2 and 3 fraud represents the point at which victims have discovered sufficient evidence that they recognize—or at least suspect—that they may be fraud victims. It is also the point at which their examination efforts tend to change from proactive to reactive. Prior to that point they had no reason to suspect that they had been fraud victims. The area between groups 1 and 2 represents the point at which the victims have accumulated sufficient evidence to know with sufficient certainty that they had been fraud victims to satisfy a prosecutor and may make a decision to prosecute the suspected perpetrators.

SIGNIFICANCE OF FRAUD UNIVERSE PERCENTAGES

It is worthwhile to contemplate the significance of the 20/40/40 percentages. These percentages are based on a fraud control environment wherein proactive fraud-specific auditing is virtually not practiced and where fraud-specific internal controls are virtually unknown. The fraud that is surfacing is being discovered, for the most part, by accident. Think how those percentages would change when (not if) entities at risk emerge from their complacency and engage independent auditors, and/or employ internal auditors and provide them with the necessary training and experience, and direct them to perform reasonable levels of proactive fraud-specific auditing.

Slowly at first, but then more rapidly, the fraud universe will begin to shrink in size. The increased level of auditing will introduce a higher level of risk for perpetrators that many will find unacceptable. For that reason many will choose not to commit the frauds they might otherwise have contemplated. The proportions of the fraud universe also will change as auditors acquire improved proactive fraud-specific training and, more important, the necessary experience.

As more auditors become better at their fraud-specific jobs, the number of fraud cases in group 3—known only to the perpetrators—will begin to shrink, through either improved deterrence or detection. Although group 3 frauds will never be eliminated, their proportion could easily shrink to 20 percent of the fraud universe. Also, as auditors become more skilled in collecting the necessary evidence to support prosecution, the size of group 2 fraud—that known but not prosecuted—will diminish as more and more cases are prosecuted successfully. One school of thought holds that many business entities do not prosecute because they wish to avoid the publicity. Although this may be true in a few cases, in the author's experience, most often prosecution was not pursued because the entity did not have sufficient evidence to assure conviction.

NOTES

1. G. Jack Bologna and Robert J. Lindquist, *Fraud Auditing and Forensic Accounting,* 2nd ed. (New York: John Wiley & Sons, 1995), p. 39.

2. Joseph T. Wells, "Six Common Myths about Fraud," *Journal of Accountancy,* February 1990, pp. 82–88.

3. Todd Shields, "The Lifestyle Was too Good to be True." *Washington Post,* March 2, 1997, pp. B1, B4.

4. American Institute of [Certified Public] Accountants, Statement of Auditing Procedure No. 1, *Extensions of Auditing Procedure 1939,* slightly modified in *Codification of Statements on Auditing Procedure,* 1951, pp. 12–13.

5. American Institute of Certified Public Accountants, *Statement of Auditing Standards 54,* April 1988, p. 3.

6. Howard R. Davia, Patrick C. Coggins, John C. Wideman, and Joseph T. Kastantin, *Accountant's Guide to Fraud Detection and Control,* 2nd ed. (New York: John Wiley & Sons, 2000).

2

FRAUD COMBATANTS

In the vast confused word of fraud, it is sometimes difficult to identify who the main fraud combatants are, who is doing what, and—despite self-serving declarations of responsibility and competence to the contrary—who can be relied on to combat fraud and/or who is best qualified. To consider these questions properly, it is necessary first to categorize the unwieldy and diverse fraud world into homogeneous components. There are two types of fraud:

1. Financial statement balance (FSB) fraud
2. Asset-theft (AT) fraud
   a. AT fraud that is not suspected by victims
   b. AT fraud that is known or suspected by victims

The three principal fraud combatants are:

1. Independent auditors (certified public accountants [CPAs])
2. Internal auditors
3. Criminal investigators

Of these fraud combatants, independent auditors clearly accept responsibility for proactively detecting significant fraud that may distort financial statement balances. At the present time, they do a very dependable job. However, contrary to popular understanding they do not accept responsibility for discovering AT fraud—nor do they engage in audit procedures designed to detect it. Internal auditors normally are the resource of choice, responsible for the proactive detection of AT fraud. However, the effectiveness of their efforts differs from entity to entity, depending on the support they receive from entity management for proactive AT fraud-specific auditing. Generally speaking, although most internal auditors are very enthusiastic about fraud-specific auditing, often they are inadequately staffed and inadequately trained to accomplish this task satisfactorily. Criminal investigators rarely if ever become involved in proactively searching for evidence of fraud. However, once evidence of fraud is discovered, frequently they are engaged to search for corroborating evidence and compile evidence necessary for prosecuting any fraud cases discovered.

FINANCIAL STATEMENT BALANCE FRAUD

As the name implies, financial statement balance fraud includes all fraud in which one or more of an entity's financial statement balances, as reported on the entity's financial statements, has been intentionally misstated. The balances usually are misstated for the purpose of deceiving one or more external entities as to the reporting entity's net worth or prosperity or for some other similar self-serving purpose. The false statements typically involve the overstatement of an entity's assets, such as accounts receivable and inventory, or sales. The practice, when it is intentional, is a criminal offense.

When FSB fraud occurs, the reporting entity involved normally suffers no loss of assets. The fraud, which is almost always perpetrated by management, is performed not to steal assets from the reporting entity but to deceive one or more external users of reported FSB information. For example, a prospective purchaser of an entity is likely to consider the entity's reported net worth in determining a price offer. A fraudulently inflated inventory value would deceive the purchaser into believing that the entity is worth more than it actually is, resulting in a higher offer. Note that the entity does not lose any assets as a result of the FSB fraud.

Land Flipping

Perhaps the most significant of recent FSB scandal was the savings and loan bank scandal of the 1980s. The U.S. government's bank deregulation, beginning in 1980, became literally an opportunity for many savings and loan banks to practice fraud on a grand scale. Before it was over, the cost to American taxpayers who insured depositary accounts was estimated at $500 billion. Although many different fraudulent acts were involved, one that caused considerable distress among the CPA firms that had audited the banks, and were subsequently sued for negligence, was a practice termed "land flipping."

The practice, perpetrated by bank management, involved the purchase of real estate and its subsequent resale a number of times between conspiring associates, each time with the selling price raised substantially. In one instance reported, a property purchased for $874,000 in 1977, with only an $80,000 down payment, was resold to a savings bank seven years later after flipping for $55 million. Accordingly, a property worth around $874,000 came to be falsely valued in the bank's loan portfolio at $55 million. In another instance, a Texas real estate salesperson described a land flipping event as follows.

"It was in the hall of an office building. The tables were lined all the way down the hall. The investors were lined up in front of the tables. The loan officers would close one sale and pass the papers to the next guy. It looked like kids registering for college. If any investor would raise a question, someone would come over and tell them to leave, they were out of the deal." At the end of the day, huge loans based on the inflated values created by the flip sales, would be taken out on the properties.[1]

Land flipping was and is enabled as a result of the generally accepted appraisal practice of determining property value based on past sales prices. There is no problem with this appraisal method where the sales are legitimate and arrived at in the open marketplace. However, when property sales are contrived, at ever-increasing prices, they fraudulently raise the apparent property value and are an illegitimate basis for determining value. In the 1980s scandals, straw borrowers subsequently would receive mortgages from the savings banks on the properties involved and loans of perhaps 80 to 90 percent of the appraised value would be disbursed. These mortgages, rather than being 10 to 20 percent under the market value of the mortgaged property, as is usual, could easily end up being several times the properties' market value. When the mortgaged properties went into default—as dishonest bank managers planned—the financing institutions were left holding substantially unsecured loans. Or, as sometimes happened, brokers who had purchased the unsecured loans based on certified financial statements issued by independent auditors—who did not detect the land-flipping practice when they negligently confirmed the value of the overvalued mortgaged properties—were left with relatively worthless mortgages. Independent auditors who failed to detect the overvalued mortgaged properties became liable to charges of negligence brought by the brokers and were sued to recover the brokers' losses. Although huge sums were lost on the land-flip deals, the bank entities involved lost nothing because losses became the liability of depositors, who were insured by the federal government.

$28 Million Inventory

It is important to understand exactly when independent auditors are responsible for discovering fraud and when they are not. For example, consider the following case, which occurred in the early 1970s. A company intentionally falsified records to make it appear that an inventory worth $28 million had been scrapped. The inventory was even physically removed from the entity's premises. Some time later the supposedly scrapped inventory was taken back onto the accounting records as newly purchased inventory and moved back into the company's warehouse. In this instance the financial statement inventory balance representing inventory on hand was always stated correctly.

Questions: Was the independent auditor responsible for discovering this fraud? At any time in its life cycle? Answers: No! and No! Not under the current AICPA auditing standards. The accounting records at all times reflected the correct inventory balance possessed by the entity. These records would not deceive any outside user of the entity's certified financial statement balance or as to the value of the inventory reported and certified. The fact that the same scrapped inventory was subsequently repurchased and recorded as a $28 million inventory addition is irrelevant.

The entity, however, suffered an AT fraud loss of $28 million at the time the charge to scrap cost was recorded. Of course, the perpetrators literally stole the $28 million inventory at that time and converted their fraud to cash when the entity repurchased the inventory. However, at all times the financial inventory balance reflecting the value of inventory in the entity's warehouses was reported accurately.

Whose responsibility was it to find the $28 million inventory fraud? Answer: Under existing AICPA audit standards, independent auditors were not responsible since they were not required to perform those audit procedures that would be necessary to find the fraud. If anyone can be considered responsible, perhaps it is the entity's internal auditors or accountants. Perhaps they should have questioned the accounting entry and the justification for scrapping the $28 million inventory—that is, just before they were fired. They also had a second chance when the repurchase was made.

$250,000 Petty Cash Fund

This very interesting case was documented during a U.S. Senate hearing and is described fully in Appendix H. It illustrates in vivid detail how Touche, Ross and Company, a predecessor company of the Big 5 CPA firm Deloitte and Touche, satisfactorily verified the existence of a $250,000 petty cash fund—in accordance with generally accepted auditing standards—without seriously questioning why such a large cash fund was being maintained, or what appeared to be clear indicia of fraud.

Fraud Dilemma

On January 6, 2000, Case 2.1 surfaced. It illustrates the dilemma faced by independent auditors in abiding by AICPA auditing standards while needing to meet the expectations of users of audited financial statements (including the Securities and Exchange Commission).

CASE 2.1 Auditors Miss a Fraud and SEC Tries to Put Them Out of Business

California Micro Devices Corp., a highflying chip maker, disclosed that it was writing off half of its accounts receivables, mostly because of product returns. Its stock plunged 40% after the announcement on Aug. 4, 1994, and shareholders filed suit charging financial shenanigans. Nonetheless, a team from Coopers and Lybrand, which was auditing Cal Micro at the time, gave the chip maker's books a clean bill of health the following month. Within weeks it became clear they had missed an audacious accounting fraud. An internal Cal Micro investigation uncovered "preposterous" revenue numbers "almost immediately" . . . One third of the company's $45 million of fiscal year 1994 revenue was spurious. . . . [at least a portion of it due to] booking bogus sales to fake companies for products that didn't exist.

. . . In a rare move that is sending shivers through the accounting world, the Securities and Exchange Commission is seeking to bar the two main Coopers auditors on this job from signing off on public-company audits. . . . The auditors maintain they followed the rules and did their jobs properly. . . . Auditors aren't doing what shareholders think they're doing, says Stuart Schube, a Cal Micro director.[2]

Although all of the details on this case are not known now, once again the problem seems to involve the infamous expectation gap that exists between the expectations of the different users of financial statement balances. Although the Cal Micro director said "auditors aren't doing what shareholders think they're doing," it is quite likely that they were doing exactly what they were expected to do. That is, if the Cal Micro write-down of one-half of its accounts receivable reduced them to the actual value of the reported receivables, and the independent auditors verified the ending balance of receivables reported, they did what was expected of them under the AICPA's auditing standards. The Cal Micro director had good reason to be disturbed over the auditors' failure to question the huge write-off of accounts receivables but clearly misunderstood their audit responsibility. It can be argued that they were not expected to question the write-off, only to verify the ending financial statement balance, which apparently was correctly stated.

ASSET-THEFT FRAUD

Asset-theft fraud sometimes is referred to as the "other fraud" since it does not have a generally recognized name. Accordingly, it will be referred to in this text simply as AT fraud, a term that aptly describes what distinguishes it from FSB fraud: It does not involve the intentional mis-statement of financial statement balances. It is also useful for discussion purposes to further subdivide AT fraud into:

1. Fraud known only to the perpetrators and not suspected by the victims of the categories:
2. Fraud known or suspected by victims usually as the result of the discovery of indicia or evidence

Where AT fraud is involved, there is always a loss of assets, but external financial statement users are rarely, if ever, deceived. Consider, for example, an illustration of AT fraud. If an entity has a $5 million inventory, and $1 million of the inventory is stolen by a fraud perpetrator, who causes the amount stolen to be written off as scrap expense, the entity has lost $1 million in asset value. However, the scrap write-off will correctly adjust the inventory value to $4 million. Accordingly, no FSB fraud is involved since the financial statement inventory balance will be correctly stated at $4 million, and no external users of the financial statement will be deceived.

Asset-Theft Fraud Audit Examinations

AT fraud audit examinations can be designated as falling into one of two groups, proactive, and reactive, each of which requires different audit skills and tactics.

Proactive audits consist of examinations performed in environments where fraud is not suspected. No indicia of fraud has been detected and the victim has no reason to believe that fraud has occurred. Reactive audits consist of examinations performed to compile validating and/or corroborating evidence for fraud that is suspected because of the discovery of indicia of fraud, which raises suspicions that fraud exists.

Audit work that is performed while proactively searching for indicia of fraud will be the primary subject matter of much of this text and will be discussed in considerable detail in subsequent chapters. Accordingly, the discussion is limited here.

Known or Suspected Asset-Theft Fraud

Fraud in group 2 is all the fraud that is known, or suspected, because some indicia of fraud has been detected—no matter how comprehensive, weak, or valid the evidence may be. Work done in connection with fraud in group 2 is mostly known as reactive auditing, because the auditor or criminal investigator normally is reacting to the evidence detected.

Generally, internal auditors are best equipped to pursue group 2 fraud in the early stages of case development, that is, when the available evidence is scant and suspicions of fraud are uncertain. Once case evidence accumulates, however, and as doubt as to the validity of the case diminishes in favor of certainty, it is advisable for internal auditors to hand further case development over to individuals trained in criminal investigative techniques or at the very least to solicit their advice. This, of course, assumes that internal auditors have not been cross-trained in investigative or paralegal skills. Criminal investigators are literally paralegals trained in the nature of evidence needed to meet the needs of a prosecutor and in appropriate methods for collecting that evidence.

FINANCIAL STATEMENT BALANCE AUDITS VERSUS ASSET-THEFT AUDITS

Independent auditors basically do not search to discover fraud in financial statement balances as directly as a fraud-specific auditor would. Rather, they search for it indirectly. When they do discover fraud, it is accidental, or incidental to their not being able to verify a reported financial balance. Proactive fraud-specific auditors, on the other hand, are not likely to be concerned with verifying how accurate the financial balances are that have been reported by their client and are likely to devote little or no time attempting to verify them. Rather they will examine selected accounting transactions that entered into the determination of the financial balances reported. Consider the $28 million inventory FSB fraud mentioned on page 18.

Essentially the case involved a situation where entity management physically removed $28 million of inventory from the entity's premises. *If no accounting entries were made to charge the amount to expense,* this action would have left a glaring discrepancy between the actual inventory on hand and the recorded inventory. Under current audit standard guidelines, an independent auditor would be very likely to detect the $28 million inventory discrepancy, investigate, question the discrepancy, and discover the fraud. However, the inventory discrepancy was eliminated when accounting entries were made charging it off as scrap expense, an act that brought the physical inventory and the book inventory into balance. Accordingly, after the scrap inventory was recorded, were independent auditors to examine the entity's reported financial balances, it is not likely that they would have discovered that the inventory theft had occurred, nor would they be expected to discover the fraud under current generally accepted audit guidelines. A physical inventory observation count would do little more than verify that the remaining financial inventory balance reported did in fact exist and was correct. Case closed. However, a proactive fraud-specific auditor would be likely to examine large transactions, such as the $28 million scrap write-off, find the write-off suspicious and unsupported, question it, and detect the theft.

Beneficiaries at Fraud

In attempting to comprehend the limited role of independent auditors in detecting fraud, it is essential to understand precisely who the beneficiaries of their audit services are. Although independent auditors are engaged by entities to examine their financial reports, many entities would be unlikely to seek their services were it not required by parties (the SEC, public stockholders, and creditors) external to the entity involved. Accordingly, independent auditors perform their work to satisfy those external users. And fraudulent financial balances would be on their audit agenda, while AT fraud would not be.

It is important to note in passing that, should independent auditors detect and disclose fraudulently misstated financial balances, such findings are unlikely to surprise entity management. In fact, where FSB fraud has occurred, management usually hopes that CPAs will be negligent and not detect it. On this point, an FBI bulletin once noted that where "auditors detected material problems and corporate management refused to take action, the CPA firm simply withdrew from the assignment. Subsequently, the company passed the job to another firm that either did not conduct as diligent an audit or employed a 'more creative' approach."[3]

On the other hand, when engaged or employed by and for the entity to be audited, AT fraud auditors serve the entity's needs exclusively. It is the entity that benefits from AT auditors' examinations, and the entity that normally is surprised by any AT fraud detected.

Entities and/or public users of independent auditors' services generally do not understand this distinction. For example, many entities believe that independent auditors perform an AT fraud audit service for them during their periodic examinations, and as a result—much to their detriment—they do not attempt to engage or employ AT auditors to perform this service.

Independent Auditors

Independent auditors currently accept responsibility for the discovery of FSB fraud. They do not accept responsibility for discovering AT fraud and do not attempt to search for it. However, much of the general public and many clients of CPAs are not aware of, or are unsure of, this exclusion: "What are the legal duties of auditors? For years auditors of troubled companies have washed their hands of any legal responsibility, saying they can't be expected to root out fraud by corrupt managers . . ."[4]

Independent auditors trace their roots back to 1887, when they organized as the American Association of Public Accountants (AAPA). Its successor today, the American Institute of Certified Public Accountants (AICPA), notes that the AAPA was formed: "just as a new urban-industrial setting was dawning . . . At the turn of the century big corporations were under pressure to accept independent annual audits and began to publish their financial statements in stockholder reports."[5]

The requirement to publish financial statements in reports to stockholders necessitated the need to assure stockholders that the financial balances included therein fairly presented the corporation's net worth. Providing this assurance became essentially the independent auditors' reason for existing. Although factors other than fraud were involved in auditor determinations of fair presentations of company financial balances, certainly the fraudulent representation of financial balances was uppermost in minds of many users of entity financial statements. However, prior to

1937, the principles and standards that guided independent auditors' examinations of financial statements were not well defined, leaving considerable latitude to the professional judgment of individual auditors. All that changed in 1937, however, with the widely publicized McKesson Robbins case.

In 1937 the company reported assets of $87 million. Price Waterhouse & Co., which audited the company's financial statements, did not physically verify the amount of inventory or accounts receivable claimed by McKesson, and did not discover that it was materially nonexistent. Subsequently, the Securities and Exchange Commission discovered that $19 million of the asset balance claimed was made up of false inventories and accounts receivable that did not exist.

The SEC investigation that followed disclosed that the company's lucrative foreign crude drug division existed only on paper. The fraud was discovered when the treasurer became suspicious after noticing that profits from the division were always reinvested in purchases. No cash from the operation ever accumulated.

The principal perpetrator was a Frank Donald Coster, the company's president. The SEC's investigation disclosed that Mr. Coster was in reality a Mr. Phillip M. Musica, an ex-convict who had been incarcerated for bribing customs officials to avoid import duties for a family-owned cheese business. He was convicted of grand larceny for defrauding 22 bank lenders out of $600,000. Mr. Musica was assisted by his three brothers who were also using false names and who occupied top executive positions at McKesson Robbins. The SEC found that the foursome pretended to buy crude drugs from dummy concerns in Canada, paying for the drugs with McKesson money. Over a 12-year period Mr. Musica and his brothers had stolen about $3 million from the company. In 1938 Mr. Musica committed suicide. The audit company voluntarily refunded about $522,000 in audit fees.[6]

The American Institute of Accountants (AIA) responded quickly to the McKesson Robbins scandal, by publishing Auditing Procedure No. 1 in 1939 calling for the observation of physical inventory counts and the confirmation of receivables. The case also forced the independent auditing profession to recognize that a dynamic program for developing audit standards was badly needed.

In a codification of auditing pronouncements issued in 1951, the American Institute of [Certified Public] Accountants declared:

> The ordinary examination incident to the issuance of an opinion respecting financial statements is not designed and cannot be relied upon to disclose defalcations and other similar irregularities. . . . In a well ordered concern

reliance for the detection of such irregularities is placed principally upon the maintenance of an adequate system of accounting records with appropriate internal control. If an auditor were to attempt to discover defalcations and similar irregularities he would have to extend his work to a point where its cost would be prohibitive. It is generally recognized that good internal control and surety bonds provide protection much more cheaply. . . .

This position seemed to many readers to disavow all but an incidental concern for fraud detection, even though the disavowal pertained to "defalcations and other similar irregularities."[7]

However, Auditing Procedure No. 1, replaced in 1951 with slight modifications, and substantially repeated in November 1972 as the AICPA's *Codification of Auditing Standards and Procedures 1,* was—to say the least—confusing. Although it obviously sought to clarify and remedy independent auditors' responsibility for detecting fraud such as the McKesson and Robbins falsification of inventories and accounts receivable, the language of the AICPA guidance was unclear. For example:

§ 110.06 Reliance for the prevention and detection of fraud should be placed principally upon an adequate accounting system with appropriate internal control. . . . If an objective of an auditor's examination were the discovery of all fraud, he would have to extend his work to a point where its cost would be prohibitive. Even then he could not give assurance that all types of fraud had been detected or that none existed, because items such as unrecorded transactions, forgeries, and collusive fraud would not be uncovered. Accordingly, it is generally recognized that good internal control and fidelity bonds provide protection more economically and effectively [than auditing].[8]

This sort of imprecise language led many independent auditors to be uncertain as to what their fraud detection responsibilities really were. Was the AICPA saying that independent auditors should not audit to discover fraud? Should audited entities rely exclusively on adequate accounting systems and internal control?

This uncertainty was recognized in the Cohen committee report in 1978. The report stated:

Independent auditors have always acknowledged some responsibility to consider the existence of fraud in conducting an audit. Nevertheless, the nature and extent of that responsibility have been unclear. Court decisions, criticisms by the financial press, actions by regulatory bodies, and surveys of users indicate dissatisfaction with the responsibility for fraud detection acknowledged by auditors. . . . Significant percentages of those who use and rely on the auditor's work rank the detection of fraud among the most important objectives of an audit. . . .[9]

The Cohen committee summarized various pronouncements by the AICPA and other authorities with the observation that they "contributed significantly to an evolving attitude among auditors of minimal concern for detection of fraud." In fact, this auditor attitude, based largely on the provisions of SAS No. 16, persisted until April 1988, with the issuance of the AICPA's SAS No. 53, which modified the guidance provided by SAS No. 16. The provisions of Statement on Auditing Standards (SAS) No. 16 —as are evident in the observations of an AICPA official that follows— persisted up until 1988, a fact that raises serious credibility issues regarding independent auditors' efficacy in discovering even financial statement balance fraud prior to that time: "Most auditors believed that SAS no. 16 entitled them to assume that management was honest unless information came to their attention that specifically contradicted that assumption. SAS 53 throws that comfortable notion on the heap of discarded audit folklore. Auditors can't assume that management is either honest or dishonest [anymore]."[10]

In its March 1993 report titled *In the Public Interest,* the Public Oversight Board (POB) of the AICPA SEC Practice Section noted, "Attacks on the accounting profession from a variety of sources suggested a significant public concern over the profession's performance. Of particular moment is the widespread belief that auditors have a responsibility for detecting management fraud which they are not now meeting."[11]

SAS No. 53, however, although well intentioned, still failed to comprehend the true nature of the "expectation gap" between the limited fraud detection service that independent auditors have been authorized to provide and the fraud detection service that their CPA members, their clients, and the public expected. For example, in the following quotation from an official AICPA publication, when the AICPA refers to "fraud" it clearly means only fraud in financial statement balances. The AICPA does not recognize the existence of—or make any allowance for—AT fraud: "In a nutshell, the public looks to the auditor to detect material fraud, and Statement on Auditing Standards No. 53, *The Auditor's Responsibility to Detect and Report Errors and Irregularities,* recognizes that responsibility. The SAS requires the auditor to assess the risk that errors or irregularities may cause the financial statements to contain a material misstatement."[12]

The latest AICPA solution to the controversy over independent auditors' fraud detection responsibilities is SAS No. 82, issued February 1997.

However, it does little to clarify the confusion that has existed for these many years, and independent auditors are not happy with it. It still does not close the expectation gap.

The AICPA's failure to solve this problem is difficult to comprehend fully, although it appears to stem from the almost exclusive dedication of CPAs to serving financial statement user needs that are external to a client's operations. At the risk of oversimplifying this situation, consider that financial statement fraud would be injurious primarily to external users of financial statement balances. Stockholders, creditors, and potential buyers would be deceived by nonexistent assets, for example. Accordingly, independent auditors assume a responsibility to ensure that the balances reported for use by these external users are accurate. However, if material assets are embezzled, and the embezzlement is charged off—thereby leaving the residual assets correct as stated—any asset balances reported will not be misstated. They will be stated correctly even though perhaps somewhat depleted by fraud. Accordingly, external users are not deceived, and independent auditors are not charged with finding the AT fraud that may have occurred. AT fraud is primarily an internal concern.

The problem seems to be that the AICPA, in its guidance to independent auditors, does not outwardly and clearly articulate this policy. However, the policy is unquestionably clear in the context of AICPA auditing standards that constitute the generally accepted audit guidance which individual auditors must abide by.

To convey this AICPA ambiguity, for example, consider carefully the definition of fraud that is provided in SAS No. 82, paragraph 3, as excerpted below. Its definition of fraud—with no adjectives modifying the term—excludes AT fraud. It provides a typically strong clue as to the underlying causes of what has become known as the expectation gap—that is, the gap that exists between the fraud discovery responsibilities assumed by independent auditors (limited to FSB fraud) and client and public audit expectations (FSB including AT fraud): "Although fraud is a broad legal concept, the auditor's interest specifically relates to fraudulent acts that cause a material misstatement of financial statements."[13]

SUMMARY

In its many official pronouncements on the fraud detection responsibilities of independent auditors, the AICPA has tended to avoid stating what fraud independent auditors are "not" responsible for detecting. However, a rare and very explicit unofficial declaration was included in an article published in its May 1987 issue of the *Journal of Accountancy:*

> The primary objective of the detailed audit, which dates back to the 19th century, was the search for defalcations; the primary objective of the balance-sheet audit, which was becoming established at the turn of the century, was to provide assurance that the balance sheet and the statement of profit and loss were appropriately set forth. The objective of today's GAAS [Generally Accepted] Auditing Standards audit is to provide an opinion on the material correctness of the financial statements. *The auditor's current responsibility for detecting fraud is* explicit, but *limited to a single type of fraud—deliberate, material misstatements of financial statements.*[14]

Merging Proactive Fraud-Specific Auditing with Financial Statement Balance Auditing

Little, if any, advantage would be gained in performing a proactive fraud-specific audit as an adjunct to an independent auditor's traditional financial statement balance audit. Performing such an audit would save little or no audit time, since the procedures needed to perform each type of audit differ significantly. Any attempt to combine the two examination types essentially would mean that the two audit types would run concurrently. Nor would doing one type of audit offer any direct benefits to the performance of the other audit. The audit requirements for each are substantially different.

Providing a More Comprehensive Audit Service

Most independent auditors are qualified in the general discipline of auditing and have excellent knowledge of accounting practices. They lack only two things.

1. Generally accepted auditing standards to guide their practice of a full spectrum of proactive fraud-specific auditing
2. Necessary training and experience

Once they have these two prerequisites, they can offer service to all clients in need.

However, many entities at risk that are clients of CPAs do not recognize that their independent auditors are not providing them with a comprehensive fraud-specific audit service, including an examination to detect AT fraud. Many entities that do become aware of this fact are not at all pleased with the gap in fraud audit service. "Court decisions, criticisms by the financial press, actions by regulatory bodies, and surveys by users indicate dissatisfaction with the responsibility for fraud detection acknowledged by auditors."[15]

Need for AT Fraud Auditing Standards

Many independent auditors are deeply disturbed when they must explain to their clients why they did not, and could not, provide an AT fraud detection service. Besides feeling responsible to offer the service, they also regret losing the significant revenue that would result from its provision.

Independent auditors are well aware that their audits—if conducted within generally accepted audit standard guidelines—offer them a measure of protection in the very litigious society in which they conduct their work. For them, audit standards formally define the difference between what constitutes generally accepted performance and what might otherwise be alleged to be negligent performance. Without appropriate and generally accepted guidelines for AT fraud auditing, any independent auditor choosing to provide such a service would be in serious jeopardy of charges of negligence for any failures to detect material fraud.

The jeopardy independent auditors face when using their judgment alone, without generally accepted guidelines, is well illustrated by the 1937 McKesson & Robbins case. In that instance, (Price, Waterhouse & Co.,) the independent auditing firm,—without guidelines for what might be considered generally accepted procedures and relying only on their own judgment—apparently did not verify inventory and accounts receivable balances, and as a result failed to notice the significant disparities between reported balances and actual amounts. Subsequently Price, Waterhouse was very fortunate in only having to refund the $522,000 audit fee—a lot of money in 1937—to the company. On the positive side, however, the experience awakened independent auditors to the need for generally accepted auditing standards to define what constitutes generally accepted obligatory performance. A series of comprehensive statements on auditing standards emerged over the ensuing 60 years.

Rather than requiring a McKesson & Robbins case to motivate the development of proactive AT fraud-auditing standards, it would be a good idea to begin the development of standards for proactive fraud-specific auditing immediately. The AICPA, as parent organization of hundreds of thousands of independent auditors throughout the United States, would be well advised to begin their development immediately.

Although AT fraud auditing standards could not, and should not, be published without appropriate study and deliberation, one standard in particular is strongly recommended because it constitutes a significant deviation from the audit philosophy that currently guides independent auditor examinations of financial statement balances. The first AT fraud auditing standard must embrace a firm declaration by the auditor that he or she does not accept any responsibility for detecting fraud, material or otherwise; nor does he or she guarantee it will be detected. Current auditing standards adopted by independent auditors who audit financial statement balances declare that they are responsible for detecting all material errors in the balances.

Why Asset Theft Fraud Audits Should Be Performed

The primary objective of a fraud audit is to search an entity's operations to detect fraud. The actual detection of fraud should not be the objective. If, however, the AT audit is performed competently, and the audit scope is sufficiently thorough, all or most material fraud will be discovered, and a powerful deterrent to fraud will have been established. AT fraud audit standards should state clearly that a client will receive audit service performed by auditors trained and experienced in fraud detection and certified as competent by the AICPA, or whatever other organization may assume a parenting role. The scope of their audit is dependent on whatever effort the client is willing to finance. Unlike financial statement audits performed by independent auditors, which are relatively fixed in scope, the scope of a fraud-specific audit should vary and be based on client wishes and what they are willing to pay for.

With the elimination of a requirement that they discover fraud in their audit examinations, what level of resources should auditors devote to the engagement? What should a fraud-specific audit cost? It seems appropriate that the client entity should determine what level of review it wishes, or more appropriately, what level of examination it wishes to pay for. The answer could easily be expressed in terms of the dollars. Any level of fraud-specific auditing would be beneficial. And, up to a point of diminishing returns, the more auditing, the better the results.

In the future after performing an introductory survey of a prospective client's fraud exposure, an AT audit practitioner might recommend a range of fees that would be appropriate for that client, to include a minimum and a maximum review level. The maximum review would offer more comprehensive coverage of the client's operations and offer better odds of detecting material fraud. In addition to seeking to detect fraud, any proactive fraud-specific audit activity could also provide recommendations for improving the client's internal controls.

NOTES

1. Stephen, Pizzo. *Inside Job, The Looting of America's Savings and Loans* (New York: McGraw-Hill, 1989), p. 207.

2. Elizabeth, MacDonald. "Auditors Miss a Fraud and SEC Tries to Put Them Out of Business," *Wall Street Journal,* January 6, 2000, pp. A1, A8.

3. "The CPA's Role in Detecting and Preventing Fraud," *FBI Law Enforcement Bulletin,* 68, no. 7 (July 1999), p. 1.

4. Richard B. Schmitt. "Cendant's Woes Highlight Legal Role of Auditors in Finding Fraud," *Wall Street Journal,* July 22, 1998, p. A6.

5. Robert K. Elliott and Peter D. Jacobson. "Audit Technology: A Heritage and A Promise," *Journal of Accountancy* (May 1987), p. 214.

6. Elizabeth, Macdonald. "Ghost of Scandal Past," *Wall Street Journal,* June 30, 1999, pp. B1, B4.

7. AICPA, "The Commission on Auditor's Responsibilities: Report, Conclusions, and Recommendations," 1978, p. 35.

8. AICPA, "Statement on Auditing Standards: Codification of Auditing Standards and Procedures." November 1992: 3.

9. AICPA, "The Commission," p. 31.

10. D.R. Carmichael. "The Auditor's New Guide to Errors, Irregularities and Illegal Acts," *Journal of Accountancy* (September 1988), pp. 41–42.

11. AICPA, "Exposure Draft, Proposed Statement on Auditing Standards, Consideration of Fraud in a Financial Statement Audit, and Amendments to Statements on Auditing Standards No. 1," May 1, 1996, p. 7.

12. "The CPA Letter," AICPA (January 1994), p. 5.

13. "Statement of Auditing Standards No. 82," AICPA (February 1997).

14. Robert K. Elliott and Peter D. Jacobson. "Themes in the Development of Audit Technology: Concepts and Procedures," *Journal of Accountancy,* (May 1987), p. 214, emphasis added.

15. AICPA, "The Commission."

3

INTRODUCTION TO PROACTIVE FRAUD AUDITING

FRAUD AUDITING DEFINED

Fraud auditing is a unique auditing specialty that involves the use of auditing techniques developed for the sole purpose of detecting evidence of fraud. There are basically two stages to fraud auditing, each of which requires a different operating methodology by the auditor as well as a different mind-set: the proactive stage and the reactive stage.

As implausible as the analogy may be, the practice of proactive fraud auditing is not unlike the practice of medical doctors who examine their patients for signs of malignancies even though the patients appear to be in good health and have no symptoms, solely because they are in special risk categories. Basically this is what proactive fraud auditors do. They examine entities at risk of fraud but that have no symptoms that the entities already have been victims. The intensity of a proactive fraud audit is based on the degree to which an entity is at risk, not on any evident symptoms of fraud. The reactive fraud auditor's job essentially begins when the proactive fraud auditor has discovered indications—often called indicia of fraud—that fraud may be present. Returning to the analogy involving medical doctors, this is quite similar to the medical doctor who discovers a suspicious lump in a patient. The discovery often means nothing by itself, but it is usually sufficient reason for the doctor to react and investigate further.

At the point of the detection, however, the nature of the doctor's examination changes from a relatively blind examination of areas at risk to a very specific examination of the detected lump or nodule. He or she is likely to perform specific tests to determine the nature of the finding. So it is with the reactive fraud auditor. With the detection of indicia of fraud, the auditor changes the nature of his or her examination from a blind search for indicia, to a specific search for evidence that will validate whether the fraud indicia discovered is malignant or benign.

Although the practice of medicine has many doctors qualified to assist their patients, the comparison ends there. The practice of fraud auditing is in its infancy and is not widely practiced—to the delight of millions of fraud perpetrators throughout the world. There are far too few qualified auditors to practice fraud auditing adequately.

Fraud auditing generally is thought of as a specialty of the general practice of internal auditing, since it is practiced only by internal auditors, if at all. However, given the proper circumstances, fraud auditing could and should be performed by independent public accountants (CPAs) on behalf of clients interested in the benefits of fraud auditing. The association of fraud auditing with internal auditing undoubtedly results from the greater freedom from regulation that internal auditors enjoy in performing their audits. Whereas CPAs must perform only in accordance with generally accepted auditing standards published by the American Institute of Certified Public Accountants (AICPA)—standards that, in effect, preclude fraud auditing—internal auditors are not similarly restrained, at least not from a regulatory standpoint. However, fraud auditing is not generally practiced by internal auditors, although they appear to have a strong interest in doing so. Many of those who do are not always provided with the necessary resources or freedom to engage in the practice to the degree they would like, and their opportunities for learning the skills needed are limited. Also, many employers, complacent in their belief that they are fraud-free and/or have adequate protection by virtue of their periodic independent audits by CPA firms, make a grievous error, in the interests of cost cutting, by restricting internal auditing resources that might otherwise be better spent on proactive fraud-specific auditing. Internal auditors normally perform a widely diversified, somewhat nondiscretionary mix of activities, ranging from routine obligations to ensure entity compliance with internal control requirements to entity operational auditing. Although undoubtedly some entities have internal auditors with the resources and interests to be aggressive in proactive fraud auditing, such firms probably are in the minority.

The good news is that the practice of fraud-specific auditing does appear to be emerging.

THREE OBJECTIVES OF FRAUD AUDITING

Fraud auditing has three basic objectives;

  1. In the proactive stage: To search competently and persistently for indicia of fraud. The hunt for evidence continues to the point when

the auditor is reasonably confident that he or she may have discovered fraud, or feels that sufficient testing has been done. In a more practical vein, the auditor must stop searching when time runs out.

2. In the reactive stage, to search for validating evidence. To react to any indicative evidence discovered in the proactive stage. And, if found, to compile the evidence necessary to be reasonably certain he or she has discovered fraud and to support prosecution. In the reactive stage, if the auditor is not sufficiently trained or experienced in criminal investigations, he or she is advised to join with a criminal investigator at some point to develop the necessary evidence to support prosecution.

3. To deter fraud by increasing the risk of detection.

The first objective is to search for evidence of fraud. Although the detection of fraud is an intention of proactive fraud auditing, it should never be the measure of audit efficacy. Whether or not auditors detect evidence of fraud should never be a criterion of how effective the audit was or how well it was conducted.

At the outset of the first stage—the proactive stage—auditors must begin from point zero, with nothing in the way of fraud evidence to guide them in the initiation of audit procedures. The only guidance proactive auditors may have in deciding what to audit is their survey of the entity being audited and any operational areas the survey may have highlighted as being at a higher risk of fraud, which would draw auditors' attention. Proactive fraud-specific auditing is, without question, the most difficult stage of fraud auditing.

When performing proactive fraud auditing, auditors usually begin audit search procedures in areas selected at their discretion, with no guidance regarding any fraud that actually may have occurred. They must look for evidence that has not yet become apparent and that may never become apparent. Their main concern is to remain alert to the faint indicia of fraud they are searching for. Fraud auditors are like fishermen who stand for hours casting a hook at the end of a line into the water, patiently waiting for a successful strike. The fact that any given day is a bad fishing day does not deter them. Ask any fisherman. Eventually they will have the thrill of the catch, which will make all the unproductive days worthwhile.

Contrary to a popular impression that a case of fraud is readily evident when encountered by auditors, many if not most cases begin with the detection of a single clue and ends as a collection of bits of evidence that all had to be found and assembled individually, any one of which was likely to be indistinguishable as evidence of fraud when first seen. If fraud auditors are tired, or rushing through their search, they could easily miss minuscule clues and not detect the case. The first bits of evidence often indicate or prove nothing by themselves, except to suggest—to the trained eye—the possibility of fraud, and that a search for additional evidence is a viable course of action.

PROACTIVE FRAUD AUDITING

The proactive stage of fraud auditing often involves two indistinct stages, which could be described as the pre-discovery stage, and the post-discovery stage. Where there are two stages, the latter stage occurs as the result of the discovery of some indication of fraud, but it is so weak that the auditor is unsure whether or not it is indicia of fraud. In this post-discovery stage auditors are reluctant to suggest a reactive criminal investigation based upon what often constitutes little more than their suspicions, and chooses instead to continue the proactive audit to search for additional evidence to confirm the suspicions. If no additional evidence of fraud is discovered, the auditor's finding is dropped. If sufficient additional evidence is found to enhance the auditor's suspicions, the case will enter the reactive phase.

In the post-discovery stage, the auditor will attempt to envision what sort of fraud is suggested by the evidence discovered. These stages involve the use of methods very much like the procedure followed in working a jigsaw puzzle. Once a picture is envisioned, missing pieces that fit the envisioned image are easier to look for and find. When a possible fraud is envisioned, audit search programs can be designed to search efficiently for the exact sort of evidence needed to either validate or nullify the suspicioned fraud. This fraud auditing technique is often called end auditing. The method is not always successful, but is better than searching for validating clues without having at least an idea of what is being sought. At this point even though they have anticipated what the fraud may be, auditors still don't have a solid fraud lead, only a deep down feeling of being on a hot trail.

If the search produces sufficient validating evidence that auditors think enhances the probability of fraud, they will schedule it for reactive audit development work. Auditors are well aware that many of the leads discovered in this stage of the audit—and the fraud cases visualized when the first evidence was found—will die from a failure to discover further validating evidence. Of course, this fact does not mean that the initial clue discovered was not indicia of fraud—only that no additional evidence could be discovered. After conducting a reasonable search for validating evidence, the file on the finding will be closed, and auditors will move on to search for or to pursue another clue. If in pursuing a lead auditors find sufficient additional validating evidence to confirm initial suspicions, they will designate the finding of fraud a case and either continue the review or refer it to a criminal investigator, to gather the additional evidence necessary to support prosecution. At this point any further work can be clearly termed reactive, depending on how certain auditors were that a bona-fide case of fraud had been found and how trained or experienced they may be in the investigative skills necessary to prepare a case for prosecution.

Deciding when a proactive case becomes a reactive one is a matter of judgment and is likely to vary from case to case, depending on personal experience. Unfortunately, often auditors' self-assessment of their qualifications varies in inverse proportion to the their training and experience. Many times auditors retain audit authority far beyond the most opportune point when the case should be relinquished to trained investigators. The decision often depends on how large and dollar significant a case may be, and what paralegal and investigative skills the auditors have or can call upon. Of course, all good fraud auditors are a bit paranoid, and the fact that they failed to find additional evidence to support their initial observations oftentimes to them only means that either the perpetrator was very clever and was not careless in leaving an evidence trail or that they missed finding it.

Less experienced fraud auditors prolong preliminary casework unnecessarily, thereby delaying entry of skilled criminal investigators and/or prosecution counsel. It is always desirable for criminal investigators to be brought on the scene on a timely basis to take necessary affidavits from witnesses while their memories are fresh, and before critical evidence is lost or destroyed. Early assistance from prosecutors is highly desirable if it appears the case is likely to be prosecuted, to assure that continuing audit/investigative work is relevant to case requirements.

Many private and governmental entities have a system that allows employees and others to anonymously report irregularities, some of which turn out to be fraud. These reports normally are received with little or no documentation and very few particulars. However, they should never be ignored; the fraud audit staff should consider them for their lead value.

CASE 3.1 The Office Supply Store Fraud

One large government fraud case began with a barely legible handscribbled note that was mailed to the U.S. General Services Administration by the jilted girlfriend of one of the perpetrators. The note described how her ex-lover—the manager of an office supply store—was involved in criminal activity, and how he had been cheating on her with another woman. When the note was received, the first reaction was to ignore it as the product of a rejected lover attempting to make trouble for the man who rejected her. However, the lead was taken seriously, and it turned out to be the loose thread that unraveled a widespread fraud in federal office supply stores across the country. Typical of the many frauds that were uncovered was a scheme that generally involved office supply brokers who would visit store managers and propose a conspiracy to commit fraud. Interestingly, they had many takers. The visiting broker would propose that store managers purchase merchandise that would never be delivered—perhaps something like $5,000 in ball-point pens. If the store manager agreed—and many did—he or she would issue a purchase order to the broker, who would then generate all the necessary paperwork that would accompany a legitimate order and shipment of merchandise, including shipping documents and an invoice—but no merchandise. The store manager would process the invoice, certifying that the merchandise had been received, and the invoice amount would be paid to the broker. Subsequently the broker and the store manager would divide the cash received. The retail inventory method in effect at the time at the stores facilitated the fraud by not highlighting irregularities in specific items in store inventories, such as the ball-point pens, but would spread the inventory shortages over the entire merchandise line, diminishing its apparent significance. A fraud case would have been difficult to prove without the woman's report. Adding to detection difficulty was the fact that store managers also had considerable latitude in setting unit sales prices. Accordingly they would increase the prices of legitimate items being sold to increase sales revenue, which in turn tended to cover the shortages. The case eventually was prosecuted successfully due to the excessive greed of the perpetrators and an abundance of evidence discovered.

Reactive Fraud Auditing

Reactive fraud auditing consists of searching for and compiling the evidence necessary to support prosecution. The term "reactive" is derived from the fact that auditors literally are reacting to validated evidence of fraud discovered in the proactive stage, or from some other source, and set an audit examination path that focuses on the evidence to which they are reacting. As more and more evidence is discovered—or not discovered—the audit path varies depending on any new case insights gained. Often mitigating circumstances that tend to negate the presumptions of fraud previously held are discovered in the reactive stage of an audit or investigation. Auditors should keep open minds regarding this possibility.

Usually the difference between proactive and reactive audit work is clear. When auditing proactively, auditors initially have no indications of the type of fraud that may be present, and follow audit procedures designed to detect evidence to confirm or deny speculation. Once indicia of fraud is detected, regardless of how slight, suspicions are enhanced but auditors still are not certain of the existence of fraud. However, when validating evidence is discovered, and auditors become convinced that the case being pursued is a bona-fide fraud discovery, the audit tends to change to a reactive one. Further audit procedures are designed to concentrate on those factors that will improve the prosecutive worth of the finding. Such factors include determining who the perpetrators are, whether other cases involving the perpetrators have occurred previously, proving their intent to commit fraud, and determining the total loss to the victim resulting from the fraud.

The roles of proactive auditors and criminal investigators are also reasonably clear. Criminal investigators rarely work proactively to discover fraud. They almost always begin their investigative tasks with a request from the victim, who has either come by evidence of fraud or has strong suspicions of fraud that he or she wishes to be investigated. These suspicions include requests from proactive auditors who require assistance after concluding that sufficient evidence has been accumulated to be reasonably certain that fraud has been discovered.

Depending on case circumstances, often this referral point is delayed to keep the fraud finding confidential. Regrettably, once criminal investigators begin their work, any confidentiality of the discovery of fraud is usually lost. The presence of investigators usually is associated with a suspected criminal act, and the office gossip begins. An entity's employee population becomes accustomed to the presence of proactive auditors while searching for evidence of fraud that may not exist, and rarely attributes their presence to the detection of fraud. By the time criminal investigators come on the scene, most employees realize that the situation has changed and begin to gossip. In addition, investigators usually interview suspects and potential witnesses, and asks pointed questions regarding the suspected fraud. Sworn statements are also usually taken, and leave office onlookers with little doubt as to the specifics of the crime and the probable suspects. The danger here, of course, is that innocent or unproven suspects will be defamed, and investigative procedures should not be started prematurely.

The reactive stage of fraud auditing is also marked by a new perspective to work undertaken. That is, with evidence of fraud in hand, the review team focuses on gathering the necessary evidence to prosecute the suspected perpetrator(s) successfully. They seek to obtain corroborating evidence. If the case is dollar significant and difficult, auditors should enlist the assistance of team members who have criminal investigative and/or legal (prosecution) experience, and who can proceed without alarming the office community.

Readers are advised not to be overconfident when seeking prosecution. Having a case declined by a prosecutor for lack of evidence is a frustrating experience, especially when auditors have collected what they believe to be overwhelming evidence of fraud. Case 3.2 relates such an experience.

CASE 3.2 Trucking Firm Engages in Defective Delivery Fraud

One such case that was nearly lost due to a lack of the right sort of evidence involved a trucking firm that had a contract to deliver supplies from a government warehouse to various government agencies in the Chicago area. The firm skimmed merchandise from large deliveries over a period of time. Apparently people at the firm noticed that some customers did not check the quantities of merchandise deliveries received and took small quantities of merchandise from each delivery to them. When they had accumulated a truckload of stolen goods from this skimming practice, they would deliver it to a dealer in stolen merchandise. There were no apparent suspicions that these thefts were taking place, in that no customers had reported any shortages in the merchandise received. However, as sometimes happens, fate entered upon the scene. A significant snowstorm occurred.

During the snowstorm, a truck laden with stolen government property was found abandoned on a Chicago street that had been designated a vital snow route and where parking was prohibited during snowstorms. To clear the street, the Chicago police had the truck towed to a police impound lot, where it was later examined, and the government property was discovered. The federal police who investigated found it simple to trace the trailer's registration to the trucking firm involved. There was no doubt that the trucking firm had been engaged in criminal fraud, and shortly after, the case was presented to the U.S. attorney's office for prosecution. Tried before a federal judge, the trucker was found guilty. However, after the trial, the U.S. assistant attorney who prosecuted the case told the auditors that the judge involved was very disturbed. Apparently he had little, if any, doubt that the defendant was guilty but was uncomfortable with the prosecutor's scant demonstration of the trucking company's intent to defraud the government. He was uncomfortable in concluding intent—a prerequisite for conviction—from the one truckload of stolen merchandise that was presented as evidence. Upon reflection, the investigation should have sought evidence that this trucker had practiced this particular fraud on prior occasions. Apparently the judge wanted to see this; undoubtedly such information would have been a factor in sentencing the defendant.

Deterring Fraud by Increasing Risk of Detection

Perhaps the most significant objective of proactive fraud auditing is the internal control effect that it establishes, if done properly. Regardless of how unsuccessful a proactive fraud audit may be in detecting fraud indicia, this objective always is accomplished if the audit work is done visibly, and if it is performed in areas that fraud perpetrators may be considering. Fraud auditing, done well, puts an unavoidable and often intolerable risk into the practice of perpetrating fraud. Most, if not all, fraud perpetrators do not want to be caught. In those cases in which an entity fails to practice routine proactive fraud auditing, would-be fraud perpetrators are assured that, if they are careful and plan their fraudulent acts well, they run a minimal risk of discovery. However, if fraud auditing efforts—particularly proactive auditing efforts—are expended periodically across a wide spectrum of an entity's operations, regardless of the purpose of the searches or their success in detecting fraud indicia, would-be and actual perpetrators will be on notice that any perpetration in those areas runs the risk of detection. Where there is little or no risk, only moral restraints keep people with few or no moral values from the easy money. Even though a fraud audit examination may fail to detect any evidence of fraud, the risk of detection it imposes is an effective deterrent.

The 20th century posed few insurmountable obstacles to fraud. With few exceptions, little effective proactive fraud-specific auditing was performed, and would-be perpetrators surely were encouraged by the low risk of detection. In contemplating fraud, it is relatively easy for a perpetrator to become aware of the internal controls in effect and to find ways and means of avoiding them. Many internal controls are relatively naive and especially ineffective where conspiracy is part of the scheme. Frequently even skilled fraud auditors do not find fraud that is cleverly hidden, so deterrence becomes a main objective of fraud auditing. Contrary to what some criminologists suggest, most fraud perpetrators do not wish to be caught and are very cautious. However, the presence of skilled fraud auditors who periodically comb through an entity's transactions constitutes an ever-present threat and will deter many otherwise thoughtful perpetrators.

Fraud auditors selecting areas for audit are well aware that their activities will be observed by many people, and will be the subject of office gossip. Accordingly, they take care to avoid signaling to onlookers any unusual interest in specific subjects or individuals, where there is a need to maintain confidentiality. But, by the same token, clever fraud auditors take advantage of others' interest in their review subjects by intentionally giving the impression that they are examining a variety of operational areas, even though they have no intention of spending their precious time on them. For example, they may request that a variety of files be provided for examination in the privacy of their offices and subsequently may not examine those files requested. In doing so, they have projected a deterrent effect far beyond what available audit time allows. The onlookers, of course, do not know that the files requested are not examined.

ADVICE FOR INEXPERIENCED FRAUD AUDITORS

Beginning fraud auditors should follow five rules:

1. Avoid becoming prematurely entangled in developing endless facts and circumstances of a case of fraud, to the exclusion of identifying a perpetrator or perpetrators, and proving their involvement. As puzzling as this suggestion may appear at first, many auditors become obsessed with developing the interesting details of a fraud case and tend to forget why they are doing what they are doing. Many auditors fully document sensational details of a fraud case, then, when asked "Who did it?" cannot answer.

   Most auditors are basically nice people who feel comfortable with the impersonal aspects of their work. When describing incidents of waste, for example, most internal audit reports fail to mention who was responsible for the waste being reported. In fact, the Office of Auditing of the U.S. General Services Administration

(GSA) once experimented with putting the names of people who had knowledge—but were not the guilty parties—of the events described in their audit reports, and the practice drew an angry reaction. Accordingly, internal auditors tend to be trained to report a finding on the order of "There is inadequate underlying support for the $12,000 payment to the Jones Company," without ever determining the names of the people who were responsible; they seem to consider that an irrelevant personal detail. During a lecture, a group of mid-level managers and auditors of an international corporation were told that, in pursuing a fraud examination, they must identify a list of perpetrator suspects as early as possible in the examination, and examine all the transactions those people may have been involved in. Several of those in attendance remarked that they would have difficulty intruding into the affairs of innocent people. They were asked if they ever heard of the expression "Nice guys finish last."

Fraud does not just happen of its own accord. Someone is always involved. Accordingly, once auditors find the first indicia of fraud, they must begin speculating as to who the perpetrators are likely to be.

2. Fraud auditors must constantly strive to prove a perpetrator's intent to commit fraud. Countless fraud cases in the group 2 (discovered but never prosecuted) category are there and will remain there, because some auditor or investigator failed to prove clearly who did the crime and that the accused perpetrator intended to commit fraud. Proving an accused perpetrator's intent to commit the crime he or she is accused of is often extremely difficult, but it is an absolutely necessary requirement for prosecution in the courts. Without a clear demonstration of intent, a case is not likely to be prosecuted, regardless of the weight of evidence regarding the crime itself. The purpose of the courts is to judge people, not to hear detail-rich stories of the crimes involved.

3. Be creative, think like a perpetrator, do not be predictable. When searching for evidence of fraud, particularly when proactively searching, fraud auditors have considerable license to vary search methods, objectives, parameters, and locations. Some of the most successful discoveries have been achieved by auditors who literally asked themselves "What would a perpetrator do in a situation such as this?" and then proceeded to test whether they were correct.

The federal GSA used to have an internal control requirement that all contracts $200,000 and over had to be examined by internal auditors for any obvious improprieties. Predictably, few if any exceptions ever were discovered. However, one day an auditor, while proactively searching for evidence of fraud, decided that any serious perpetrators would most likely be aware of the $200,000 internal control requirement. Thus, if they were going to attempt fraud, it would be more likely in contracts just under $200,000. Accordingly, the auditors decided to lower the audit threshold to $150,000 without notice. The result: multiple infractions were discovered, many of them easily found and obviously intentional, surely because perpetrators expected that the auditors would not examine the contracts. Obviously the internal audits had been painfully predictable.

4. Fraud auditing detection procedures must take into account that much fraud involves conspiracy—either true conspiracy or pseudo conspiracy. Many internal control systems are designed to prevent unauthorized acts by people acting alone. However, no internal control system can prevent illegal acts by two or more people from acting as co-conspirators to evade the internal controls.

Accordingly, when planning fraud discovery strategy, although fraud auditors must consider the fraud-specific efficacy of internal controls in place, they should not depend on them excessively. At one time the collusion of two or more people in fraud was rare, and auditors depended heavily on that assumption. Collusion is no longer rare, and auditors must learn to put far less dependence on internal controls intended to prevent people acting alone from committing fraud. Adding to the fraud auditors' dilemma is the fact that many perpetrators have discovered that individuals charged with maintaining internal controls are often negligent or poorly trained, and can be tricked into failures equivalent to lowering fraud barriers. Accordingly, it is appropriate to classify collusion into two categories, conspiracy and pseudo-conspiracy:

a. Ordinary conspiracy involves the willing cooperation of two or more people intent on committing fraud.

b. Pseudo-conspiracy occurs when one or more of the people cooperating in the fraud scheme is innocent of any intent to commit fraud, or has no knowledge of the fraud scheme, but fails to act—or acts in a negligent manner—so as to make fraud by another person or persons possible. Pseudo-conspirators are never aware that they are a party to fraud and have no intent to commit criminal acts.

Pseudoconspiracies often occur, for example, when perpetrators must evade internal controls designed to prevent unauthorized acts from occurring and require the cooperation of an innocent person responsible for maintaining the control feature. Usually the innocent parties are somehow tricked into cooperating. Most frequently this occurs when entities employing pseudo-conspirators do not select and train key internal control employees adequately, and/or do not refresh their training adequately. Similar internal control lapses also likely to occur during vacations, sick outages, days off, and rest breaks when temporary personnel replace regular experienced control clerks. See Case 3.3.

CASE 3.3 The Negligent Internal Control Clerk

The following actual fraud, involving a pseudoconspiracy, totaled over $900,000 and required the participation of an internal control register clerk in a large automated payment system. The automated system involved was designed to accept only transactions that were submitted by authorized people. To demonstrate that they were permitted to use the system, all authorized users authenticated their accounting documents submitted for processing by including the lowest unused number from a series of ascending numbers issued only to them. Each number could be used only once and, when used in ascending order, assured the processing system that the person submitting them was approved and that all transactions submitted had been processed—and no more. No duplicate numbers would be accepted, and any missing numbers resulted in a search for the missing documents. The system seemed reasonably secure and, theoretically at least, precluded unauthorized people from using the system. Any possible payment fraud would be limited to a small circle of authorized users. However, the key to the control system was the clerk who was in charge of issuing the blocks of control numbers to authorized users.

From time to time, a friendly charismatic man-about-the-office who had gained the friendship and trust of many employees explained to the clerk that one of the authorized system users had asked him to pick up a new block of numbers for him. Not realizing the significance of issuing the control numbers only to authorized users, the clerk would comply and issue a block of numbers logged to whoever the man named. The man subsequently used the numbers to submit phony documents for building maintenance services that allowed him to steal over $900,000.

The innocent control number clerk became a pseudo-conspirator when she gave out the control numbers and in so doing made the man's fraud possible. The clerk had no knowledge of the fraud scheme or the man's criminal intent, and so was not guilty of a criminal act. She was not even found to be negligent, since her employer could not demonstrate that she had been adequately trained or refreshed as to the internal control significance of the control numbers.

In other instances similar to the one described, even though control clerks may, in fact, be adequately trained in the internal control role, occasionally they are absent. Whether for vacation time, sick absences, lunch breaks, coffee breaks, or rest periods, substitute clerks must be assigned, and all of them must be trained adequately if the control system is to work effectively. Alert perpetrators will watch for undertrained, careless, insecure, or underattentive clerks and take advantage of any lapse in control.

---

5. Proactive fraud detection strategy must consider that fraud may appear in the accounting records as distinct entries or hosted entries, and in some instances may not appear in the records at all.

Some fraud, not a lot, appears in accounting records as distinct accounting entries. If a fraud auditor randomly selects a fraudulent entry to be tested, the entire amount of the transaction will be the amount of the fraud, and discovery is likely. It is perhaps the simplest of the three to discover. Multiple-payment fraud, duplicate-payment fraud, and shell fraud are all examples of fraud cases that involve distinct entries.

Assume that a random audit test includes a $5,000 payment to ABC Contractors for construction work. The auditor discovers that the entire item contracted for is a total fabrication. It was never delivered by ABC Contractors. Further investigation reveals that it is fraud. The entire $5,000 will be the amount of the fraud. There will be no legitimate support whatsoever for the disbursement. There is nothing to justify the payment, no question as to the amount of the fraud or who is responsible.

Most of all fraud that occurs is hosted entry fraud. When it occurs, the amount of the fraud is masked by an apparently legitimate transaction that hosts it. Accordingly, if auditors select, at random, a payment for $50,000 for 1,000 widgets, they may find what appears to be a perfectly proper payment. The paperwork is all correct, and all 1,000 widgets appear to have been received, signed for, and placed in inventory. Do the auditors pass the transaction as being fraud free? Not necessarily. At least several different frauds can be possible despite the audit tests performed.

Although the receiving records indicated that 1,000 widgets had been received, in fact, something less actually may have been actually received. Or the transaction examined may have been the second of two, the first legitimate, the second fraudulent. In both cases there would be a legitimate order for 1,000 widgets at $50,000, which would pass most audit tests. It would be confirmed that all 1,000 widgets had been received, and all the paperwork would have passed ordinary scrutiny. Only in the unlikely event that auditors happen to select both transactions would the fraud have been obvious, and then only perhaps. The legitimate entry would in effect host and mask the illegitimate entry.

A kickback is another example of fraud which is hosted by an otherwise legitimate transaction. The kickback amounts are always included in the price the victim pays for the product or service received. Reconsider, for example, the circumstances described in Case 1.2, page 9, The Arrogant Kickback Solicitor. Note that the would-be perpetrator indicated that he would allow the contractor to inflate the price offered on future contracts to finance the kickback amounts.

In such contracts, auditors reviewing contract details would find that a properly authorized and legitimate product or service was delivered. The only problem would be in determining whether the price was right. In many cases this is a very difficult determination. Subsequent chapters discuss kickback fraud and suggest audit and internal control techniques for dealing with it.

Another type of fraud is that which is off the books. Inexperienced fraud auditors must note that selecting transactions for examination from the accounting records does not always ensure an opportunity for examining all fraud that may have occurred. Consider accounts receivable that have been written off as bad debts and subsequently collected. A perpetrator has the opportunity to divert payments for bad debts with no record on the books that the debt had been paid. Scrap inventories that were never capitalized can be another off-the-books fraud. Frequently, manufacturers generate scrap inventories that have considerable value. If those scrap inventories are sold without having been capitalized, the revenue the sales generate could be diverted and never appear on the accounting records for auditors who did not go beyond the accounting records in their search for fraud. For example, one organization followed the practice of reclaiming the silver content from discarded X-ray films. Occasionally the considerable silver that was generated would disappear. No examination of accounting transactions would ever disclose the theft. No one could ever say with certainty the value of the inventory that may have been stolen. The theft was deterred by periodically capitalizing the silver inventories that were generated.

4

PROACTIVE FRAUD AUDITING

Proactive fraud-specific auditing bears few similarities to traditional auditing. To understand fully what proactive fraud-specific auditing is and is not, traditional auditing practices also must be understood. In the simplest terms possible, it is fair to say that whereas traditional auditing seeks to verify things that are known to be, proactive fraud-specific auditing seeks to determine the existence of things that are not known to be and may not be.

Admittedly, this simple definition sounds very much like a riddle, and will be explained in the paragraphs that follow. However, using a somewhat generally accepted analogy involving a needle and a haystack, consider how each auditor type would react if the haystack were somehow involved in their audit objectives. Whereas traditional auditors would be likely to look upon the haystack and see only a need to verify the quantity and quality of hay in the stack, proactive fraud auditors would be likely to ignore the quantity and quality of the hay and to ponder, instead, how to find the needle(s) that might be in it. Although neither auditor type spends much time looking at haystacks, the illustration depicts the mind-set and objectives each auditor type takes in his or her endeavors and the relative difficulty each faces in accomplishing those objectives.

Determining the amount and quality of hay in the stack is a relatively straightforward and positive task. Auditors begin with something tangible. There are no doubts that it exists. All that is left for them to do is measure it and perhaps test it, both tasks being very doable. However, determining if there is one or more needles in the haystack, and finding it or them, is obviously a much more difficult task, and requires methods quite different from those employed by traditional auditors. To begin with, there is no tangible evidence to suggest that the fraud—the needles—actually exist. And—for fraud auditors—most of the time no evidence is ever found that it did exist. However, there is also no evidence that it does not exist. Accordingly, fraud auditors frequently search for things that, most of the time, simply are not there. In fact, if fraud auditors could be assured that they were searching for something as tangible as needles, their job would be greatly simplified.

There are, however, methods proactive auditors can use to maximize their fraud detection probabilities. In the following sections, readers should note the differences between proactive fraud auditing and traditional auditing. And they should attempt to understand why traditional auditors, particularly independent ones, cannot possibly be expected to accomplish dual audit objectives of searching for indicia of fraud during ongoing verifications to verify financial statement balances or accomplish routine audit tasks without a significant increase in resources and time expended. In fact, independent auditors attempting to perform proactive fraud-specific audits without the unique training and/or experience needed generally find their well-intentioned efforts at fraud detection less than productive.

The great difficulty in proactive fraud auditing is that auditors are literally auditing blind. The traditional audit normally begins with an assertion of some kind by the entity being audited that something—a financial statement balance or a condition—is correct. The traditional auditor's task is basically to verify that assertion. The proactive fraud auditor is not as fortunate. There are no assertions to be verified, other than the beginning presumption that there is no known fraud—but fraud may exist. Proactive fraud auditors would surely endorse mystery writer Agatha Christie's remarks when she wrote that: "a crime is like a fine omelet. You get your first clue of what's in it, when you put your fork in it."

This is very much the case in proactive fraud auditing. Auditors first must choose what to examine for fraud from the myriad of options that are available and then search for the clues that may signal the possibility that fraud is present. If auditors simply search for clues without any specific agenda, their chances of ever discovering fraud are minimal, if they exist at all.

Once, as I lectured young CPAs on fraud, I asked if any of them ever searched for evidence of fraud in their audits. One young man raised his hand and replied that he had. I asked if he would discuss the methods he used when looking for it, and he replied that occasionally, when he was engaged in a client audit, he would take a few moments to simply look around for fraud. He could not explain what techniques he used, or what he was looking for, but he stated that he would know fraud when he saw it. This is not intended to be a humorous story. There exists a general lack of training and experience among auditors who are otherwise very interested in searching for fraud. Of course, as an independent public accountant, the auditor who volunteered his response could not officially search for fraud under AICPA generally accepted auditing standards. Nevertheless, many CPAs who attend my lectures admit off the record that they spend some time searching for evidence of fraud, even though they lacked the authority, training, or experience.

ART OF FISHING

The practice of proactive fraud auditing can be illustrated best by comparing it to the art of fishing. Proactive fraud auditing is very much an art in that detection success depends on the auditor's exercise of his or her intuitive and creative talents. Whereas traditional auditors tend to be very methodical in their work—that is, "left-brain" oriented, relying on carefully considered generally accepted audit standards and tried and true audit procedures—experienced fraud auditors tend to be less inhibited in the conduct of their examinations and often rely substantially on their instincts and gut feelings; theirs is a "right-brain" orientation.

People who are not skilled fishermen think of fishing as a simple matter of hooking a worm, attaching the hook to the end of a line tied to a long pole, and dropping the hook into the water. It is possible to catch some fish this way, and many auditors search for fraud this way. But anyone who has done any serious fishing knows that this it is not the way to maximize the catch or to catch the fish of choice. Fishermen actually begin first by deciding what type of fish they wish to catch. Most game fish require very different fishing methodologies, fishing locales, and fishing gear, and the fisherman who elects to catch any one type of fish is unlikely to catch any other type of fish using the same methods, equipment, and technique. For example, the fisherman seeking to catch brook trout is unlikely to catch bass while fishing for brook trout.

The same is very true of fraud. Fraud auditors must begin by selecting a fraud type to attempt to detect. Once selected, fraud auditors design a program to detect the specific type of fraud selected, and only that type. Often the audit programs utilized are so specific to a particular type of fraud that the auditors are unlikely to detect any other type of fraud. For example, the auditor seeking to detect multiple payee fraud is unlikely to detect duplicate payment fraud, even though the latter fraud may be present in the transaction selected for examination.

There is one exception in the favorable comparison of fishing with proactive fraud auditing. In fishing, fishermen take pains not to scare the fish away. They want to catch fish, and quietly go about the sport. If the trout fisherman scares the trout away, he or she goes home unhappy. In proactive fraud auditing, just the opposite is true. Fraud auditors frequently make their audits as visible and noisy as possible in order to scare/deter fraud perpetrators away. If they can deter perpetrators from committing fraud with the threat of detection, the audit can be said to have been successful.

HOW PROACTIVE FRAUD AUDITORS THINK AND WORK

Proactive fraud auditors must cultivate a mind-set that is different from that of traditional auditors. To be proactive fraud auditors, traditional auditors must ignore all the rules they have learned in practicing their craft. It is difficult to illustrate this without returning to a whimsical comparison on how both auditor types—using techniques learned in their auditing professions—would approach a fishing challenge. For example, assume that a traditional auditor and a proactive fraud auditor both set out for a day of fishing. The objective of each was to catch as many walleye pike—a delicious freshwater fish—as possible.

After arriving at the lake, the traditional auditor, influenced by customary audit methodology to accomplish this task, proceeded to divide the lake into equal gridlike sections, to eliminate any bias, and throughout the day fished equally in each grid segment, carefully recording the number of walleye pike caught in each. This fisherman caught no fish. In fact, based on a statistical sample, which was calculated to provide a 98 percent confidence level, there were no walleye pike in the entire lake. He decided that it was futile to spend any more time fishing and went home to feast on chicken.

The fraud auditor, on the other hand, influenced by a methodology she was familiar with, was not interested in the numbers of walleye pike in the entire lake. She was interested only in catching enough for her dinner that evening. Accordingly, she programmed her search in such a manner as to maximize her chances of catching the wily pike. She would not search randomly in every part of the lake, as did the traditional auditor, because she knew that walleye pike did not inhabit all parts of the lake. Rather, she fished only in those parts of the lake where she knew the walleye pike would be, if there were any. Doing this allowed her to eliminate much of the center area of the lake, where she knew that the walleye pike spent little time. Why? She knew they have weak eyes and prefer the cooler, shady shorelines. She was also aware that the fish detested the bright sun and the heat of the day, and actively fed only in the early-morning and late-evening hours. Whereas her friend the traditional auditor slept late and had a late breakfast, she got up at sunup and missed breakfast to be on the lake when the fish were feeding, thereby increasing her chances of catching fish.

She did other things to catch her dinner as well, and when she left the lake in midmorning, she had enough fish to feed her entire family. Note that the fraud auditor here eschewed statistical sampling and was totally biased in choosing locations and times of the day to maximize her catch.

Returning to the real world, whereas traditional auditors normally are concerned with confirming the overall value and/or condition of something—such as a reported inventory balance or reported accounts receivable, proactive fraud auditors are less concerned with confirming the accuracy of an inventory balance or accounts receivable balance reported than they would be with analyzing the transactions that enter into determining the inventory or accounts receivable balance. Traditional auditors, on the other hand, are minimally interested in the inventory transactions, as long as the value of the inventory amount reported to be on hand is materially correct. A determination that the inventory on hand may have been materially depleted as a result of fraud several months earlier is not an audit objective of traditional independent auditors. For example, independent auditors engaged to verify financial statement balances—which included an inventory reported to be worth $100 million—would likely be satisfied if they were able physically to determine that the client actually possessed $100 million worth of goods. They would be likely to overlook a $1 million discrepancy in the reported balance as being immaterial. Fraud auditors, on the other hand, are less concerned with the correctness of the $100 million balance reported—because they know that although correctly reported, it nevertheless could have been fraudulently depleted—and would be very concerned with the $1 million inventory discrepancy.

Although both auditors routinely use statistical sampling, each is likely to use it somewhat differently. Traditional auditors make every effort to avoid bias in conducting and/or siting their audit testing to ensure that final test results are representative of the whole. As a result in their verification process, usually they are willing to accept values or test results with a predetermined confidence level of less than 100 percent—perhaps 95 to 98 percent. Fraud auditors are concerned that a determination of asset value through a statistical sampling process tends to eliminate any anomalies in the data universe that may be immaterial in terms of the total asset but that are of special interest to them. To fraud auditors, so-called anomalies may be the faint clues, or fraud indicia, that will lead them to the detection of fraud.

Fraud auditors rarely, if ever, use statistical sampling to detect fraud and normally thrive on their intuitive inclinations and hunches based on any threads of evidence that may be detected. However, fraud auditors do use statistical sampling for tasks such as testing the occurrence rate of known fraud that is allowed to continue. Allowed to continue? Yes. From time to time, recurring fraud is discovered that—strange as it may sound—an entity chooses not to stop. Entities sometimes choose not to eliminate an ongoing fraud that has been discovered because the control measures that would be required to stop or materially reduce the fraud would exceed the amount that it is estimated the entity is losing as a result of the fraud. Assume, for example, that it is estimated that a fraud that seems to be recurring is cumulatively resulting in a $50,000 annual loss. Assume further that it would cost $100,000 to stop it. How many entities, do you think, would be willing to spend $100,000 to stop a $50,000 loss? Annually? Most entities would not. In this instance not stopping the fraud is a sound business decision. However, if the victims did not, they would very likely wonder, and grow increasingly concerned as to whether the fraud that was discovered was diminishing or increasing. Statistical sampling often is used to monitor the fraud in the instance. Fraud auditors, when necessary, do monitor the size of such fraud losses annually by statistically sampling the occurrence rate of the fraud discovered. In this instance, a 95 percent confidence level may be acceptable, which would require a rather small audit effort. If auditors discover that the cumulative loss remains significantly under $100,000, they will very likely recommend that further fraud control action would not be cost beneficial. If the loss is determined to be near to or to exceed the $100,000 cost of controlling it, the auditors would very likely recommend that further control action be considered.

BEGINNING THE PROACTIVE FRAUD AUDIT

Proactive fraud auditors do not simply enter an employer's or client's office location and begin looking for fraud. To begin searching for fraud proactively, auditors must select a specific type of fraud to hunt for. Some proactive fraud auditors are specialists and search for only one type of fraud. By concentrating in one type of fraud, they become expert at catching their quarry. Those who search for fraudulent insurance claims are an example.

Whichever variety of fish the fishermen may choose to fish for, they are well aware that it will require specific unique methods, special equipment, a special place to fish, and fishing only at certain hours of the day. If they are looking to catch trout, they know that only special gear suitable for catching trout will do. They also have to know where the trout are feeding—perhaps a pool of water off a fast-moving stream—and when the trout are likely to be feeding, and on what. Also, fishermen know that, if they are not careful, their mere presence in the area will alarm the fish and diminish their chances for catching any. In fact, even when fishermen have done everything correctly, there is no assurance that they will be successful. Many fishermen believe that fish are wily creatures that possess a natural intelligence that allows them to survive.

Everything that fishermen must do to catch fish applies to proactive auditing. To begin with, fraud auditors who simply search for fraud without having something specific in mind before beginning will not be very likely to find any fraud. Like fishermen, proactive auditors must decide in advance of their search what type of fraud they are going to search for. It may be duplicate payment fraud, multiple payee fraud, shell fraud, defective delivery, defective shipment, defective pricing, contract rigging, unbalanced contracts, or any of dozens of others, including countless variations of those named. Once having decided which variety of fraud they will search for, auditors then have a better idea of what, where, and how to perform the examination and what sort of clues to look for.

Whatever type of fraud auditors choose to look for, doing so will require unique methods, perhaps expert assistance, a special place to look for the chosen fraud, and a special time to look. If auditors decide to search for defective delivery fraud, they may choose to forgo a detailed examination of any documents and go directly to the item that was allegedly delivered. If it was delivered in accordance with the purchase order or contract specifications, that may be all that is necessary for them to accomplish their audit program objectives. If the item that was allegedly delivered requires a technical determination of adequacy, auditors will have to acquire whatever technical assistance may be necessary to make that determination. They may engage a technical specialist to assist them, or provide samples of the product delivered for laboratory analysis. Also, auditors may choose to examine transactions only in a certain time period, such as at the end of a fiscal period, when bogus transactions are more likely to occur and organizational units may have excess budget authority to spend. Or they may choose to select their audit samples from the period immediately subsequent to their last audit.

SELECTING A FRAUD TYPE

Selecting the type of fraud that will be the object of search in a proactive fraud audit can be relatively simple or relatively involved. It can be arbitrary and decided literally by the toss of a coin on the spur of the moment.

However, more experienced auditors carefully schedule fraud types to be audited a year or more in advance, to ensure that ultimately they address all fraud types they wish to visit. Because auditors cannot look for everything, they must choose what type of fraud to look for at any given time. Whatever type of fraud they choose to search for, they understand that the procedures needed to detect it will likely miss another fraud type that may be thriving. However, to minimize the possibility of missing a fraud type completely, proactive fraud auditors, over a set time period, attempt to include a mix of all fraud types to which the entity being audited is vulnerable. Auditors also usually consider preparing a proactive fraud audit schedule, the entity's prior experience with fraud, either suspected or proven. If the entity has had prior cases of suspected fraud, auditors give that fraud category higher priority in the annual audit program. For example, if the entity has had a disturbing experience with duplicate payments to vendors or contractors, that fraud type should definitely be included in the upcoming schedule of audits.

FRAUD AUDIT PROCEDURE

The following is the basic procedure that would be followed in performing a proactive—and subsequently reactive—fraud-specific audit. For demonstration purposes the example case selected is hypothetical, and extremely simple. Nevertheless, the basic procedure is substantially the same for more involved and higher-dollar-value cases.

Decide the Type of Fraud to Search For

Let us assume that auditors choose to search for multiple payee fraud, which involves paying a legitimate vendor's invoice two or more times but issuing the additional checks to different payees. Usually each fictitious payee name chosen is different to preclude the accidental detection of duplicate payments to the same payee. Chapters 5, 6, and 7 discuss common frauds that auditors may have chosen.

Select a Suitable Accounting Transaction

Select a suitable accounting transaction that has been paid some time within the past year that distinguishes the fraud type selected. Obtain relevant underlying document records and files for the transaction selected and become familiar with contract or purchase order terms and product or service requirements, as may be appropriate. No verifications need be done at this point in the examination.

Perform the Audit Procedures

Multiple fraud payee is similar to duplicate payment fraud but is several degrees harder to detect. In duplicate payment fraud, the basic detection process involves scanning the payments made to a single vendor and identifying payments of like amounts for further examination. Any duplicates that are detected will be either unintentional errors—which do happen from time to time—or possibly fraud.

In seeking to detect multiple payee fraud scanning a single vendor's account for identical payment amounts will not reveal the fraudulent payments being sought. The perpetrator will have selected different payees as the recipients of record for whatever product or service justified the payment(s) to make accidental discovery less likely. Multiple payee fraud is the fraud of choice of many perpetrators because it is relatively simple to perpetrate and it is not as easy to detect as duplicate payment fraud. Perpetrators find multiple payee fraud convenient in that all of the justification underlying a payment to legitimate Contractor A—including a satisfactory receiving report—may be used to justify an identical payment to Contractor B and possibly Contractors C, D, and E. For example, inexperienced auditors who might select the payment to Contractor B for examination would not be likely to dwell on it because a legitimate project is involved, and it would be found to be properly authorized and satisfactorily delivered. What else is there to determine? However, the legitimate purchase order or contract could have been easily changed to insert Contractor B's name—or a similar name used—and a phony invoice prepared.

Multiple payee fraud is likely to be detected only if auditors are looking for it. If so, they will know that a limited examination of underlying documents will not disclose the fraud, nor will an inspection of the actual work or goods delivered. Accordingly, auditors limit or omit critical examination of the documents. They may visit the worksite, if it is a construction project, not to inspect the work but to attempt to elicit information from employees who witnessed the work being done, asking "Who did the work?" If it were goods or a service that was delivered, the same tactic may be useful. The questions "Who was the distributor?" or "Who was the service provider?" would be asked of possible witnesses.

One advisory is appropriate here. Auditors must never underestimate the cunning of fraud perpetrators even though some of them do turn out to be inept. Truly clever perpetrators will be aware of audit methods to detect them and will not select unlike names for the fictitious payees, such as, for example, Contractor A and Contractor B. Rather, they will be more likely to select phonetically similar names, such as the Smith Company versus the Smyth Company, or to make an insignificant character transposition in the multiple payee names so that it seems that a typographical error was made. They do this to throw off auditors who seek to determine who delivered the service or product involved. If someone tells them the Smith Company did the work, auditors could accept that to mean the Smyth Company was the real contractor or vendor. It is also done to throw off auditors who use computers to display all the work performed by only the Smith Company. Any names that are not spelled exactly, such as S-m-i-t-h, will not be displayed.

If no indicia of fraud are discovered, auditors must decide whether to pass the transaction selected, for audit time is valuable, or to go on. The decision is up to them, and they may do either. However, if they were to pass the transaction, they would have missed an opportunity to discover fraud here. Many auditors neglect to utilize auxiliary information systems for verification. For example, if the transaction represents payment for a maintenance or repair project, it is very likely that any expenditures are posted to recurring maintenance project ledgers. The entity's building maintenance department may maintain a record of the maintenance performed on each building—how many times and when a building or its rooms were painted, for example, or when the roof was resurfaced and when the floors were recarpeted. These sorts of data are essential for planning purposes. Since these nonaccounting records very likely are posted from invoices paid, any multiple payments would be likely to show up as duplicate postings to these records. If the multiple payments were for inventory items, quite possibly a review of inventory control records would show the duplicate postings. In fact, auditors may well consider initiating multiple payee fraud audits from records of item shortages disclosed by physical inventory counts. Obviously, if a multiple payee fraud involves paying two or more times for the purchase of a single item of inventory, a subsequent physical inventory count will reveal a shortage.

If Indicia Is Not Found

If no indicia of fraud is discovered, auditors pass the transaction and go on to another selection.

If Evidence Indicia Is Found

If indicia of fraud is found the auditor must seek additional evidence to validate the finding. For illustration purposes assume that the transaction selected involved a payment of $25,000 to the Smith Company to resurface employee parking lot number 3. On inquiring further, the auditor discovered that the Jones Company may have performed the work, and a review of payments to the Jones Company discovered a paid invoice for $25,000 for resurfacing employee parking lot number 3. Further, the auditor visits the address given for the Smith Company and discovers an empty lot.

In cases such as this when strong evidence of fraud is discovered, the auditors must take extra care to assure that their findings remain confidential, and begin to discreetly search for additional instances of the same fraud. Although, the evidence given in the illustration is strong enough to indicate that fraud has occurred, if prosecution is to be considered, it would be advisable to attempt to detect corroborating evidence. With just one case in evidence, the perpetrator(s), particularly if they are first time offenders, are not likely to be convicted in a lenient court, or may be convicted and be given a lenient sentence. However, experience has shown that when perpetrators are successful and are not detected, they will attempt other similar frauds and often will not change their successful modus operandi. That is, there is a good chance that—for the case given— the Smith Company will again be the bogus recipient of multiple payments. Accordingly, auditors' continuing examinations should begin with a search for any and all payments to the Smith Company. If any are found, they should be investigated. Note: One reason why perpetrators are likely to keep using the Smith Company is that they may have established a bank account under that name, and it is convenient to clear all checks through it. Other transactions involving the perpetrator suspect(s) should be examined for similar bogus payments or other frauds, under the theory that once auditors have found a thief, other thefts are likely. Consider once again the fishing analogy. Once fishermen have caught a fish—and may have identified a fishing hole at the point of the catch—they will fish the hole repeatedly in the expectation that they may have found the mother lode.

Auditors should discuss their initial finding of fraud by the Smith Company with the audit committee, if there is one, or whatever other company official has been designated as their confidante. Every chief auditor should have one. If there is no audit committee, usually the controller or chief financial officer is designated. During this meeting the engagement of an investigator to pursue case development should be discussed. The investigator should be brought into case development after the danger of any premature publicity is minimized. The investigator should be provided any evidence developed during the audit. After he or she has finished work, the case will be reviewed by council and a decision whether to prosecute will be made.

When prosecution is considered seriously, a prosecutor should be contacted. All fraud cases in which the sum of evidence is sufficient to eliminate reasonable doubt should be prosecuted.

SUMMARY

In carrying out a fraud audit plan, auditors must be resourceful and know that all audits will not be as successful as the case described. However, auditors will seldom be bored. In keeping with the old adage that "If something could possibly go wrong, it will!" an internal auditor attending a fraud lecture once told about an interesting actual experience he had.

Case 4.1 presents the auditors tale.

CASE 4.1 The Phantom Renovations

The auditor once attempted to verify approximately $450,000 in renovations and other improvements made to an older medical clinic building in Minnesota. Were he the typical internal auditor, he probably would have examined the underlying documents, found them all to be in order and all properly signed by medical administrators, including attestations that the improvements had been delivered satisfactorily. The average internal auditor would have taken no exceptions to the $450,000 project. However, he was an exceptionally good fraud auditor and chose to visit the site of the improvements to see them for himself. But when he went to inspect the work that had been done, he found that the building had been demolished, and a new building stood in its place.

Astounded, he reasoned "Why would anyone spend $450,000 in improvements to an old building that was soon to be demolished?" Of course, he reasoned "Why indeed?" and suspected fraud. However, he was at a dead end as far as the fraud evidence was concerned.

What would be your reaction were you to discover these circumstances? How do you verify that the $450,000 in improvements claimed were actually made? Sounds very suspicious. Ways and means of verifying delivery of the improvements were considered, as was the engagement of a private investigator. The auditor involved planned to begin interviewing the various people who may have had knowledge of the improvements, including contractors, workers, medical clinic employees, and so forth. It was our mutual supposition that clinic administrators attempted to cover a $450,000 unexplainable loss, very probably fraud, by charging it to the old clinic building, knowing it would be torn down within six months. The question that had not been answered was "What explanation would the contractors named have when asked about what they delivered for the $450,000 paid?" Because of the blatant nature of the circumstances, it is quite possible that medical management in this case "did not want the $450,000 expenditure investigated" and the auditor who was involved may have been told to "forget it." Auditors sometimes are faced with this sort of dilemma and must decide how to react. They have the hard choice of either "forgetting about it," as they may be instructed, and becoming a part of a cover-up, or pursuing it and being fired.

5

ELEMENTARY FRAUD TYPES

THREE ELEMENTARY FRAUD TYPES

This chapter begins the fraud auditing practice segment of the text with three elementary fraud types. They are rather simple to understand and are immensely popular with perpetrators who have limited opportunities to commit fraud; hence, fraud auditors cannot ignore testing for them periodically This chapter defines and discusses three fraud types: duplicate payment fraud, multiple payee fraud, and shell fraud.

Perpetration is relatively simple, which is perhaps why these frauds are practiced so widely. Many entities inadvertently make duplicate payments that are detected only when honest creditors return the duplicate checks. Although these three fraud types are relatively simple to commit, they are not always equally simple for auditors to detect, and all require very different detection methods to reveal them. However, using the appropriate detection procedures, on a comparative scale, all are among the easiest of frauds to detect. Each fraud type is discussed further and includes detection techniques and difficulties therein. Each fraud type discussed requires different detection methods. For that reason, fraud auditors must designate which type of fraud they are going to search for before beginning.

Duplicate Payment Fraud

As the name implies, duplicate payment fraud involves the issue of two or more identical checks to pay the same debt. One serves to pay the creditor, while the other(s) are recovered and cashed by the perpetrator.

Normally the fraud occurs when an employee of an entity, with criminal intent, initiates the necessary documentation to cause an additional payment(s) to be made to a vendor or contractor to satisfy a debt. The employee may act alone or in collusion of an employee of the vendor or contractor. The perpetrator arranges to intercept the second check, and any additional checks that may be issued, and cash them.

Multiple Payee Fraud

Multiple payee fraud is similar to duplicate payment fraud with a most important difference—the payment checks are not identical. This fraud involves two or more payments to different vendors or contractors for the same debt. One of the payees usually is the one that actually delivered the product or services being paid for. The other(s) are either fraudulent or conspirators in the fraud. The fraud probably was invented by someone familiar with fraud detection methods, in that multiple payee fraud is not detected as easily as duplicate payment fraud.

Shell Fraud

Shell fraud involves payments to vendors or contractors—real or fictitious—in payment of alleged debts for fictitious projects, materials, or services. All underlying documentation is forged. It may or may not involve conspiracy with contractors or suppliers. All of the payment money generated is pocketed by the perpetrator(s).

DUPLICATE PAYMENT FRAUD

Every entity has had the experience of unintentionally paying an invoice two or more times during the rush of business. It can happen very easily. Sometimes when payment is delayed, the vendor or contractor sends a second invoice, and both get paid. When duplicate payments occur, they usually happen very innocently on the part of all parties involved. Most times duplicate payments are returned by the recipients or credited to the paying entity's account.

However, when fraud is involved, an employee of the paying entity normally initiates whatever procedures are required to cause one or more checks to be issued that are identical to a check that already has been issued in payment of a legal debt. The duplicate payment(s) are intercepted or otherwise acquired by the perpetrator. If the paying entity's internal control is weak, the perpetrator simply takes the check out of the outgoing mail. Or the perpetrator will telephone the payee and explain that a duplicate check was inadvertently sent and that she would appreciate it if it would be returned to her attention when it is received. The fact that the payee's name is indicated on the check is usually no problem for a clever perpetrator. For example, it was reported in 1999 that a taxpayer's check made out to the IRS was stolen out of the IRS's mail and altered to read I R Stevenson.

The employee perpetrator may initiate the duplicate payment with a second copy of the vendor's invoice, which is easy to get simply by asking for one, or simply photocopying the original invoice. Copy machines may be used to reproduce any number of copies of an invoice—in faithful color—with no problems. Purchase orders, receiving documents, and the like prepared for the original invoice may be copied to "document" the duplicate payments. All approving signatures and initials can be forged easily. Internal controls may or may not be a deterrent.

Sometimes a dishonest employee will conspire with a vendor's employee, in which case the conspirator will provide second invoices, simplifying the preparation of a second check in payment, and assure acquisition of the duplicate payment check. If due care is taken in perpetrating duplicate payment fraud, the duplicate payment is rarely noticed, provided the perpetrating employee is not particularly greedy or careless.

Unless auditors are specifically looking for duplicate payment fraud, it is unlikely that it will be detected. Each of the duplicate payments is a complete and separate transaction, and each documentation package is complete and authentic, without flaws, and ordinarily will survive audit testing not designed to look for duplicate payments. If any one of the payments is selected for examination—either the original or one of the duplicates—traditional auditing practice will find the documentation package to be in perfect order. If auditors attempt to verify the product or service involved, they will find it was fully delivered with no exceptions to be taken. Unless they accidentally happen to select both payments for transaction testing an extremely unlikely event—either transaction will not be likely to attract traditional auditors' attention. In addition, audit testing performed to discover any of the other elementary frauds discussed in this chapter will not discover duplicate payment fraud.

However, if auditors have chosen to search for duplicate payment fraud, it is relatively easy to discover. Auditors look for identical payment amounts made to the same payee. Their scan of payment amounts can be done manually, for small businesses, visually using a computer monitor if the capability exists, or by using an automated search program, allowing a computer program to select out identical payment amounts made to the same payees. In the unlikely event transactions are numerous, appropriate parameters can be imposed, but normally the business volumes with any one vendor are small enough that a manual scan would be effective.

If two or more identical payment amounts to the same vendor are noted, auditors often can resolve the duplicates expeditiously by eliminating the duplicates where the time span between payments exceeds 30 days or by examining the underlying documents. If the documents bear identical dates, product items, and other characteristics, auditors can fairly well assume that they are duplicates. Most entities discovering duplicate payments automatically assume that error was involved. However, that can soon change when the payee insists that it received only one payment. A payee acknowledging that it received two payments generally—but not necessarily—indicates that the payment was not fraudulent. Some vendors, or more likely one of their employees, have been known to conspire in this type of fraud.

Before or after contacting the payee, auditors who suspect a duplicate payment also may verify the apparent duplicate receipt—or nonreceipt—of goods or services by consulting information system records such as inventory, maintenance or, housekeeping records, and the like, which usually are used to record the receipt of goods or services. A physical inspection of the items or services purchased is useful only if it is possible to inspect both apparent purchases. If any discrepancy is discovered, it is probably advisable to expand the verification procedure. Sometimes common sense alone will tell auditors that it is unlikely that two of a unique product, such as two roofs, were installed on warehouse number 3 during the same time period.

A word of advice to auditors. Be as cunning as the perpetrator is likely to be. If perpetrators are intelligent and aware of your discovery methods, they will make adjustments to frustrate your search. For example, if they make the slightest change in a duplicate payment amount—as little as 1¢ in applying a cash discount, for example—a computer matching of payment amounts will not recognize $12,397.14 as a duplicate of $12,397.13. To a computer they are two different numbers.

MULTIPLE PAYEE FRAUD

Multiple payee fraud involves two or more payments to different payees for the same item or service. One of the payments will be to the legitimate creditor; the other payment will be fraudulent.

Perpetration of multiple payee fraud is relatively easy in that, as in duplicate payment fraud, most of the supporting documentation underlying the legitimate transaction can be switched to support the bogus transaction(s) and will serve to give the bogus transaction(s) the appearance of legitimacy. Supporting documentation for the bogus payments usually utilizes the same purchase authorizations, purchase orders, and receiving reports as were used for the legitimate transaction. Most will allow the bogus transactions to pass all but the most exacting of examinations including confirmation with entity requesting or ordering officials.

The multiple payee fraud perpetrator may work alone. A bogus vendor name may be used, with an address or post office box controlled by the perpetrator to receive all payments. Multiple payee fraud is relatively detection resistant if the employee perpetrator works in collusion with an existing vendor or an employee of an existing vendor. In such cases they can use legitimate invoices and mailing addresses.

Multiple payee fraud is not difficult to discover—if it is being looked for—but it is a bit more difficult to detect than is duplicate payment fraud. If traditional auditors were to, by chance, select a transaction involving multiple payee fraud for examination, the transaction undoubtedly would pass most customary audit tests without any exceptions taken. Either of the payment files would have a fully documented support file that would satisfy most auditors. And audit procedures designed to detect duplicate payment frauds would not detect multiple payee fraud since no one vendor listing would have more than one of the payments on it, so scanning would not disclose any exceptions. If either payment is compared to the product or service that is being paid for, no exceptions are likely to be noticed.

Perhaps the quickest and easiest way, although not the surest, for auditors to search for multiple payee payments is to:

1. Select payments of goods or services to verify
2. Visit the site of where the project, goods, or services can be examined

At the site, the auditor can inspect the items in question in an attempt to determine if the performing contractor or vendor signed or marked the item delivered in any way. Many contractors do sign their work, and vendors usually mark the cartons delivered. If auditors can determine who delivered the items in this manner, and can match it to the payee selected, the test is over. Of course the auditor may have been unlucky enough to have selected the payment to the actual performing contractor or vendor, and missed the bogus payment. It is the luck of the draw.

However, if it appears that a contractor or vendor other than that whose name appears on the payment voucher actually delivered the item, the auditor may have found evidence of multiple payee fraud, where two or more contractors were paid for the one service, product, or project delivered. The finding should be considered indicia of fraud, and the auditor must check it out. To do so, it will be necessary to go back to the disbursement or contracting files and attempt to find the payment made to the new contractor or vendor name identified with the project, goods, or service examined. If the auditor can locate the payment made to the contractor or vendor who it appears actually delivered the item in question, the auditor may have proven at least one example of multiple payee fraud.

If the auditor cannot find the delivering vendor or contractor's mark on the item inspected, inquiries should be made of persons who might have knowledge of who supplied the product or services. It's auditing by conversation, but it is acceptable if it accomplishes the audit purposes. For example, if it's a construction job, when the construction site is visited, the project may be discussed with entity employees who may have observed the work when it was being done. Of course, the auditor's line of questioning need not convey the conversation's real purpose, but might start with a conversation with people in the area, and innocently remark "Nice work. Do you know who did it?" If it involves services delivered, the same conversation is usually effective if the person the auditor speaks with is aware of who the contractor is. But, discretion is called for. The auditor should not be so obvious as to make it appear fraud is suspected.

Queries frequently bring out the name of the real contractor who performed the work, with a remark such as "Yeah, the Charlie Company knows what they're doing." Not exactly high-tech auditing, but it can be effective. If supplies are involved, auditors can visit the storage area and examine the supply boxes. Often the packages bear the supplier's name or advertising. If the source names agree with the name on the payment document being examined, auditors may consider dropping the item and moving on to another. If the payment has been made to Delta Company, and it appears that Charlie Company shipped the goods, indicia of fraud that must be resolved may have been found. If auditors' suspicions of multiple payment fraud are strong enough, they must begin a search for the other payees, one of whom will be the vendor or contractor who actually delivered the product.

Depending on the accounting and information systems in use, other verification options may be available to auditors. Where multiple payments may be a possibility, they are likely to bear the same accounting codes. For example, if an item selected for examination bears an accounting code 2100, which let us assume is the code for exterior maintenance, a machine or visual scan of accounting code 2100 items may limit the transactions that auditors will have to review. For example, auditors can use a computer system to retrieve and display all account 2100 transactions for the 90-day period surrounding the date of the transaction being examined, or the number of transactions may be not be too excessive to scan all of them visually for similarities of amounts, or even the names of suppliers or contractors.

Additional testing auditors might employ to detect multiple payee fraud depends on the information systems in use by the victim and their reliability. In all proactive fraud audit examinations, auditors should be reasonably familiar with all nonaccounting information systems that may be available and know how they can be used to reveal information that the accounting records do not. For example, if the entity being examined maintains logs of maintenance performed on plant buildings or maintains a record of painting, which many entities do, a review of the records may reveal that the building involved was painted twice, or more often, in a short span of time. A review of these records may indicate a suspicious level or frequency of work performed, which can lead auditors to a review of applicable payments. It is also possible that if auditors were to select a bogus painting contract accidentally, by checking it to the information system, they might find that the painting was never posted to the painting record—an omission that should be questioned.

Why not scan the payments register for identical payments to discover multiple payee fraud? If a new warehouse roof was installed for $75,000, wouldn't detection result if $75,000 payments were scanned? Not if the perpetrator was at least moderately clever. First remember that, unlike duplicate payment fraud, payee names will be different, so any scanning would have to be with regard to amounts only. Further, there is nothing to prevent the perpetrator of multiple payee fraud from varying the amount of the payment. One of the new roof payments could be $75,000 and the other could be $71,500.

SHELL FRAUD

Shell fraud probably got its name from the old carnival game where con artists very obviously place an object under one of three half shells, each of which resembled half of a tennis ball. They would then move the shells around in such a manner that the victim was always certain that the object existed under one of the shells and was always sure where it was. The victim then would bet a sum of money that he or she was right. Of course, the con artists were expert on making the object disappear, so that it was not under any of the shells. No matter which shell the victim selected, it would be the wrong one. Shell frauds are so called because, like the object under the shells, the item that was purchased and paid for did not exist and never existed. Shell frauds are totally fictional. In some instances they are easy to detect; in some cases they are not.

In executing shell fraud, the perpetrator conceives of a fictional purchase and prepares all the necessary paperwork and accounting entries, forging whatever signatures are necessary and making all the necessary entries to acquire an item or services. Initial requisitions, authorizing documents, purchase orders or contracts, and receiving reports—whatever is needed to complete the document files—are all forged and fictitious. Finally, all the perpetrators have to do to obtain payment is submit a simple bogus invoice at the proper time.

Depending on the size of the entity and the internal controls in place, a perpetrator can work alone to accomplish a shell fraud, particularly if he or she is in a key position. Normally, however, shell frauds are best accomplished using an actual vendor or contractor serving in a conspiratorial role.

The federal government has experienced many cases of shell fraud. One case involved the government's office supply stores operated in various cities throughout the country, for the convenience of government agencies. Supply store managers were given the authority to purchase various items from commercial sources in wholesale quantities and to resell them to government customers on a retail basis. One day the government agency involved received a note from a jilted girlfriend of a store manager telling of his fraudulent practices. Subsequent audit and investigation initially discovered that, in the Baltimore store, brokers wholesaling various products were conspiring with store managers to purchase office supply products without any intention to deliver them or for the store to sell them.

All that was necessary was for the store manager to prepare a purchase order to buy $5,000 worth of ball-point pens through the broker. Two or three weeks later the store manager would prepare a receiving report to confirm that the pens had been received, even though they had not been. A short time later the broker mailed an invoice to the servicing government finance office. With the purchase order, the receiving report, and the vendor's invoice in hand, the automated payment system would mail a $5,000 check to the invoice address. At no time were the pens shipped. The cost was absorbed by charging higher prices on other merchandise sold. Because the stores, at that time, were operating on the retail inventory method of accounting, control of the fraudulent practice was difficult. Since it was impossible to determine what individual inventory item levels should be at any given time, it was not possible to take physical inventory counts and compare them to book inventory levels to detect shortages. Subsequently, automated item bar coding was implemented for inventory control and sales, making the fraud much more difficult to perpetrate.

Many other instances of shell fraud also have been disclosed. Building maintenance projects seemed to be a target of choice among perpetrators. There were paint jobs that were never done, walls that were never constructed to divide large rooms, and buildings that were never built. However, all were well documented with forged papers and bogus computer entries, and all fictitious vendors were paid promptly.

In another instance, fraud auditors testing an agency's automated supply control system detected what they believed to be an internal control weakness that would have permitted shell fraud. Testing it, utilizing a remote computer keyboard, they were able to enter an electronic purchase order into the system for $98,000 in tool kits, with an imaginary tool kit distributor. After delaying for about three weeks for the imaginary distributor to "deliver" the tool kits, the auditors used the same computer keyboard to "advise" the inventory control system that the tool kits had been received in the warehouse. The auditors then mailed a custom-printed invoice to the agency billing them $98,000, allowing a 2 percent cash discount for prompt payment. Within two weeks the auditors had a check in their hands for about $96,000. The cash discount had helped speed payment.

The best way to obtain assurance that shell fraud has not occurred is to determine that the project, supplies, or service has been delivered as claimed, at or about the time claimed, if at all possible. It simply involves selecting a payment transaction, selecting one or more line items from it, and going wherever is necessary to verify that the item has, in fact, been delivered. Reviewing maintenance records will not work.

To illustrate that shell frauds can be dollar significant, in a case in Chicago a perpetrator submitted totally fictitious purchase orders, receiving reports, and invoices for building cleaning services that were never performed. The services were for things such as carpet cleaning, washing walls, and cleaning Venetian blinds, and each invoice averaged about $10,000. The total aggregate fraud committed in this manner over several years was over $900,000. Luckily, the fraud was discovered accidentally. If the accidental discovery had not occurred, the fraud may never have been disclosed through auditing unless the auditor had the exceptional good fortune to select one of the perpetrator's invoices for fictional services soon after the service had been delivered and found that the carpet or the blinds had not been cleaned. It is difficult to verify nondelivery in this type of shell fraud when too much time has passed. Also, where a consumable or fungible commodity has been purchased, or a service is involved, it is not possible to see, touch, or feel it to confirm its delivery. In many instances it is not reasonably possible to inspect the work allegedly done.

Consider the difficulty in verifying that a dedicated electrical service line had been installed after a wall covering had been installed over it. The question always is how to verify that the service was delivered. The more ingenious the auditor, the more successful he or she will be in finding fraud.

Shell frauds can involve very large dollar amounts. Chapter 4 presented a case where the auditor of a medical clinic in Minnesota discovered $450,000 in payments to improve an old clinic building. When he went to inspect and verify the improvements, he found that the building had been demolished to make way for a new one. Although the final case results are unknown, the case described bears all the indications of being a shell fraud. In another instance, government auditors searching for defective delivery fraud selected a $1 million payment made to a contractor who had supposedly installed new floor tile at the super-secret CIA building on the outskirts of Washington, DC. The auditor found that no new tile had been installed. In fact, upon his inspection of the area in the corridors in which the tiles were said to be installed, he found the tiles were in excellent condition. He was about to "pass" on his defective delivery fraud under the presumption that they were the new tiles. Only later did he realize that the tiles were 9 inches square, whereas the new tiles were the then standard 12-inch square variety. The 9-inch tiles had not been manufactured for a number of years. Soon after, the case unraveled very quickly and the building manager and the contractor involved were charged with fraud. It was a totally bogus shell fraud.

There is no easy way to determine whether various products, projects, services, or supplies have been delivered when they cannot be readily identified and inspected. And, of course, clever perpetrators can be expected to select this sort of item to commit fraud because verification is a bit more difficult. Not all perpetrators are stupid. Where inspection is not possible, fraud auditors must attempt to verify that the items were delivered by contacting the supplier or contractor. This, of course, assumes that the suppliers or contractors are not in a criminal conspiracy with the internal perpetrator. But auditors must—at first, at least—trust that there is no conspiracy, and talk to the other party. If that person says that no such job was performed the auditors are lucky. In many cases there will not be a conspiracy, and the supplier or contractor named will quickly deny that anything was delivered. In contacting the supplier or contractor, auditors should not raise suspicions that anything improper is suspected. Rather, they can ask circuitous questions that verify the project was delivered, such as: "We are reviewing the X Company's relationship with suppliers. Were you paid on a timely basis for project X?"

Also, internal information system records—receiving registers, receiving documents, or even personnel records—which will vary from entity to entity, may offer avenues for verification. Auditors must become acquainted with them. For example, if Henry Jones signed for the receipt of the delivery of a large project, ask: "Was Henry Jones on duty the day the receipt was signed?" Auditors must be imaginative, perhaps even groping at straws, and look to auxiliary records for corroborating information sources if suspicions are aroused.

Consider Cases 5.1 and 5.2 examples of shell fraud based on actual fraud cases.

CASE 5.1 The Refurbished Water Tank

Government GSA auditors specifically looking for shell fraud selected a $5,000 payment that had been made to a general contractor for refurbishing a 10,000-gallon water tank located atop a 10-story building. The contract called for the contractor to drain the tank, scrape and clean the interior, coat the walls with a sealant, and refill the tank with water.

Since the auditors were searching for evidence of a shell fraud, they proceeded directly to the work-site to determine if the work had been accomplished. At the auditors' request, the building manager who had signed the receiving report attesting that the work had been done, showed them the tank high atop the building, and laughed, saying they would have a hard time inspecting the work, for the tank was full of water. But the auditors, who were experienced in fraud detection, anticipated the problem and had engaged the assistance of a technician who was qualified to inspect the work.

The technician rode the elevator to the building's roof and climbed the steel ladder attached to the side of the tank. At the top, he swung the access hatch aside, rolled up his sleeve, reached into the tank, and felt the interior surface. Next, he dragged his hand—fingers rigid—up along the side of the tank and withdrew it from the water. He held a handful of rusty scale proving that the tank had never been refurbished. It was a shell fraud.

CASE 5.2 The Phantom Building Services

In a federal government agency responsible for the management and maintenance of federal buildings in six states, an accounting clerk with access to the financial plans of all the buildings systematically forged the necessary documents to cause payments for building cleaning services that were never received. For example, he would prepare a purchase order requesting a cleaning service and forge a building manager's name. The document would be duly recorded in the automated accounting system as a purchase in process. The clerk used a fictitious contractor's name and a post office box address, which he controlled. Two or three weeks later, the clerk would forge a receiving report to advise the automated system that the service had been performed satisfactorily. Shortly thereafter he would mail a simple invoice for between $10,000 and $20,000. The automated system, noting that all prerequisites for payment had been satisfied, would mail a check to his post office box. He was eventually caught, accidentally, and prosecuted for perpetrating $300,000 in fraud. Privately, the auditors estimated his total theft was closer to $900,000.

A likely discovery strategy: This was a shell fraud that was discovered accidentally when a cash-short building manager, operating during a period of austerity, was challenged for performing discretionary maintenance at a time when he was seeking additional budget authority for necessary maintenance. In better times the fraud may not have been discovered. However, in this case, had an auditor happened to select one of the many fraudulent cleaning payments and asked the building manager if the cleaning service was performed, he would have said no. Of course, if the building manager had been the perpetrator, he would have said yes. In the actual case the building manager was among the prime suspects, and direct questions of that sort were not considered.

In Case 5.2, as in many shell fraud cases, the perpetrator used a fictitious contractor's name in submitting building services invoices. However, had one of the invoices submitted to gain payments been selected for shell fraud testing, a simple test—that is, determining if the contractor was legitimate—would have disclosed the fraud. Reference to telephone directories, Dun & Bradstreet credit directories, chambers of commerce directories, and similar business reference directories could have provided the clue that the payees were fictitious.

Where usual sources do not confirm the existence of a vendor or contractor, resourceful auditors always find another way. In one instance where the auditor was suspicious of a machine parts supplier allegedly located in a distant city, the auditor telephoned an acquaintance in the city where the vendor was supposed to be located and asked the associate to drive by the address to at least verify that there was indeed a business there. The auditor was not surprised to learn that the address given was that of an empty lot.

6

FRAUD DEFECTIVES

DEFECTIVE DELIVERY FRAUD

Defective delivery fraud involves the delivery of products or services that are inferior in some manner by a perpetrating vendor or contractor. Further, the vendor or contractor (1) intentionally caused the delivery to be "defective" in some way, (2) does not disclose the defect to the customer, and (3) does not offer a corresponding decrease in price to compensate the customer for the defective products or services. The products delivered may be less in quantity and/or of inferior quality to that ordered and paid for. Defective delivery fraud occurs very frequently and should be a regular proactive fraud audit pursuit.

Defective delivery fraud is undoubtedly one of the most common types of fraud that is perpetrated. Defective delivery fraud involves the secret substitution of such things as cheaper material, less material, a lesser quantity, cheaper labor, and/or less labor than the buying entity bargained for, without disclosing the substitution to the contracting entity and without giving a corresponding reduction in price. The perpetrating contractor or supplier profits to the extent of the reductions or substitutions that have been made. The classic defective delivery fraud involves the building contractor who cheats on the sand and cement mixture used in constructing bridges and buildings. The resulting concrete eventually crumbles and the bridge or building collapses.

All proactive fraud-specific audit schedules periodically should include procedures designed to detect defective delivery fraud. They occur in an infinite number of variations. The better part of this chapter is dedicated to communicating a comprehensive understanding of this fraud type and illustrating some of its many variations.

Usually conspiracy between the contractor or vendor and a key entity employee is necessary for defective receipt fraud to work. That is, normally a vendor or contractor considering defective delivery fraud would be deterred by a competent loyal employee of the victim, who would be charged with determining whether delivery met the employer's requirements. However, if the victim's employee who normally would determine whether the delivery met purchase order or contract requirements was dishonest, and in collusion with the delivering vendor or contractor, then the delivering vendor or contractor has nothing to fear—unless, of course, someone is proactively looking for defective delivery fraud.

In some instances, predictable negligence by some entity employee may be involved. Most internal control systems require that designated employees must complete a receiving report, or other attestation, certifying that the product or service was delivered in accordance with applicable purchase order or contract specifications before a vendor's invoice is processed for payment. However, if the employee responsible for accepting the delivery is noticeably negligent and easily distracted in performing this responsibility, a vendor or contractor may exploit this loophole. Sometimes vendors or contractors are known to be generous with Christmas gifts to key employees or to lavishly entertain them. Their payback is often a perfunctory examination of incoming goods or services received from those contractors. Anyone who wishes to see proof of this need only visit a large company's chief purchasing officer around the holidays. They will see cases of fine scotch whiskey and gifts piled high.

Defective delivery fraud can involve defects in materials or services. Materials delivered may be defective in quality and/or quantity. Instead of a high-quality material ordered, a cheaper material may be substituted. Instead of delivering 1,000 widgets, as were ordered and paid for, only 900 may have been delivered. Services delivered may be defective in one or more of several ways. Where the contract involves time and materials, for example, instead of 1,000 hours of service invoiced, only 900 may have been expended. And whereas the hours may have been billed as involving a senior technician's time, 300 of the hours may have been the hours of an apprentice, who earns one-third of the senior technician's wages.

To illustrate further, consider the following examples taken from actual cases of defective delivery fraud.

Defective Delivery of Services

A common example of defective delivery fraud involves interior painting. Many entities defer painting interior office space for an interval of five or more years to avoid the disruption of business that it causes. However, when painting is performed, it is common for building managers to contract for two coats of paint to be applied, to satisfactorily cover five or more years of wear, and to obtain full brilliance of any new colors applied. And, of course, the application of two coats of paint requires the expenditure of more labor and paint than does one coat; hence the cost is significantly greater than that for one coat.

The problem is, where two coats of paint are required by a contract, after the painting has been completed, how can anyone determine how many coats were applied? Perhaps more apropos, how does a company prove it received only one coat of paint? The problem is a very real one since dishonest painters do cheat by applying one coat when two were contracted for. In a rare public admission reported by the *Washington Post,* a painting contractor, Robert Lowry, told a reporter of his experience painting for the GSA:

> In exchange for kickbacks, GSA . . . paid for phantom paint jobs, for two coats of paint when only one was painted, for thousands upon thousands of square feet of nonexistent painting, plastering and repairing, thus hiking prices so that they and the contractors benefitted. . . . There were certain hitches, such as regulations that the building manager had to get three bids. So a kick-backing company merely made up companies. . . . The Washington Post disclosed that while Levcon had painted only 1.9 million square feet of wall and ceiling space in the GSA headquarters, it was actually paid for painting 2.4 million square feet.[1]

The government, with its millions of square feet of office space periodically in need of redecorating, has long been a victim of this variety of fraud. And every so often a government building manager has been a willing conspirator of the dishonest painter. In the Constitution Avenue building of the Department of Interior in Washington, DC, on one occasion a painter had completed a very extensive interior painting job, which required two coats for all interior wall surfaces. As was normal practice when the work was completed, he sought out the building manager to verify the satisfactory completion of his work, only to find that the manager he was accustomed to dealing with was no longer employed at that building. Nevertheless, he approached a young man who had newly assumed the manager's duties and asked that he sign for satisfactory receipt of the painting. He had applied only one of paint but offered the new manager $5,000 in cash for his certification acknowledging that two coats of paint had been applied, stating that the $5,000 payment was the customary amount expected in these circumstances for the job completion signature. Unsure of what to do, the young man said he wanted to think about it, and agreed to meet the next day. He later contacted the agency's criminal investigation office, which arranged to tape record the next day's conversation with the contractor. When the painter again offered the $5,000, he was arrested and charged with bribery.

What is especially noteworthy in this illustration of an actual crime is that the painter solicited the new building manager's signature without any concern for what was a criminal act. It was the customary way of doing business. He appeared to be not at all reticent or concerned with exposing his crime.

Ordinarily, an auditor performing a defective delivery fraud audit who attempts to determine if two coats of paint were in fact delivered as required will have a problem. Even if obviously only one coat of paint has been applied, it is the auditor's opinion against that of a skilled tradesman. The problem is particularly compelling if the examination is made months after the work is completed. And fraud auditors always must be concerned with compiling adequate evidence to support possible fraud charges against a painter. Their opinion would have very little worth in a court proceeding charging the painter with fraud. Merely eyeballing a newly painted wall is insufficient for alleging fraud or to claim a refund. In fact, it would be difficult even for an expert painter to conclude with certainty that only one coat was applied when two coats were required. How then can people protect themselves in this situation?

The answer is that there is no way that auditors can verify the application of two coats of paint under normal circumstances. However, they should not despair. There is a way to detect this specific fraud—with a little advance planning. What might it be?

The method for determining whether one or two coats of paint were applied lies within the contracting entity's internal control system. Consider, for example, the control effect if all painting contracts involving two coats of paint were to specify that the first coat must include a certain tint. How easy it would be then to determine at any time after the paint had been applied whether the new surface included two coats. A simple scratch in an obscure place would show two colors. Much of the government's painting now includes the requirement that the first coat be tinted to its specification.

Defective Delivery of Goods

Many vendors or contractors cheat by delivering less product than was ordered. This is done in a variety of ways. For example, a paint manufacturer in New Jersey used to "short fill" the paint cans he delivered to customers. Instead of putting 5 gallons of paint in a can, he would consistently put in something less. He was discovered, prosecuted, and convicted. A dairy farmer in Wisconsin diluted the milk he shipped to dairies by adding water. He was discovered, prosecuted, and convicted. On a consumer level, individuals are cheated on defective deliveries in a variety of ways all the time. One company would add finely crushed black rock resembling black oil sunflower seeds to its 50-pound bags of black oil sunflower bird seeds. Birds discovered their crime. They would eat the seeds and leave the added black rocks.

Defective delivery frauds are not always perpetrated by the vendors who supply the materials involved. Not infrequently, middlemen render defective the delivery of supplies. That is, a distributor may ship a customer's entire order as specified by the customer. But a truck driver delivering merchandise, for example, may deliver less than a customer's full shipment.

If the victim's receiving personnel are not careful in counting the entire shipment—they may be busy or shorthanded—a count shortage may go unnoticed. For example, a truck driver required to deliver 100 cases of a certain product may deliver only 90. If the shortage is noticed, the truck driver can readily acknowledge it and offer a plausible explanation. He or she may find the other 10 cases among other freight in the truck. Or, more likely, the truck driver may be involved in a conspiracy with the victim entity's receiving dock personnel. When the 90 cases are delivered, they are signed for as if 100 cases were delivered. If the victim's internal control system is not tightly structured, the 10 missing cases will always be a mystery, and warehouse theft will be most likely suspected.

An actual example of this occurred in a government warehouse in Maryland. The theft was discovered accidentally, when an alert government auditor, on his day off, happened to be shopping for bargains at a surplus sale in a commercial warehouse. While examining surplus furniture that he might have a personal use for, he noticed several new telephone secretary desks that he liked. On examining them further he noticed that the cartons bore standard government federal stock numbers (FSNs). He purchased one. When he returned to work the next day, he researched the FSN numbers and learned that the furniture items had only recently been introduced into the government's supply system and had never been sold as surplus. Further investigation revealed a conspiracy between the freight carrier and government receiving dock personnel. If 100 of something were to be delivered, for example, the delivery service would drop off a lesser quantity, say 90. The conspirator on the receiving dock would certify that 100 had been received, the book inventory would be increased by 100, and the vendor would be paid for shipping 100—which the vendor did. The discovery of the scheme solved a long-standing mystery and explained the discrepancies noted for several years between physical inventory counts and the book inventory. It had been thought to be caused by thefts from warehouse stocks and/or defective shipments.

Defective Delivery of Labor

This fraud involves substitution of less-qualified labor than specified and invoiced. When an entity contracts for a specific category of skilled labor and is invoiced for that skill level, but receives a skill level lower than that agreed to, that is fraud. For example, if an entity wishes to have electrical work performed in a building and enters into a contract with an electrical contractor that specifies estimated hours of work by a master electrician at an hourly rate of, say $75 an hour, any work performed by an electrician of a lesser skill level could be fraud, if the less-qualified person was billed at the master electrician's rate. Consider Case 6.1

CASE 6.1 Contract Wage Costs Fraudulently Increased

A large computer software company contracted to provide data processing system engineers to design a sophisticated new government automated system. It was agreed that the contractor would be reimbursed on a time and material basis. The contract price was to be determined on the basis of the actual number of hours required, to be billed at agreed-to hourly rates for the various skill levels of computer engineers who would be actually assigned to do the work. That is, senior engineer hours would be reimbursed at, for example (not actual), $150 an hour, intermediate engineers at a rate of $100 an hour, and junior engineers at a rate of $75 an hour. As with all government contracts, it reserved the right to examine the contractor's records. The rates included overhead and profit.

A typical progress billing for hours expended resembled the following:

Period: January 20XX
Senior engineers:

J. P. Jones	160 hours @ $150 =	$24,000
Intermediate engineers:		
Al Smyth	200 hours @ $100 =	$20,000
Thomas Jepson	190 hours @ $100 =	19,000
Sheryl Upton	200 hours @ $100 =	20,000
Mary Shipp	200 hours @ $100 =	20,000
Barry Sullivan	75 hours @ $100 =	7,500
Junior engineers:		
John Maxtor	190 hours @ $75 =	$14,250
Bixby Fenster	35 hours @ $75 =	2,625
Total Costs January 20XX		$127,375

When government auditors examined the computer company's records, they discovered that computer engineer skill classifications for Jones, Smyth, Shipp, and Sullivan were all correct as billed. However, Jepson and Upton were junior engineers and should have been billed at the $75 rate. This illustration is fictitious, but the fraud was real, and simplified here only to illustrate the finding. The actual fraud involved hundreds of thousands of dollars. The contractor, a nationally known company, was prosecuted, and convicted.

Defective Delivery of Building Construction

Over the years there have been many examples where building construction contractors have substituted inferior materials, or taken other money-saving but harmful shortcuts, in the supporting walls and supports of bridges and buildings under construction. When the bridges and buildings fail, the loss of lives can be catastrophic and the architects and contractors involved are disgraced. Of course, they normally come to the public's attention only when they fail. See Case 6.2.

CASE 6.2 Building Construction Quality Degradation

In a major U.S. city today, there exists a functioning government high-rise building (which must go unnamed; sorry) that contains several serious defective deliveries, the most serious of which is that the poured concrete walls of the structure were "cold poured," whereas the construction contract required that the concrete walls be poured continuously. When concrete is poured continuously, all of the concrete—regardless of how much is poured—fuses together to form one solid very strong block of material. This is most desirable for concrete walls to maximize their structural strength. The process is expensive, however, when much concrete must be poured, because considerable overtime and night differential wages must be paid over as many days as may be necessary to finish the wall.

The alternative is cold pouring the concrete. Basically this means that concrete is poured into the forms until a convenient time to stop is reached. This may be the end of a regular workday or at that point when it is necessary to erect additional forms. The concrete pouring process is resumed the next day. The problem is that the concrete that is poured the first day hardens before the next day's concrete can be poured. When pouring is resumed the next day, it is poured on top of the previous day's pour. Where the two pours meet, no fusing occurs, and a fault line is created. In effect, what happens is that two or more huge blocks of concrete are created, one sitting on top of the other. The fault line between the slabs weakens the structural strength of the wall, and under the right conditions—perhaps a mild earthquake—the wall can collapse. Or perhaps it will never fall. However, fault line(s) in a building over 10 or more stories high are very serious. In addition, the building contractor further weakened the walls by discarding scrap lumber into the wet concrete mix. Hundreds of people work in this building today. The government chose never to pursue the defective delivery. The remedy would be literally demolishing the structure and starting over.

There was an interesting complication to Case 6.2. The government, to ensure that the contractor complied with contract specifications—which required wet-pouring the concrete walls and no construction debris discarded into the concrete mix—assigned a government building engineer to spend full time at the site to maintain surveillance over the construction process. This required the engineer to travel to the building site from his home, a considerable distance away, and return home each week. In effect, the on-site engineer was to be the government's quality control representative. His purpose was to ensure that the contractor complied with contract requirements. Foolproof? No. It seems the engineer had a mistress in a third city whom he chose to spend his weeks away from home with. His absence from the construction site allowed the building contractor to deviate from contract specifications as he chose.

Active internal controls, depend on the integrity of the people who operate them, and they cannot always be relied on. The conclusion of this story is that the wayward engineer's deeds were discovered—after the building had been erected. He was allowed to resign without prosecution after he agreed to repay the travel and subsistence expenses he was given during the period he spent with his mistress.

A variation on defective delivery fraud requires a little advance planning on the perpetrators' part to include superfluous specifications in a contract or purchase order. As the product or service is being delivered, the superfluous features are eliminated. However, the vendor's invoice still includes the cost of the superfluous specifications required, and the victim pays for them. The result is the delivery of a perfectly satisfactory product or service, which is not likely to raise objections—or suspicions of inadequacy from users. In other words, although a defective delivery fraud may be involved, the product or service delivered is in no way defective or otherwise unsatisfactory. The victim merely ends up paying for superfluous contract specifications never received. Since no defects are involved, unless a proactive fraud auditor is clever and looks for this fraud, it is never discovered and there are no complaints.

Detection Tips

Ordinarily defective delivery fraud is very easy to detect. All auditors need to do is to determine that the product or service that was contracted for was delivered in all significant respects. Doing so requires a review of the contract or purchase order that was issued to determine exactly what was required of the vendor or contractor and a comparison of one or more of the line items on it to the actual product or service delivered. Often this process is more difficult to execute than it is to describe, but it is what is required. There is rarely a substitute for auditors' verification of actual delivery.

In some instances, especially where fraud may be involved, verification of delivery is not always so easy. In Chapter 5, under shell fraud, an example was presented where $450,000 was apparently spent remodeling an old medical clinic building. When the auditor went to verify the improvements, he found that the building had been torn down, eliminating his opportunity to see for himself what was done. In such instances—each of which will have differing circumstances—auditors must be resourceful in verifying the satisfactory delivery of goods or services.

Internal controls will not receive major coverage in this text. However, as they specifically apply to audit topics under discussion, they must be mentioned. In some instances internal controls can be considerably more effective than proactive auditing to control fraud, and auditors should identify opportunities where new internal controls would be beneficial in deterring or detecting fraud.

To control instances of one coat of paint being substituted for two coats, as was described previously, the tinted first coat idea is what is know as a passive or risk internal control. The term "passive" is derived from the fact that once the control is initiated, it does not have to be maintained constantly. It just exists and continues to serve its intended control purpose without any continuing cost or additional effort.

The tinted first coat of paint requirement, which costs little if anything to accomplish, does not prevent painters from applying only one coat.

However, should they do so, the evidence of defective delivery of services remains an ever-present and effective indicia of fraud. It is an unavoidable indicator of defective delivery just waiting to be discovered. Painters who claim that they did apply two coats of paint as required but simply forgot to tint the first coat, if not fraudulent, at the very least lose their proof that they applied two coats and should be reimbursed only for applying one coat. One mistake normally is insufficient basis for alleging fraud. However, if auditors find that painters have "forgotten" to apply the tint more than once, those painters are very much in jeopardy of being charged with fraud.

In a sense, passive controls are analogous to land mines. Once the mines are buried on the perimeter of anything that must be protected, it is no longer necessary to actively guard that area quite as intensely. There is peril, or risk, for anyone choosing to enter the prohibited area. Another passive internal control that most accountants and auditors are familiar with are so-called audit trails. Audit trails do not prevent fraud from happening, but they do allow auditors to backtrack a transaction trail to the one that originated an entry of interest. Hence a perpetrator initiating a fraudulent accounting entry is always at risk of being identified through the audit trail that was left as a part of the permanent record. Passive internal controls do not prevent fraud but they do put perpetrators at risk, which often is sufficient to deter them.

Defective receipt fraud is similar to shell fraud in that victims pay for something that they do not receive. Often verification procedures similar to those used to detect shell fraud can be used to detect defective deliveries. However, there is a significant difference between the two fraud types. In shell fraud a fictitious purchase is involved, and detection is normally relatively easy. Nothing is delivered, and often that fact can be determined readily. In defective receipt fraud, a legitimate purchase is involved, and a product or service is newly delivered, but victims do not get the full measure of the product or services ordered.

For example, if a contract called for carpeting an executive dining room, and shell fraud was involved, the dining room would not be newly carpeted, and a quick inspection would quickly establish this. In defective delivery fraud, the contract might require carpeting the dining room with $100-a-yard carpeting. The contractor's invoice would indicate that the dining room was carpeted with $100-a-yard carpeting as specified, and the victim would pay for the $100-a-yard carpeting price if a substitution was not detected. But let us assume that the dining room was, in fact, carpeted with $50-a-yard carpeting. Whereas in shell fraud auditors would only need to look to see if new carpeting had been delivered, if defective delivery fraud had occurred, auditors would have to go beyond looking for a new carpeting installation to determine whether the contractor actually had delivered the $100-a-yard carpeting. To do this auditors probably would have to obtain a sample of the carpeting and take it to an expert for appraisal, or engage an independent carpeting expert to visit the site. It also might be a good idea for auditors to recompute the number of square yards of carpeting required to carpet the dining room. Determining that the entity involved actually received the full quality and quantity of product required and invoiced often requires the services of experts. Auditors should not hesitate to hire such experts if verification of product or service delivery requires it.

DEFECTIVE SHIPMENT FRAUD

Defective shipment fraud involves the shipment or provision of products or services, by the victim, that (1) are superior in some manner and (2) do not include a corresponding increase in price to compensate the victim. The victim, of course, is not aware of the excess products or services being shipped or otherwise provided. Defective shipment fraud may involve everything from relatively petty fraud to large sums. Perhaps the greatest incidence of defective shipment fraud occurs in shipments from victim's warehouses. Whereas a shipping order may call for the shipment of 100 of some product, 110 are shipped. Whereas a grade B product should be shipped, a grade A product is substituted. See Case 6.3.

CASE 6.3   The Diamond Caper

In a transaction that suggests the possibility of defective shipping fraud, although fraud was never charged, in 1975 the custodian (GSA) of the U.S. strategic materials stockpile entered into a negotiated contract with Country X to sell it 300,000 carats of industrial diamond stones. The regulations that allowed the negotiated sale, as opposed to normal advertised sales, provided that the quality mix of diamonds sold be consistent with that previously sold at advertised sales. The reason for this was to provide a market basis for negotiating prices. No price advantage was to be given to the buyer. Also, it was U.S. policy that the quality mix sold was to include a suitable blend of high-quality as well as low-quality diamonds so as to assure U.S. stockpile retention of as many high-quality diamonds as possible, while still obtaining maximum competition in advertised offerings. The total price for the 300,000 carats sold was slightly over $9 million.

The sale appeared to be consummated without incident. However, subsequent to the sale, representatives of the diamond industry questioned the quality mix of diamonds delivered to the buyer. In short, they charged that a disproportionate amount of higher-quality diamonds were included in the batches delivered. And, if the allegations were true, the loss to U.S. taxpayers was the difference in value between the disproportionately higher-quality diamond batches delivered—which was not authorized by the U.S. Congress—and the $9 million paid for the standard-quality mixes included in diamond batches previously advertised.

This illustration was taken from a GSA internal audit report. The internal auditors noted that the mix of diamond quality sold to Country X, as compared to past sealed bid sales, was:

	Diamond Mix Sold to Country X	Diamond Mix Sold at Past Sealed Bids
First Quality:	71.3%	25%
Second Quality:	27.5%	35%
Third Quality:	1.3%	40%

The negotiated price for the noncompetitive sale to Country X was required to be based on the per-carat price realized in past sealed bids. For the price of a 25%/35%/40% diamond quality mix, Country X received a 71%/28%/1% mix. This was contrary to the wishes of Congress and to the U.S. government's official requirements.

Who was the victim in this case? The American public, of course.

Retail merchants are frequent victims of defective shipment fraud, which may involve undercharging the customer (a conspirator) for products. Sales clerks are known to undercharge friends for items purchased. The widespread use of product UPC codes limited the practice of this fraud somewhat. However, any enterprising thief need only have available the UPC code from a cheaper product at the time a confederate presents an item for payment and to scan it to register a cheaper selling price. Accordingly, a confederate presenting a $220 item at a cash register may be charged only $20 if the cashier scans a product code for the $20 item, resulting in a $200 loss in revenue for the merchant. Some merchants attempting to control this fraud routinely have a guard at exit doors to verify that the products sold were correctly charged.

In other instances trusted employees substitute more costly materials or labor than those that were contracted for. The fraud type always involves conspiracy between an employee of the shipping entity and the recipient of the supplies or services that are being purchased. In some cases victim entities are defrauded when dishonest employees fatten legitimate outgoing shipments from warehouses. This is possible because of weak internal controls or lax or dishonest employees responsible for administering controls, coupled with the victim entity's over reliance on the effectiveness of internal controls without periodic audit verifications. In illustration of how serious this can be, a fraud that occurred in the 1970s was reported by construction workers in Chicago. They told of an individual who periodically visited building construction sites to "take orders" for power tools available for sale through catalog departments of a company. Any construction workers wishing to purchase tools needed only to browse through a catalog to pick from a wide selection that were available, noting the stock order numbers of the items they wished to buy. When the man returned the following week, the construction workers would provide him with the necessary stock numbers for the items they wanted. They would get the exact tools they ordered delivered to their worksites the following week at one-half of the catalog price.

Because of the regularity and precision of the man's delivery schedule, it is reasonable to assume that the items were obtained from a large catalog warehouse then located in Chicago. How was it done? The most probable answer is that they were being added to legitimate orders being shipped out the warehouse door. Someone responsible for ensuring that only legitimate orders left the warehouse obviously was not doing his or her job. It must be assumed that the company had tight internal controls in place to prevent anyone from simply walking away with merchandise of their choosing, especially expensive small tools normally categorized as sensitive inventory. However, internal controls are totally dependent on the honesty and integrity of the people charged with maintaining the controls, and entities who rely on them totally are asking for trouble.

Active internal controls are the first line of defense against defective shipment fraud. However, active controls are much like chains: They are only as strong as their weakest links. Accordingly, although active internal controls are strongly advocated to prevent defective shipment fraud, they must not be totally relied on. Auditing, as a passive internal control procedure, designed to periodically test the efficacy of active internal controls is the most effective way of ensuring the prevention and/or deterrence of defective shipment fraud.

Accountants or auditors must periodically, on a surprise basis, observe or otherwise test internal control efficacy. They should determine that control personnel are rotated periodically and should periodically check the materials and/or supplies in the process of being delivered to determine that they are in agreement with warehouse shipping orders or sales orders. Where services are involved, auditors should periodically match invoices with personnel time cards to determine that the personnel services as billed were correctly billed.

DEFECTIVE PRICING FRAUD

Defective pricing fraud usually involves charging the victim a price higher than the price that was agreed on or falsely representing prices so as to deceive the victim. The fraud does not appear to be widely practiced and often is easily detected by proactive fraud auditing. An inside conspirator is almost always involved.

In most instances, defective pricing fraud works very simply. A contractor and a contracting entity will enter into a contract to provide goods or services over a period of time, in accordance with prices set by the contract. The contractor periodically invoices the contracting entity at a higher price than that provided by the contract, and a conspirator—an employee of the contracting entity—approves the amount requested. If the conspirator is strategically placed, excessive billings are rarely questioned.

Usually the scheme is more complicated than simply agreeing to charge a set sum for some specific unit of services or goods. For example, the contract will not be so easily verifiable as to stipulate that the price for widgets ordered will be $150 each or the price of services delivered will be $100 per hour. Rather, more often these term contracts set the contract unit prices at something that reflects the market price, such as the contractor's most current published or catalog price for widgets, or an hour of service, all less 40 percent. Accordingly, contract negotiation usually dwells on the amount of the discount allowed rather than the unit prices charged.

As the contractor is called upon to provide goods or services in accordance with the contract, the goods or services are delivered in an acceptable manner. Subsequent billing, however, usually is flawed so that the contracting entity is overcharged. Often the overcharging is so cleverly done that if it is discovered, it is assumed to be an honest mistake or plausible error, and the person finding the error is given a pat on the back. This sort of overcharge happened in a northern Virginia city in 1999. A city clerk who was checking invoices received from a company that provided services to the city on a regular basis happened to discover what was subsequently described as an "unintentional careless error" by the company that had happened for several months in a row. The company apologized and refunded the amount of the overcharges, the clerk discovering the error was given a commendation, and the incident was quickly forgotten.

In another case, government auditors found a similar "careless" pricing error. The auditors—who were not trained or sensitized in fraud auditing—were examining payment transactions, and had selected a payment of about $5,000 for cleaning Venetian blinds. The cleaning had been performed in accordance with the provisions of a term contract, which stipulated that the contractor would be paid based on the square feet of blinds cleaned at the price per square foot advertised in the contractor's most recently published catalog. The auditors checked the square feet cleaned and found the contractor's claim correct. Next they checked the contractor's most recent catalog and found the unit price correct. They were about to go on to another payment when one of the auditors remembered that the total prices, determined as described, were subject to a 25 percent discount. The contractor had forgotten to apply the discount, and the government supervisor who approved the invoice for payment had not noticed that the invoice did not include the discount. The auditor promptly reported his finding to building management, who notified the contractor of the overcharge. The contractor apologized for his error and promptly refunded about $1,200. The auditor was commended for his discovery and resultant savings.

In the postaudit review of the way this transaction was handled, the auditors were commended for detecting the overcharge and then counseled on the fraud audit opportunity they missed. Their mistake was not being properly sensitive to the possibility that fraud might have been involved. Had they been sensitized, they would have kept their finding of the overcharge confidential and treated it as if it were indicia of fraud. As indicia of fraud they would have examined other cleaning jobs performed by the same contractor and involving the same supervisor who approved the invoice. If no additional similar overcharges were noted, the error possibility could have been accepted, and management could have been notified to obtain a refund for the overcharge on the invoice examined. If more were found, fraud charges could be considered, depending on the circumstances. At the very least, the finding of more incidents of this nature would have increased the refunds due. Also, the supervisor who approved the invoices without requiring that the discount be applied could and should have been disciplined for negligence. And the entity involved could have considered barring the contractor from further business.

In some instances a vendor or contractor simply charges higher unit prices than those agreed to in the contract. Although most internal control systems require someone to review and approve an invoice before payment, many individuals charged with this responsibility tend to trust the companies submitting the invoices—especially if they have been periodically rewarded with generous gratuities—and give the invoices a cursory review, if any at all. This is one of the hazards faced by employers who allow their employees to accept gratuities from vendors or contractors. To avoid the problem at least partially, companies are well advised to adopt a zero gratuity policy.

Does defective pricing fraud only involve relatively small amounts? No. In Case 6.4, the government almost lost $1 million on a defective pricing fraud. The fraud involves a government purchase of about $10 million in office furniture.

CASE 6.4 The Disappearing Discount

The case began with a visit by Manufacturer X to the government's furniture procurement agency to solicit a large furniture contract. The manufacturer had been a producer of furniture for the government in the past and made essentially this offer:

> "In return for a furniture contract for approximately $10 million, which would be our cost of production, we will waive our normal 10 percent profit of $1 million on the order. We make this offer to keep our factory busy, recover our overhead, and retain our employee workforce."

The government, which normally warehouses the furniture items offered for issue to government agencies, thought it was good business for both parties and gave the manufacturer the contract requested.

During the production period there were several changes to the design of the furniture being manufactured, which resulted in the need to hold a price renegotiation conference after the production required by the contract furniture had been completed, about two years later. Government personnel as well as those representing

Manufacturer X sat around the negotiating table, while the manufacturer presented his price recapitulation. In addition to his total manufacturing costs of about $10 million, Manufacturer X added about 10 percent, or $1 million in profit. The government's contracting personnel reviewed the contract file, saw no reason to question the manufacturer's price summary, and adjourned the meeting for several days to prepare the final documents.

As luck would have it, an auditor had the opportunity to witness the renegotiation proceeding. He vaguely remembered the manufacturer's offer to waive his $1 million in profit but wasn't certain. The next day he returned to his office and reviewed the audit file on the contract. The auditor was a pack rat. He had saved a copy of everything that had taken place since inception of the contract—including a photocopy of the document signed by both parties agreeing to waive the $1 million profit. The manufacturer had substituted a similar document in his file that did not show that profit had been waived. Interestingly, the copy of the document waiving his profit was also missing from the government's official file. The auditor's copy of the document prevailed, and the manufacturer's claim for $1 million in profit was denied.

At the time this all happened, the question that seemed to defy solution was: Why didn't the government's file include the document that the auditor had in his file? An unrelated event that occurred six or seven years later suggested the answer. One of the officers of Manufacturer X was involved in the prosecution of another firm. During his questioning, it was revealed that Manufacturer X had been paying a government employee $500 a month to perform certain favors. Could he have removed the critical document from the government's files?

In pursuing defective pricing fraud, auditors always should become thoroughly familiar with the contractor purchase order terms and specifications. When examining invoices, auditors must make certain that all the terms were correctly applied to the invoice and that the contract or purchase order specifications agree with the contractor's or vendor's invoice.

For large contracts, auditors occasionally should extend the audit procedures to determine that the contract specifications are correct. That is, they should ensure that contract specifications were not altered after the contractor's proposal was accepted. This can be accomplished by examining

the detailed price proposal submitted by the contractor when responding
to the invitation for bids (IFB)—if it is an advertised contract—or reviewing the records of negotiation if it is a negotiated contract.

NOTES

1. Myra MacPherson, "The Making of the Whistle Blower: Robert Lowry's
   GSA Scandal Stories," *Washington Post,* September 20, 1978.

7

CONTRACT RIGGING FRAUD

DEFINITION

"To rig" is defined by the *American Heritage Dictionary* in the context of contract rigging fraud as "to manipulate dishonestly for personal gain." The term "contract rigging" is generally used to describe those clandestine and intentional acts that serve to give an unfair advantage to the contractor or rigger.

Although contracts are rigged, or manipulated, for criminal purposes in a multiplicity of ways, they always tend to involve a two-stage process. Stage 1 involves doing whatever is necessary to obtain the contract award. Stage 2 involves the actual mechanics of defrauding the victim. Contract rigging almost always involves conspiracy between an employee of the contracting entity and the contractor. Where contracts are rigged, the resultant fraud is usually very significant in terms of dollar cost to the victim.

OBTAINING THE CONTRACT

The necessary first objective of a perpetrator engaged in contract rigging fraud (CRF) is to obtain the award of the contract. This is absolutely necessary if the perpetrator is to gain the opportunity to fleece the victim.

Advertised Contract Awards

Most entities believe that the best way to protect themselves from fraud—and to ensure that they have obtained the lowest price for whatever it is that they wish to acquire—is to advertise their intentions and to allow the marketplace to respond to their invitations to bid. They then may select the lowest qualified bidder from those vendors or contractors who responded. The theory is that this practice allows the marketplace to determine the best contract price and ensures that the contractor will be selected impartially. Most entities, public and private, require the use of this advertising process in the naive belief that it protects their interests. They believe that interested contractors will sharpen their pencils and, in competing with each other, offer their lowest prices.

In the perfect world, this process probably would work very well. However, we do not live in a perfect world, and the process is badly flawed. Undoubtedly many honest contractors do respond to entity invitations to bid on proposed major acquisitions. However, dishonest contractors are also likely to respond. And there are several ways that dishonest contractors are able to submit low price bids and win contract awards. Some involve plans to engage in defective delivery fraud to lower their cost expenditures by substituting cheaper materials and labor. Or they may engage in contract rotation fraud, wherein a number of contractors will conspire to submit bids in response to an advertisement, allowing a chosen one of their number to submit the lowest bid, and to give the appearance of competition. On large contracts, however, contract rigging is a favorite practice of dishonest contractors.

Advertised Acquisition Process

When entities decide on a major acquisition, such as a construction project, for example, and are ready to select a contractor, they usually publish their intentions in a newspaper or other appropriate regional media, to invite all prospective contractors who may wish to compete to make their interest known to the advertising entity. Those contractors who express their interests are given IFBs, which include a complete set of blueprints, related specifications, and all information that may be necessary to allow each contractor to prepare cost estimates. Usually they are instructed to submit a sealed price proposal. Normally the advertising entity makes it known that the sealed bids submitted will be opened at a specified time and place. The low bidder determined to be qualified will be awarded the contract.

Getting the Contract Award

To gain the opportunity to rig the contract, any contractor intending to engage in contract rigging fraud must underbid all other bidders in order to be awarded the contract.

Submitting the lowest bid is rarely a problem for contractors planning CRF. There are two ways to ensure that they submit the lowest bid. The simplest way, if possible, is to have a confederate—usually a key employee of the contracting entity—who will provide the amount of the lowest bid received from the other bidders. The contractor, of course, must delay submitting a bid until the very last moment. Then the contractor to take advantage of this information, need only to bid a small amount under the lowest bid to obtain the contract award. No one ever questions a bid that is close to the other bids. In fact, this is often regarded as a sign of a very competitive marketplace.

However, this procedure is rarely possible because most entities require that all bids received be sealed, to be opened in a forum including all interested bidders, at a previously announced time and place. In such instances there is no opportunity for a confederate to observe the lowest bid and inform the dishonest contractor of other prices that were offered.

Where perpetrating contractors do not have the advantage of knowing the other bids submitted in advance, their submission of the lowest bid is made more difficult. However, they have an advantage in that they do not have to submit a price proposal that will make a profit. In contract rigging fraud, the profit is realized in stage 2. Accordingly, preparation of a price proposal is dominated not by computations of what production costs are likely to be but by estimates of what other interested contractors are likely to bid, so that perpetrators do not bid so low that the bid appears totally unrealistic. Many bids submitted by CRF contractors would result in their financial ruin if they were required to complete the contracts ultimately awarded to them without the rigging opportunities contemplated in stage 2.

Where inside conspirators are sufficiently influential, one scheme gives conspiring contractors an opportunity to know the prices other contractors have bid and gives them a second opportunity to adjust their prices after a sealed bid opening. In a large contracting action, the government sought to lease about 400,000 square feet of office space for a large government agency. The specifications for their space needs were delivered to approximately six property owners who had expressed an interest in participating in the leasing action. About four property owners responded with sealed bids offering satisfactory office space, together with proposed rental rates. The four bids, expressed in terms of the square-foot rental rates per year, were: Bidder A: $18.95; Bidder B: $17.80; Bidder C: $17.50; and Bidder D: $17.17.

When the bids were opened and reviewed, someone decided that the original specifications given to the six interested landlords were unclear. To be "fair," it was directed that the ambiguity should be explained and all bidders should be given the opportunity to adjust their bids. A notice was sent out to all bidders with the clarified specifications, and all bidders were told that they would be permitted to resubmit their bids if they wished. But it became very apparent that the specifications were not too ambiguous, because three of the bids that were returned were identical to the first bids submitted. Bidder C, however, who had originally bid $17.50, changed the bid to $17.16—one cent under the previous low bid. The original bid amounts submitted were supposed to have been held in confidence and not disclosed, except to personnel having a need to know. However, it seems obvious that the new low bidder had been informed by someone as to the amount of the previous low bid.

Not all low-price bids that appear to be suspiciously low are made with the intention of committing contract rigging fraud. For example, some-times—due to a contracting entity's history of not being able to resist changing contract specifications—bidders will feel they can predict the contracting entity's future actions and will gamble that postcontract changes are likely to occur. Accordingly, they will offer a suspiciously low price, designed to win a contract award, a price they could never live with were they required to complete the contract without changes. How-ever, no inside conspiracy may be involved and no criminal manipulation. Contractors, based on past observations of the contracting entity's impul-sive behavior, are gambling that the contracting entity will continue to tamper foolishly with contract specifications. And, when that occurs, they will use the opportunity to revise their price. This is not criminal behavior. If the entity does not change the contract, as the contractors hope, they would have to perform as required at the original price bid and probably would lose money. These contractors, however, often have a fallback pro-vision that allows them to declare bankruptcy or something less drastic that enables them to escape performing under the contract.

Many contracting entities cannot resist making changes to a contract after the initial award to incorporate afterthoughts in the specifications. Auditors are advised to review the contracting records of their employers or clients for evidence of this practice and firmly advise against it. Internal control systems should firmly require a no-contract-change policy or one that requires high-level approval by management.

The federal government is famous for changing contract specifications, in many instances for the most capricious of reasons. And many contrac-tors count on those changes when offering competitive prices. On one occasion a computer software contractor who had repeatedly failed to obtain a contract with a military service expressed his frustration by remarking "I don't understand it. I've never been successful in offering a price low enough to be awarded a contract, despite many attempts. I examine and reexamine my price calculations carefully, and have cut my costs and profits to the absolute minimum, but I never win. I know I am an efficient producer. What am I doing wrong?"

It was explained to him that in all probability he was doing nothing wrong and that the contractors who were underbidding him were gambling that contract specifications would be changed, bidding low, and waiting for that open door to renegotiate their profits and costs back into the contract. This practice is especially true for contracts involving evolving technology where changes can be expected.

The first objective of the CRF perpetrator is to secure the award of the contract. Nothing else is important. At the successful end of stage 1 of contract rigging fraud, no crime has yet been committed, except perhaps the act of conspiring to commit a crime. The old expression "getting your foot in the door" might be used to describe the CRF perpetrator's objective for stage 1.

CONTRACT CHANGE ORDERS

Stage 2 of contract rigging fraud begins after the contract has been signed. Although fraudulent intent may be involved in stage 1, it is in stage 2 that the victim is actually fleeced. The contracting entity is defrauded by any of a number of practices, all of which involve contract specification change orders.

A contract is legally binding agreement between two parties. In its simplicity, the contract agreement provides that contractors will deliver a specified product or perform a specified service, in return for which the contracting entity agrees to pay an agreed-on sum.

The contracting entity often reserves the right to change the original contract specifications as necessary. When the contracting entity wishes to make a change to the contract, it prepares a document called a contract change order (CO). Sometimes, where a product is involved that is undergoing specification changes, the change order is called an engineering change order (ECO). These orders usually are numbered sequentially and are referred to as CO1, CO2, and so forth. In the contract change order, the contracting entity specifies the exact nature of the changes it wishes the contractor to make, and the contractor must proceed to make them. However, it is always provided that there will be a cost adjustment up or down, as may be necessary to effect the changes, together with a renegotiation of prices to reflect any cost increases or decreases resulting from the contract changes. The contractor's cost of making the changes is usually fully reimbursable, and left to be determined at some point after the contractor has completed the contract. Both parties to the contract are required under civil law to comply with contract change provisions, which are actionable under civil law.

Once a contract change order is issued, the contracting entity becomes exposed and vulnerable to just about whatever significant cost liability the dishonest contractor has planned. The entity initiating a contract innocently extends the opportunity for fraud in the contract changes. What the contracting entity does not know is that often, many of the changes are planned prior to the award of the contract by one or more of the entity's employees. Consider, for example, the pricing advantages available to a contractor who is aware of—and can depend on—major specification changes that will be made subsequent to the award of a contract. There are many ways contractors can adjust a price proposal to obtain the award of the contract and profit handsomely subsequent to the award. It is somewhat analogous to having a copy of the stock market section of tomorrow's newspaper today. Among the things contractors can do are:

- Bid a low price on those contract items they are assured will be eliminated during the term of the contract to get the award.
- Defer work on contract items they know will be changed and falsely claim to have invested substantial sums in time and material, for which they are entitled to be reimbursed.
- Substitute cheaper materials than those specified.
- Unbalance the bid in such a way to profit disproportionately as items are changed or eliminated.

Some entities strictly follow the practice of no changes after signing. However, most do not restrict changes as a matter of general practice. Where public entities are involved—such as federal, state, and local— officials may have a fraudulent interest in seeing that the changes are made. Other organizations in which the managing officials are not a part of the vested ownership of the entities involved—such as colleges, universities, and public hospitals—also may have similar interests and may, in fact, themselves be the inside conspirators who ensure contractors that certain changes will be made from which they all are able to profit. To avoid this fraud peril, the general rule is to not enter into a contract unless you are absolutely sure that changes will not be necessary.

Entities that do change contract specifications expose themselves to a wide variety of fraud practices and should beware of becoming victims. Of course, all contract specification changes do not have fraudulent intent, but all are risky. Obviously, there are many honest contractors who will submit the fair cost of any changes made by an entity. However, even honest contractors may find it hard to resist the opportunity to recover costs and profits that may have been lost in competitive bidding and cost-shaving.

When a contracting entity decides to alter the specifications of an existing contract, two events occur: the contracting entity must formally change the contract's requirements, and it must provide for an appropriate adjustment in the contract price. The amount of the adjustment cannot be computed until after the required change is completed. This is as it should be. However, at this point the contracting entity is at the mercy of the contractor. The contracting entity has lost any advantage originally gained when the contract was competitively advertised, when bidding contractors were constrained in price proposals by competition. Once a contract has been awarded and changes are made, there are no such natural price restraints. The contract change order is, in effect, a sole source contract. When contracting entities require changes, they no longer have the option of choosing another contractor, and the contractor can—at the very least—be expected to be generous in his or her own behalf in recovering all costs and profits. For dishonest contractors, being given a change in contract requirements is like being given the combination to the bank vault.

Change Orders to Correct Omissions

It is not uncommon for a contracting entity to fail to include all features of a construction project in the specification package mailed out to contractors. (In one large building in Washington, DC, for example, the electrical system was mysteriously missing from the specification package initially distributed.) When this occurs, and when the omission is not detected before the specifications package is mailed out to prospective bidders, bidding contractors are likely to prepare their bids for a complete all-inclusive structure often by relying heavily on statistical costs to prepare their cost estimates (e.g., $100 per square foot). After all bids are received, the lowest qualified bidder is awarded the contract and directed to proceed with construction.

After the contract award, as contract work gets under way and specification omissions are discovered and brought to the contracting entity's attention, the entity has no choice but to issue contract change order(s) to include the missing specifications in the contract. Were the change orders not written, contractors would be perfectly within their rights to construct the building as originally specified, even though the plans were deficient. Contract change orders covering the missing specifications require contractors to comply. However, since the change orders specify work that was not in the specification package that contractors bid on, they are entitled to add the cost of performance required by the change order to the contract price. Sometimes the omissions are unintentional, and in such instances no fraud may be involved.

However, if contractors were aware of the omission at the time they prepared the price proposal, this knowledge would allow them to reduce their estimated price for the construction and give them a pricing edge in the competitive bid—an edge that contractors who did not detect the omission would not have. More to the point, if the omission was not readily apparent, if perhaps it was intentionally omitted, and one bidding contractor was informed as to the nature of the missing specification, he or she would have a clear advantage over other bidders. That contractor would be able to underbid the others, knowing that there would be a later opportunity to add any costs back that were eliminated in the competition to be low bidder.

Experienced fraud auditors view all contract change orders with a sense of heightened suspicion. They will be immediately concerned whether the omission was accidental or planned. If it appears to have been planned, fraud bells and whistles will begin to sound, and the entire contract will come under a critical examination.

Assuming there were no further irregularities in the contract, at the very least, the contracting entity would have lost any advantage received through the competitive bidding for the contract award and may end up paying a costly premium for the omission. However, where significant omissions have occurred, and the omissions were planned for fraudulent purposes, it would be surprising if the contracting entity did not experience a need for more changes as the contractor's performance under the contract continues.

Specification Change Orders

Some entities, when constructing a new building, strictly follow a hands-off or turn-key policy. These terms mean that, once the contract has been awarded, the architect and/or contractor is fully responsible for delivering a fully functional building for the price agreed to. The entities take the self-protective attitude that the architect and/or contractor should have exercised due care before contract award, and by submitting the completed blueprints and/or contract bids the architect and/or contractor became responsible for performance in accordance with them. The entities want nothing to do with construction problems and avoid any involvement with the contract or the construction, until the architect or contractor gives them the keys to open the completed building. If there is a need to change a specification that was not foreseen by the architect, the entity's attitude is "It is the architect's responsibility, and his or her cost risk." Entities take these attitudes to protect themselves from cost increases, problems of any sort encountered during construction, as well as fraud. Should any problems result in contract delivery delays or cost claims, they are prepared to enforce the terms of the contract that call for a completed building at an agreed price, at a specified time. The downside of this policy is that architects and contractors who accept this degree of risk are apt to charge more for taking it, increasing the cost of the construction.

However, few entities are prepared to act in this manner. They tend to be drawn into becoming involved in the construction details, changing building features sometimes capriciously, and exposing themselves to a multitude of abuses. Sometimes their changes are the result of innocent second thoughts or omissions, and sometimes the changes are premeditated by inside conspirators to produce the opportunity to fleece the contracting entity. In case 7.1, consider what happened during the construction of a new federal building in a midwestern state. Were the changes honest and sincere or were they fraudulently inspired? This is a true story.

CASE 7.1 The Construction in Progress Specification Change

A six-story building was in the process of construction. The contract had been advertised. After several months had elapsed, the tenant that was to occupy the building stated it wanted a minor change in the building's design. After reviewing the directional siting on the property, it decided it wanted to take advantage of morning sunlight through a laboratory's windows, and insisted that the building be rotated clockwise on the site about 90 degrees. Since none of the building's foundation or superstructure had yet been built, the request was granted, and a contract change order was issued.

Much later, when the time came for the contractor to submit the costs incurred as a result of the change in plans, they were substantial. The construction contractor claimed that he had already installed all underground utilities (water, sewer, electrical), which had to be redone when the building siting plan was rotated away from its original siting. In addition to claiming the cost of installing new underground utilities, he claimed all of the costs he incurred in installing the underground utilities as originally specified. His claim was perfectly legitimate, and it had to be paid. However, it presented an opportunity for padding his expenses.

A fraud audit was never performed in response to the indicia suggested by the circumstances just described. However, had one been done, the fraud auditor would surely have attempted to resolve the following questions:

- Did the contractor actually install the underground utilities that he claimed became redundant when the new contract change order was issued? If he had reason to suspect that the building siting would be changed at the start of the contract, he could have delayed installing the underground utilities to the original site and later could have claimed that he had installed them, charging for the utilities to the original site as if they actually were installed. How could he be aware of the coming change? There are several possibilities, all of which would have required a bit of advance planning. For example, the architect may have known that the new building's tenant was vulnerable to the suggestion that the building's laboratories face toward the southeast to catch the morning sun. To take advantage of this vulnerability, he need only design the building with its laboratories facing northeast. It would be very easy subsequently to plant that idea in the tenant's mind. This scheme, of course, would require collusion between the architect and the contractor.

  A dishonest contractor would not have installed any underground utilities to the original location site if he was aware of the impending contract change order, and particularly if he were in league with the architect. He would simply delay in installing the utilities, or even perhaps install the utilities in the location needed to best serve the expected new building site. His false claim would be totally unfounded, but at the time he would be likely to file it, it would be very difficult to prove it was false.

- Was the prospective tenant a conspirator to the fraud suggested here? If the tenant was influential in the building's original siting, as can be expected, his or her subsequent change of heart is at the very least suspicious and certainly would have been enabling.

- Is there any evidence that the contractor or architect were aware of the tenant's siting wishes before the bid proposals were submitted? If so, this information could have given the contractor an unfair advantage in preparing his price proposal.

CASE 7.2 The Federal Building and Courthouse

This case involves what appears to be a simple error in assigning floor space in a new building, which did not give sufficient regard to the idiosyncracies of the judicial system. The error, however, required major changes in the architectural design of the building and incurred $50 million in extra cost. The building is a high-rise federal court house. The architectural design of the structure was guided by instructions to accommodate federal appeals courtrooms on the building's sixth floor and federal district courtrooms on the eighth floor. Construction of the building was substantially under way when members of the appeals court decided to visit the building to view its progress. And, apparently for the first time, they were stunned by the realization that a lower district court would be located higher in the building than they would be. Their objection was so strenuous that changes were necessary to reverse the floor locations of the two courts.

Although this may sound like a simple change in floor occupancy plans, it was not. The change required physical changes in the building's construction that cost many millions of dollars. Among the very costly things that had to be changed was the load-bearing strength of the floors, involving the removal of the previous floors and the installation of new and stronger floors. No fraud audit was ever performed relative to the changes described, and for that reason we must presume that no fraud was involved. However, an experienced fraud auditor's intuition would be tingling were he or she to examine the circumstances just described.

Fraud auditors must always consider the possibility that architects may be co-conspirators in fraud, designing or omitting construction features that will subsequently require contract changes that will provide the opportunity for costly, perhaps fraudulent claims. However, fraud auditors must also determine the general design specifications that architects were given by their clients. In Case 7.2, the architect's design was apparently fully responsive to the client's requirements, but nevertheless, subsequent substantial and very costly specification changes were required. The question of whether fraud or negligence was involved was never determined.

It is highly improbable that an experienced person planning the occupancy of the new building would not be aware of the idiosyncracies of higher court judges and their interests in maintaining the appearance of superiority, to include having courtrooms located above a lower court located in the same building. It is difficult to believe that serious fraud was not involved.

Something was terribly wrong in the construction of this building. The obvious questions a fraud auditor would be likely to ask include:

1. Who determined the tenant occupancy plan for the new building?
2. To what degree was the architect independent in his or her initial building design, versus responding to the contracting entity's design orders?
3. Was the contracting entity responsible for requiring unnecessary changes after construction had begun, or were the many changes the result of evolving circumstances?
4. Were changes premeditated to provide the contractor an opportunity to submit $50 million in supplementary cost claims?
5. How much of the $50 million in supplementary cost claims were bona-fide costs incurred as the result of contract changes, and how much were falsely claimed by the contractor?
6. All of the above?

Contracts are changed in the manner of Case 7.2 every day, and there is nothing intrinsically wrong with changing a contract's specifications. However, when a rigged contract is involved, the changes to contract specifications are opportunities fraud perpetrators look for. Many changes are premeditated and often initiated—directly or indirectly—by a key employee of the contracting entity. For the perpetrators, timing of any changes is crucial—they must be initiated at a point when contract work-in-progress is substantial, so the contracting entity has no practical alternatives to costly charges.

Post-Award Change Orders

Contract rigging with fraudulent intent occurs in the acquisition of personal property as well as real property. Most of the mechanics in personal property fraud are very similar to that involving real property. The fraud usually occurs in the acquisition of personal property manufactured to the entity's specifications, as opposed to off-the-shelf items. The entity's interest in purchasing custom-made personal property is made known to the relevant manufacturing community. Those manufacturers interested in competing are provided with manufacturing specifications. Manufacturers interested in manufacturing the items desired submit price proposals. The lowest qualified bidder is awarded the contract to manufacture the items. Any changes after the contract is awarded are accomplished through change orders.

Product Degradation

Surely everyone has seen old movies where someone is given a gold coin in payment for something. The recipient frequently bites on the coin to tell if it was gold. Obviously, he was concerned with someone substituting a cheaper metal for the more valuable gold. Base metals such as lead have been substituted for precious metals such as gold. Anyone who has any doubt as to the profit to be made in substituting lead for gold need only to look at the commodities market on any given day. At one point in the year 2000, for example, gold was worth about 10,000 times the price of lead. And yet a government contractor substituted lead for gold in a defense contract, claiming that there was no cost effect in recommending the engineering change to the U.S. Navy, as seen in Case 7.3.

CASE 7.3 The Fraudulent Substitution of Lead for Gold

This story begins with a contractor—Contractor X—who obtained a government contract to build an antiaircraft missile for the navy. The initial contract was sole source—given without competition—to a very capable aerospace contractor to design and build a long-range missile having certain prescribed defense capabilities not then existing in the navy's arsenal. And, of course, no specifications existed that could be advertised. Customary in such instances, the contract was fully cost reimbursable.

Contractor X labored for several years in designing and building prototype missiles. Using design recommendations provided by a major university, the contractor ultimately constructed a missile that ended up being very effective with a high target acquisition rate. As is usual with cost-reimbursable contracts of this type, no expense was spared to build the very best missile to heighten its dependability in acquiring and destroying enemy targets many miles away from the fleet. Because cost was secondary to quality, the highest-grade components were used, including nickel and gold plating on electrical circuit board pathways.

After several years and many millions of dollars spent on design, engineering, and prototype construction, the missile specifications had evolved sufficiently and were sufficiently enduring to justify a large production contract. The navy, interested in obtaining the best possible production price, decided to advertise the contract, and solicited price proposals from several major manufacturers, one of which was Contractor X.

Prior to this time Contractor X had no real incentive to reduce manufacturing costs. It had not been cost effective, and it quickly realized that its prior extravagant production experience would be a liability rather than an advantage. If it were to win the advertised contract award, it would have to offer a price that would underbid a very competitive marketplace, and that would be difficult. Nevertheless, it did. It bid what it believed to be a low competitive price—one that was considerably under its previous costs per missile produced under the cost-reimbursable contracts. Its proposed price was the lowest bid, and it was awarded a production contract of about $100 million.

However, it did not take the contractor long to realize that it would lose money if it was required to build the missile at the price bid. And, shortly after the contract was awarded, a group of Contractor X's engineers found themselves in meetings to discuss ways and means of sufficiently reducing the cost of manufacturing the missile to enable the company to make a profit. The engineers suggested various ideas for changes that would reduce costs. Many of the suggested changes eliminated parts, modified physical design of the parts, substituted cheaper materials, relaxed acceptance tolerances, and reduced prescribed testing. Generally, the changes served to make the missiles much less expensive to produce.

The problem with the cost reduction changes that were suggested—aside from the fact that the changes would result in a degraded product—was that the contract bid price for building the missiles was based on the higher missile specifications existing at the time the contract was advertised. Any cost reductions that would result from making them should have been passed on to the U.S. Navy and should not have benefited Contractor X—unless, of course, the firm's owner was deceitful, and that is exactly what it appears he was.

Government auditors discovered details which revealed the contractor's intention to cut production costs and profit from its low bid. Their report revealed that the contractor was trusted to designate which engineering changes were major in nature (Class I) and would require a comprehensive review by navy engineers, and which were minor (Class II) and not subject to extraordinary review. This of course was a rather naive internal control plan, and somewhat akin to giving the keys to the chicken house to the fox. Contractor X simply designated many of the engineering specification changes which resulted in the missile's degradation as Class II changes, thereby avoiding scrutiny of its claims that no cost reductions were involved. The changes were approved by a mid-level naval officer in residence at Contractor X's manufacturing plant, without any questions as to the serious nature of the changes or the cost effect. The office apparently had no problems with Contractor X's claim that the substitution of a tin/lead alloy in lieu of nickel/gold alloy plating would result in no cost savings. The auditors computed a $50,000 savings in materials to Contractor X from this single change. In another of the several hundred Class II changes made by the contractor, the officer apparently had no problem approving Contractor X's claim that no cost savings would result from the change from hand-soldering electrical circuit board connections, to simply passing the assembled circuit boards over molten lead (flow soldering). The auditors discovered that the change was expected to result in a 94 percent reduction in soldering labor.

In an interesting postscript to the missile illustration, the navy eventually became so alarmed at the precipitous loss of their missile's reliability in test firings that it gave an engineering study contract to Contractor X to determine the reasons for the performance degradation. After an appropriate period of time to study the defective missiles, Contractor X essentially recommended reversals of the cost-cutting changes it had made during the production of the missile inventory.

Case 7.3 is a classic case of contract rigging. Contractor X was in a unique position that few contractors enjoy. Not only did the company manufacture the missiles, it also served as the designer of the missiles. Accordingly, it was understandable that when Contractor X recommended what it described as minor engineering changes to the navy—in its authoritative role as the missile's designer—the recommendations were readily accepted. What cannot be as easily explained is why the resident navy officer approved the recommended design changes as submitted, even though they were obviously not minor, as classified, and even though Contractor X submitted them with the notation "no cost effect," although most if not all of the changes obviously involved labor and material cost savings.

UNBALANCED BIDDING

Unbalanced bidding fraud is a variety of contract rigging fraud in which contractors planning to perpetrate fraud bids a price estimated to be lower than any other bidders, and on which they probably would lose money if they were required to complete the contract advertised at the price bid. However, such contractors are counting on certain events occurring that will restore profits, and more. Unbalanced bidding fraud is similar to other contract rigging fraud discussed except for one important aspect. It is considerably more subtle and is easy to overlook.

In the other contract rigging frauds discussed, perpetrating contractors depend on contract change orders to add new requirements to open the door for price negotiations in which they expect to charge outrageous prices and recover costs and profit. In unbalanced bidding fraud contractors anticipate that the contracting entity will cancel a requirement and, as a result, leave them with a handsome profit.

In unbalanced bidding fraud contractors customarily overprice one or more line items while sufficiently underpricing other line items so that their aggregate bid is likely to be the low bid. Such bidders are anticipating that the items they bid low on will be canceled from the contract, leaving only the overpriced items to manufacture, which will provide a handsome profit.

Case 7.4 is a very oversimplified illustration of unbalanced bidding fraud.

CASE 7.4 A Simple Case of Unbalanced Bidding

Assume that the Yore Corporation wishes to have a freight transfer terminal (Building A), a warehouse (Building B), and a service workshop (Building C) constructed. All three buildings must be completed by December 31 of the current year. A penalty of $500 per day will accrue for each day subsequent to December 31 that

final delivery is delayed. The three contractors interested in participating (Contractor Able, Contractor Baker, and Contractor Charlie)
are provided with the building specifications and instructed to submit their price proposals by line item. Building A is line item 1,
Building B is line item 2, and Building C is line item 3. The Yore
Corporation reserves the right to change contract specifications or
delete items at any time, and to renegotiate prices as may be necessary as a result of any changes it may make.

The contractor price proposals received were:

Contractor Able:	
Line Item 1	$100,000
Line Item 2	$195,000
Line Item 3	$225,000
TOTAL BID	$520,000
Contractor Baker:	
Line Item 1	$105,000
Line Item 2	$203,000
Line Item 3	$229,000
TOTAL BID	$537,000
Contractor Charlie:	
Line Item 1	$132,000
Line Item 2	$135,000
Line Item 3	$243,000
TOTAL BID	$510,000

Before reading further, please take few minutes to contemplate
these bids. Keep in mind the following:

- There may not be fraud involved in this transaction. It may be a
  trick to cause readers to speculate on fraud they have reason to
  expect to be there when in fact none is present.
- Given only the above information, assuming that each contractor is
  equally qualified, to whom should the contract be awarded? Why?
- If anyone other than the low bidder was chosen, reasoning must be
  justified. Bear in mind that if you are the Yore Corporation and
  you select a contractor other than the low bidder without a good
  reason, you may be sued by the low bidder.

At this point in the contract, there is nothing apparently wrong
with the bids received. Contractor Charlie has offered the lowest
price and must be accepted. This contractor is qualified and offers a
price $10,000 lower than the next lowest bidder.

Mary Lande is an official in the Storage Division. Ms. Lande is aware that the corporation is growing very rapidly and seriously lacks adequate storage space. She was a prime mover in getting the new storage building authorized, and now realizes that it will barely meet their needs. She had known Charlie Braun, the Contractor Charlie owner, since they were in high school together, over 22 years ago. At their last high school reunion she attracted Charlie's interest when she casually mentioned that Yore Corporation was going to build several new buildings estimated to cost over $500,000. As a building contractor, Charlie was interested in getting the job, and Mary mentioned it would be advertised.

The next day Charlie called Mary and they had lunch together. Charlie reminded Mary that she had said the warehouse would probably be too small before it was completed, and asked why a larger building was not being built. Mary replied that she planned to recommend just that before the specifications were mailed out for bids. She said that since the building had been planned last year, the Yore Corporation had experienced a surge in manufacturing that predictably would continue. Charlie replied that building a warehouse twice as large would not cost that much more. Mary agreed and said that she did not think it would be difficult to sell the larger building to corporation management. She said she would begin immediately, to which Charlie replied, "Wait, I've got an idea. Why not wait a few months until after the contract is awarded, and then do it?" He explained his plan to submit a low bid, pricing the warehouse low to get the contract. Then when she was successful in selling the corporation on a larger warehouse, he predicted he could net well over $50,000 when the smaller warehouse was canceled from the contract and the larger warehouse was added. He offered to split $50,000 with Mary. Mary agreed, and everything worked according to plan. Charlie turned out to be the low bidder.

After the contract was awarded to Charlie, the Yore Corporation notified him to began construction of Building A immediately. Several weeks later Mary advised the Yore Corporation management board that the construction of Building A was proceeding well. She also voiced her concerns that given their excellent sales forecasts, the new warehouse building would very likely be obsolete before it was finished. One of the management officers suggested, "Since the new warehouse construction hasn't yet been started, we have an excellent opportunity to cancel construction and a larger building." Everyone agreed; and item 2 on Contractor Charlie's contract was ordered canceled and the contract price reduced by the amount Charlie had bid—$135,000. Mary bought a new Buick with the $25,000 Charlie gave her.

The Yore Corporation received its annual audit the following January. By chance, the auditors examined the construction contract for the three buildings, saw it had been advertised, the lowest bidder selected, and took no audit exceptions.

Choice- and Select-Grade Beef

Case 7.5 was re-created from actual events that occurred in the U.S. Army, Europe. Although the actual figures vary somewhat from the real events, they depict the essence of what actually happened. No fraud audit or investigation was ever pursued. However, this does not mean that fraud was not present in what appears to be a classic case of contract rigging fraud, only an insensitivity to clear indicia of fraud that is typical of many entities. Readers should consider the probability to which fraud may have been involved in this case, as well as ways and means by which it may have manifested itself. In a real-world situation, auditors will have to do so to pursue a successful fraud-specific examination of the circumstances.

CASE 7.5 The Unbalanced Meat Contract

It is the U.S. Army's practice to buy much of the perishable food needed to feed troops in Europe from continental sources. To accomplish this, it advertises its intentions to food suppliers, inviting them to submit price proposals. This illustration describes the procedure once used for buying fresh beef.

According to army purchasing officials, the army's stated goal in buying food for U.S. forces in Europe is to purchase only the best quality. And this was their avowed criteria when buying fresh beef. If price was not a significant factor, they said, they would have asked meat contractors to submit proposals offering to sell required quantities of only the "choice grade" of beef. However, their buying philosophy, as expressed to auditors, was that since the beef that was available to wholesalers came in three grades—choice, select, and good—if the army were to insist on large quantities of only the highest grade of beef (choice), the supply of which was limited, the competition for it alone would drive its selling price unacceptably high.

Accordingly, to obtain the best price offer for the choice grade of beef that the army wanted, army purchasing agents would solicit bid offers for a "market mix" of all grades. A market mix was calculated to be the proportion of each grade of beef that it was thought would yield the best unit prices for each grade, but was also in keeping with army intentions to buy the best grade. Accordingly, the agents solicited offers from interested suppliers of perhaps 1 million pounds of beef, of which 40 percent would be choice grade, 40 percent would be select grade, and 20 percent would be good grade. Their solicitations for bids stipulated that each grade of beef was to be unit priced separately, with the low bidder determined by the lowest total price submitted for all three grades of beef. In addition, army buyers inserted a caveat in the solicitation for bids that said something similar to the following:

> The low bid will be determined on the basis of the lowest aggregate price offered for the entire 1 million pounds of beef required. The contractor selected will supply beef to the U.S. forces on the basis of its requirements throughout the year at the unit prices stipulated in the contract. The U.S. Army guarantees to purchase a minimum of 1 million pounds of beef from the contractor selected during the contract period. However, the buyer reserves the right to order any quantity of any grade of beef at the unit price bid.

The bids that were received were similar to the following abstract of bids:

Contractor Ein

Choice beef	400,000 pounds	@ $1.00	$ 400,000
Select beef	400,000 pounds	@ $ .80	320,000
Good beef	200,000 pounds	@ $ .50	100,000
Total price bid	1,000,000 pounds		$ 820,000

Contractor Zwei

Choice beef	400,000 pounds	@ $1.02	$ 408,000
Select beef	400,000 pounds	@ $ .78	312,000
Good beef	200,000 pounds	@ $ .60	120,000
Total price bid	1,000,000 pounds		$ 840,000

Contractor Drei

Choice beef	400,000 pounds	@ $1.25	$ 500,000
Select beef	400,000 pounds	@ $ .57½	230,000
Good beef	200,000 pounds	@ $ .40	80,000
Total price bid	1,000,000 pounds		$ 810,000

Contractor Drei submitted the low total bid of $810,000 and was awarded the meat supply contract for the designated year. The actual contract from which this illustration was drawn was more complicated and perhaps a bit less obvious, but was essentially the same. Once the contract was awarded, its terms were advertised to military kitchens and commissaries throughout the U.S. forces service area. During the contract period, they were then free to order from the contract to meet their needs for beef, but still were to be guided by the military policy of only buying the best for the troops, which means they would not ordinarily requisition anything other than choice-grade beef.

Consider what the ultimate contract price is likely to be if the entire 1 million pounds of beef guaranteed by the contract and used by military kitchens and commissaries is choice grade. Why would they use anything else? At $1.25 per pound, the choice beef will cost the government $1,250,000, considerably above the price offered for choice beef by Contractor Ein and Contractor Zwei.

Fraud-sensitive readers may ask: "Why didn't contractors Ein and Zwei unbalance their bids in a similar manner?" Surely the losing bidders should have been savvy to the military policy of buying all choice-grade beef. Why then didn't they also bid high on choice-grade beef while bidding low on the other two grades to make the total come out an overall low bid? Think about this for a few minutes before reading on.

Bidders who do not have an army inside conspirator would have valid reason to be fearful of unbalancing their bidding as did Contractor Drei. Were they to bid in this manner, they would be at risk of the army choosing to take advantage of the unrealistically low prices offered for select-grade and good-grade beef. It would be a risk that, understandably, they did not want to take. Think what would have happened if the other contractors were to unbalance their bids similarly without inside help. Suppose that Contractor Ein submitted a low overall bid proposal, which included an offer to sell select-grade beef at $0.55 a pound, without an inside conspirator to protect his or her interests. Contractor Drei's inside conspirator could simply retaliate by calling attention to Ein's bid to sell select beef at $0.55 a pound, exclaiming "This price is too good to pass up. Let's direct all military consumers to requisition only select-grade beef!" Considering that the market for select-grade beef appears to be 80 cents and 78 cents a pound (see abstract of bids received), Contractor Ein would suffer a loss of about $250,000 in having to supply 1 million pounds of select-grade beef at only 55 cents a pound. As it is, Drei will make an extra profit of $250,000.

DETECTION RECOMMENDATIONS

Contract rigging fraud, if crafted carefully, is very difficult to detect and/or to take action on a timely basis. The important thing is to know that it exists and to be watchful for signs of it. Although it is often possible to discern what appear to be (1) suspicious bidding practices or (2) unbalanced bidding in Stage 1, little can be done to change anything. If a bidder chooses to offer an unusually low bid—one that will lose money—that is the bidder's prerogative. It is not the advertising entity's responsibility to ensure that the bid proposer makes a profit. However, when suspicious Stage 1 bidding practices or apparent profit-loss bids are observed, auditors should view them as possible precursors to fraud. What to do about them is the question. The answer is to watch what may come next very carefully.

In almost all instances where contract rigging fraud is suspected, contract changes are the keys to the perpetrator's success. Stop the contract changes and you will stop contract rigging fraud dead in its tracks. The contract must be changed in some way for the perpetrator to profit. And, of course, it is the anticipation of the changes that causes the perpetrator to bid low to get the contract, never expecting to have to perform at the price bid. Always remember that as long as the suspect contract remains unchanged, it is usually impossible for CRF perpetrators to profit. Accordingly, financial managers, accountants, auditors, or whoever is looking for contract rigging fraud should become a bit paranoid with regard to all contract changes, both those proposed before the fact and those executed after the fact.

If the suspicious bidding practices or unbalanced bidding are suspected, extraordinary attention should be given to any contract changes proposed. Any changes proposed by the contracting entity should be carefully scrutinized to determine who proposed the changes, the cost effect of the changes, and any other consequences on the overall contract. Every attempt should be made to determine the cost of the change, including a requirement that the contractor prepare an estimate of what the costs of making the change are likely to be. Where the changes will have a deleterious effect on overall contract cost, entity management should be made aware of the consequences.

If the changes are required because of a design error, auditors need to find out who was responsible for the error. Is it the architect? If so he or she may be responsible for any extraordinary costs incurred. Also, auditors should make every attempt to pinpoint the source of any changes originating within the entity. In other words, does the contractor have an inside conspirator who may be instrumental in generating the changes? Or is there any reason to believe that a contract change was known or could be anticipated at the time the contract was advertised, which could have been communicated to the bidding contractor to allow him or her, to lower the winning bid? In other words, is there any evidence to indicate when the idea for the change was first conceived? How does that date compare with the bid solicitation dates?

Auditors with a reason to suspect contract occurrences but who cannot prove anything might consider reviewing past contracts or purchase orders that involved the contractors and/or insiders suspected of involvement. If they are guilty of malpractices, chances are a pattern will be evident in past events. Any patterns developed may make or at least strengthen auditors' convictions.

ROTATION FRAUD

Rotation fraud is a close cousin to contract rigging fraud. It happens only from time to time, and financial managers and auditors must be aware of it. In rotation fraud, two or more contractors who dominate an industry in a region conspire to alternate the business between them, thereby defeating the advantages of advertised contracts. They obviously feel that it is preferable to share the business equally rather than to engage in cutthroat competition where all of them lose profits.

If there are three contractors involved, for example, they will conspire as to whose turn it is to win an advertised contract, Contractor A, Contractor B, or Contractor C. If it is Contractor B's turn, then Contractor B will bid a comfortable price with an ample profit, making the bidding price known to Contractors A and C. Contractors A and C will then slightly overbid, thus giving the appearance of competition. The contracting entity is pleased and believes it has received the best price available in the marketplace, which is evident in the closeness of the prices offered. Normally, when rotation fraud occurs, a conspirator is not involved within the contracting entity's ranks.

In a variation of rotation fraud, only one contractor participates in a bidding action, conspiring with the contracting entity's procurement agent to provide false documentation, giving the appearance that three or more contractors submitted bids. Anyone reviewing the procurement files after the fact will find that the procurement action was advertised, that three contractors responded with bids, and the lowest bidder was chosen. End of story!

It is very difficult to detect or to stop rotation fraud. Rarely is an insider conspiracy involved, except possibly in the situation just described. All the documentation is genuine, as are the contractors who have submitted bids. One recommendation that is worth pursuing is to determine all contractors who should have been interested in bidding on this contract. If, for example, a painting contract is involved, auditors should check who the painters in the general area are whom the entity should have received bids from but did not. If the list contains more names than those from whom bids were received, auditors might contact them and ask why they did not bid on the solicitation. Auditors should use their best and most congenial interviewing technique, give them an opportunity to talk, and listen very carefully to what they have to say. They may have never known about the solicitation, in which case auditors should find out why. There may be political reasons why they did not bid. Perhaps they were intimidated out of the competition. Auditors should get as many details as possible, and follow any leads provided.

8

ETHICAL BEHAVIOR AND STANDARDS OF CONDUCT

ETHICAL BEHAVIOR

At first ethical behavior may appear to be a strange topic for a fraud auditing text. However, fraud auditors need firm criteria for what constitutes ethical behavior when they must consider the behavior of individuals whose behavior is questionable. Accordingly, it is important to know precisely what ethical behavior is. The problem is that there is no reasonable consensus of what the term means.

The different definitions that people have for ethical behavior becomes a problem when an employer decides that an employee's behavior was not in accordance with the employer's idea of what constitutes ethical behavior and attempts to discipline the person for any violations noted. Consequently, to ensure the ethical behavior of their subordinates, many employers find it desirable, if not essential, to specify those behavioral actions that they believe are ethical and those actions that they believe are not ethical. They may be long or short lists, but once they have been prepared, employees who have been compelled to read the lists are—from that point forward—bound to comply with them, regardless of what their personal views on ethical behavior may be. The employer's published code of ethics is binding on employees during the hours of their employment. And violations of the employer's code of ethics subject the employees involved to disciplinary action and even to termination of their employment. An employer's listing of limitations on employees' behavior while in its employ is commonly known as standards of conduct.

To be effective, the standards of conduct must be required reading for all employees at least once every year to be enforceable, and employees must be required to sign that they have read and understand the standards provided.

The failure of employers to declare and publish definitive standards of conduct for their employees to follow is equivalent to allowing employees to use their own judgment. In such cases, the employing entity is literally asking for trouble, because every employee, depending on his or her own private criteria for what is right or good, driven by the wide range of differences in moral character, will have different limits—if any—on personal behavior. And, of course, some employees will stretch the limits to justify their errant behavior. The employer who has not issued standards of conduct has little or no sustainable cause for disciplinary action. Needless to say, auditors who discover questionable acts by employees often find it similarly difficult to be critical of such behavior where standards of conduct cannot be cited. Standards of conduct are not a guarantee of good behavior on the part of employees. They are, however, a criteria for their behavior, good or bad, and provide a basis for disciplinary if not criminal action when warranted.

There are many aspects to ethical behavior, most of which will not be discussed in this text because they have little or no relevance to the primary topic of fraud. However, of particular importance in any discussion of workplace ethical behavior is the acceptance of things of value by employees from entities doing business with the employer. These items of value are commonly called gratuities. They range from items of little or no monetary value, such as a calendar or a free lunch, to things of considerable value, such as large cash amounts, automobiles, and expensive vacations.

Although most employees who receive gratuities would argue that the gratuities received do not influence them to favor the entity giving the gratuity, most employers have good reason to think otherwise. It is interesting to note that although the conveniently popular understanding of a gratuity is that it is something of value given without the expectation of something in return, the formal definition of a gratuity is: "a favor or gift, usually in the form of money, *given in return for service*"[1] Employers who may be considering prohibiting their employees from accepting gratuities should ask themselves: "Gratuities given in return for what service?" And readers should ask themselves: "When was the last time someone other than a friend or relative, who was not indebted to me, bought me an expensive lunch without wanting something in return?"

Why are standards of conduct important to auditors? Because some day all auditors will find themselves pursuing questionable actions by errant employees, possibly involving fraud, and will have cases fully compiled and ready for prosecution, only to have them rejected by prosecutors when auditors cannot convincingly demonstrate that the alleged perpetrators acted inappropriately. That is, there is no demonstrable quid pro quo. Strange as it may sound to many auditors who have never experienced this situation, the mere fact that employee Jane Smith received an expensive new television set from Contractor X, shortly after Contractor X received a $50,000 order written by employee Jane Smith, does not ipso facto mean that there was a quid pro quo agreement between the two parties. The contractor could successfully argue that the television set was a unilateral gift in expression of his gratitude and a generally accepted practice in his industry. In other words, there was no quid pro quo agreement. If prosecuted, Jane Smith would very likely successfully argue that there was no quid pro connection between the new television set and the $50,000 order she wrote to Contractor X. And since her employer did not prohibit the acceptance of such gifts, she had no reason not to accept it.

In such a case, an employer's standards of conduct establish a standard with regard to what gifts an employee may not accept from an outsider. In this instance, had the employer published standards of conduct that prohibited the acceptance of gifts such as the television set, Ms. Smith would have been precluded from freely accepting the set and very likely would not have been motivated to write the $50,000 order that was not in her employer's best interests. Had such a standard existed, and had Ms. Smith written the order regardless, she would have been in clear violation of it, and the quid pro quo would have been much more easily demonstrated.

Some employers establish a standard that states that no gifts in any amount may be accepted from a company doing business with the employer. Others establish a more liberal standard, such as allowing gifts not exceeding $300 a year. In either case, if Jane Smith were to accept a television set from Contractor X, she would be—at the very least—in violation of her employer's standards of conduct and subject to disciplinary action or termination. Standards of conduct do not preclude an employee from exceeding the limitations they impose, but they do provide a basis for dealing with those who do.

In business and government, it is quite common for contractors and vendors to give expensive gifts to the employees of the entities they do business with. A gratuity may be a two-martini luncheon, a case of scotch, a Caribbean cruise, an all-expense-paid trip to Europe for the family worth thousands of dollars, an expensive fur coat, an automobile, a television set, or a large sum of cash. For readers who may find it unbelievable that gratuities of this magnitude are offered at all, consider that gratuities of $750,000 to a K-mart employee, $1.5 million a J. C. Penney Co. employee, and $440,000 to a Pentagon employee for their conspiratorial assistance in fraud by firms doing business with their employers as reported.

Gratuities are a fact of life. They happen routinely in business. And that is also part of the problem. Most are harmless, such as business lunches, even though provided to ingratiate employees. However, they cease being harmless when employees, either intentionally or subconsciously, begin to favor the gift giver. When that happens, even a minor act of favoritism meets the definition of fraud.

The term "gratuity" includes a wide range of things of value given by vendors and contractors to a customer's employees. In addition to simple gratuities, such as a free lunch, gratuities include bribes and all quid pro quo payments. It is useful to classify gratuities into two general categories: unilateral gratuities and bilateral gratuities.

UNILATERAL GRATUITIES

A unilateral gratuity is a gift provided by one party to another that does not involve or require a quid pro quo agreement, although the gift provider normally hopes for—if not expects—favorable treatment from the recipient of the gift.

This is the gratuity category that most people are likely to think of whenever contractor or vendor gratuities are mentioned. The problem is that, outside of a family setting where gifts are routinely given to loved ones, it is not normal human behavior for people to give gifts to others without expecting something in return. In the business world, businesses give gratuities only to individuals they are indebted to or from whom they expect something in return. To do otherwise is not simply good business.

Proponents of gratuities argue that the recipients have done or will do nothing extraordinary to earn any gifts received and feel no obligation to respond in any way to the giver. When questioned, they usually reply indignantly that their integrity precludes them from being influenced by gratuities. Those who oppose the acceptance of gratuities from outsiders argue that, as a practical matter, human beings are motivated by rewards and either consciously or subconsciously will favor the gift giver where they must choose. Who would argue that, in a competitive business environment, the company that takes a purchasing agent to lunch at a fine restaurant is more likely to win a purchase order than the company that gives no gratuities? Should the recipient of a gratuity be motivated to select products that are offered by the gratuity giver which are inferior to a competitor's, buy in excess of his or her employer's needs, or pay a price that is excessive, the employing entity is hurt as a result of the gratuity. In the end, the cost of gratuities given either increases the vendor's price or reduce his or her profits, and businessmen and women are loath to reduce profits.

Many employers feel that gratuities are relatively harmless gifts, trivial in value, and not likely to influence their employees' judgment. However, what may appear trivial and noninfluencing to an employer may be regarded differently by the employees who receive them. And in many instances recipients come to expect gratuities provided by vendors on a recurring basis, and the employees are likely to favor those vendors in anticipation of gifts. Thus a presumptive sort of quid pro quo relationship develops.

To illustrate, an off-line general freight agent for the Southern Pacific Railroad was known to remark how he dreaded his monthly visit to a large fertilizer company's shipping department. His job was to visit Midwest manufacturers, to sell them on shipping their products to West Coast destinations via the Southern Pacific's railways. The agent's visits, however, were an occasion that all 20 or so of the fertilizer company's employees looked forward to each month—a time when they were treated to an orgy of fine food and alcoholic beverages. Because all of the employees could not leave their worksite at once, they would arrange to go in two shifts. The railroad's agent had to accompany both shifts, and eat, drink, and make merry with them, and above all pick up the sizable check. He often complained about the ritual, explaining that the Southern Pacific had attempted on several occasions to eliminate or cut back on it. However, whenever he missed a monthly orgy, he noticed a corresponding precipitous drop in the tonnage of fertilizer products shipped over Southern Pacific's tracks in the following month. Shipments were diverted to competing railroads. The agent presumed that competing railroads were not excepted from the monthly ritual. That is, any failures to take the gang out for a gala party each month would result in a very noticeable loss of fertilizer tonnage shipped. Gratuities that had begun innocently eventually had reached the level of extortion.

Although the most common unilateral gratuities involve relatively petty things, such as free lunches, a bottle of wine, sports tickets, chocolates, and things generally costing less than $100, they can involve much more valuable things.

BILATERAL GRATUITIES

A bilateral gratuity, as the name implies, involves a mutual agreement, or a clear understanding—in effect, a contract—between the provider of a gratuity and a victim's employee, in which either party makes an offer—or requires—something of value, which the other party may choose to accept or reject. There is both an offer and acceptance between the two parties to a bilateral gratuity. The gratuity is, in fact, earned by the employee by performing in some predetermined manner that favors the provider of the gratuity. In all cases where a bilateral gratuity is involved, it can be said that the transaction is illegal since there is, in effect, a conspiracy to profit from an act detrimental to a third party, which is usually the recipient's employer.

A bilateral gratuity may involve:

- A proposal made by a contractor or vendor to a customer's employee
- An offer by an employee of the proposed victim to a contractor or vendor

CLOSED AND OPEN GRATUITIES

A closed gratuity is one that applies only to a specific contract or purchase order that the contractor or vendor is seeking. For example, he or she may offer money to an employee—a fixed sum, a percentage of profits, or a valuable prize, such as a vacation trip to Europe—in return for an order that is not in the employer's best interests.

An open gratuity is advertised so as to be known by employees in positions of trust, who then may choose to perform acts that will earn them the awards. These gratuities may consist of a fur coat for $100,000 in orders, a television set for ordering $10,000 in merchandise, or airline frequent flier miles.

The offering and acceptance of a bilateral gratuity are normally clear and obvious acts to which both parties to the gratuity are aware, and recipients have the opportunity to accept or reject. However, such is not always the case, and employees in positions of trust should beware. Case 8.1 was taken from an actual case, with names and key circumstances changed. It is presented to illustrate that at first sight all gratuities are not always presented as quid pro quo opportunities, but later it may become painfully obvious that they were. Readers should beware, because anyone could become an unintentional victim of a bribe; and if they are ever confronted by a situation where something appears to be too good to be true, it probably is not!

CASE 8.1 The Subtle Gratuity

The case involves a man named John. He was a government architect/engineer, living in the Washington, DC, area, and was the project manager responsible for overseeing the construction of a new building in California. As was normal practice, he was visiting the California construction site and had been working with the general contractor all day. The contractor suggested they go out to dinner that evening—his treat. The dinner was at a fine restaurant, and the food was superb. During the meal, an attractive woman, Marsha, approached their dinner table to chat with the contractor, who invited her to join them for dinner. She accepted. During the meal the contractor received a telephone call that appeared to disturb him. A short time later he apologized to his dinner companions, explaining that an emergency had arisen and that he would have to leave. He insisted, however, that they continue with their meal, and he arranged to pay the check before he left. John was fascinated with Marsha, who was a beautiful woman, and she appeared to be fond of him. One thing led to another, and John ended up spending much of the night with her. The next day John could not get Marsha off of his mind, and he was determined to see her again. That evening, remembering her address, he took a taxi to her home and rang the bell. When she came to the door she was surprised to see him. When he asked if he could come in, she asked him: "Who is paying tonight, you or the contractor?"

John learned very quickly that Marsha was a gratuity, and he had blundered into accepting it. He later claimed that he was not aware of the gratuity on that fateful evening when it was accepted, but the damage was irreversible. What followed is not entirely clear, but it is apparent that the contractor attempted to coerce John—a family man—into a conspiratorial role. John, however, displaying remarkable integrity, refused, and the excruciatingly painful news of his infidelity that evening got back to Washington before he did.

Open bilateral gratuities also include kickbacks and bribes. A clear example of an open bilateral gratuity surfaced as news in 1988, when it was disclosed that travel agents were involved in contests with various travel and transportation firms to win prizes offered to the agent(s) steering the most client business to contest sponsors. Prizes included $650,000 in cash from a car rental company, free trips to Hawaii and Europe, Sony Walkmans, cruises, fur coats, the use of a Ford Thunderbird for a year, maid service, and $4 million in free rooms at a Hyatt hotel in Hawaii. Ethical questions were raised about whether the contests, which were offered by everyone from air carriers to cruise lines, were in travelers' best interests. Critics observed that the promotions increased the cost of travel and influenced agents to steer customers in the wrong direction: "If I go to an agent and ask for his or her unbiased opinion between cruise ships for me, it's important for me to know whether the agent is working toward a fur coat."[2] Fears of how the contests affected service prompted a number of corporate customers to hire auditors to check on travel agencies. One found that travel agents were often booking one airline when another had a cheaper fare. The average cost difference: $113.

BRIBES AND KICKBACKS

A bribe is defined as something, such as money or a favor, offered or given to someone in a position of trust to induce him or her to act dishonestly. A kickback is defined as "a percentage payment to a person able to influence or control a source of income, as by confidential arrangement or coercion."[3]

A bribe is a gratuity—often a very large gratuity in excess of several thousand dollars—offered to a specific individual in a position of trust, to favor the donor in some way. Although cash is the usual currency of bribes, a bribe may involve the offer of a future job or literally anything of value. Consider, for example, the possibilities suggested by the following news article:

> As head of the Johnson Space Center in the 1970s and early '80s, Mr. Kraft approved paying one contractor tens of millions in bonuses for doing an especially good job of controlling costs—at the very time the contractor was being accused, by NASA's own inspectors, of defrauding the U.S. through false billing. Then when Mr. Kraft left NASA, he became a paid consultant to this contractor, Rockwell International Corp.[4]

When bribes are offered, there are almost always clear quid pro quo understandings, and they always originate with an entity interested in profiting as the result of obtaining something or some kind of favorable treatment. Bribes are most frequently associated with dishonest public officials who are given a sum of money to influence the award of a contract to the company offering the bribe. However, they probably occur more often in the private sector, where detection is more difficult. Consider the following news item.

The problem that U.S. companies have faced for many years in conducting international business is that French, German, and other firms have suffered no legal jeopardy at home for bribes they pay to get business; in fact, such bribes have been tax deductible. In 1995, for example, the Lockheed Corporation was fined $24.8 million for illegally paying $1 million to an Egyptian lawmaker in 1990 for helping to sell its C-190 aircraft to that country.

Bribes by U.S. firms are illegal, and when detected have brought severe penalties. It was estimated that in 1997 German companies paid bribes totaling as much as tens of billions of marks a year worldwide. (Two marks equal about one dollar.) The head of the Organized Crime and Corruption Department of the Frankfurt prosecutor's office stated that "as a rule of thumb, the payer of a kickback submits bills for double the amount paid."

"Kickback" is a slang term that connotes a vendor's or contractor's act of returning (kicking back) a share of ill-gotten profits resulting from the enabling employee's treacherous act. Both bribes and kickbacks are considerably more malevolent than simple bilateral gratuities.

Bribes frequently are confused with kickbacks, and the terms often are used incorrectly. They are, indeed, similar in important respects. Primary differences between the two include:

- *Timing.* A bribe is usually paid to the recipient before the illegal action takes place to induce him or her to participate in whatever scheme the entity offering the bribe has in mind. The recipient in a kickback scheme is normally a partner in crime and is willing to share ill-gotten gains as they materialize.
- *Computational Basis.* A bribe is usually a fixed sum calculated as sufficient to induce the recipient to participate in a scheme. A kickback is usually a percentage of any ill-gotten gains resulting from participation in a scheme and is likely to vary with the degree of the scheme's success.

In most cases involving bilateral gratuities, both the gratuity provider and the recipient are willing participants. In some cases, however, the gratuity provider is coerced into providing kickbacks. There was a case in New York City, for example, involving a corrupt government executive, who approached a large government supplier of stationery products and required that the supplier pay the executive a percentage of all future business received. The stationery company complied. However, after a period of time, the supplier involved had reason to plea bargain in another matter and offered the FBI details of the ongoing extortion. The executive was subsequently videotaped on a New York street handing over an envelope filled with cash. He was accused of receiving kickbacks of over $64,000.

In another case a Maryland electronic building security systems contractor was approached by a government contract employee who demanded a

10 percent kickback of all contract amounts that the contractor hoped to get. When the contractor complained that his profit margin was insufficient to provide the 10 percent kickback, the contracting employee had a solution. He would allow the contractor to increase his contract amounts by 10 percent. Rather than pay the kickback, the contractor reported the incident. An investigation followed, and the corrupt employee subsequently was found guilty of extortion. This case had its bizarre aspects. The contractor related how he was first approached by the corrupt employee's mother. He said one night during a trip to New York to negotiate the contract, he was in his hotel room when there was a knock at the door. He opened the door to find a little old woman carrying two shopping bags. She introduced herself and advised him that if he wished to do business the next day with her son, things would go better if he would buy the health foods she was selling. He said he bought everything she had in both shopping bags. The next day the son outlined the kickback proposal. In the weeks that followed, the son told the contractor that his family might enjoy a weekend trip to Washington and that the contractor should arrange it. He did. He reserved hotel rooms and paid for all their meals. After a few more weeks of petty demands, the contractor decided that enough was enough.

In many respects, the frequent flier awards offered by airlines to travelers who fly the airline's routes can be classified as simple bilateral gratuities. Employees of public and private entities often are permitted by their employers not only to schedule airline flights but to select the airline they will travel on as well. Many of the employees involved schedule unnecessary trips, destinations, and airlines, allowing them to accumulate frequent flier miles, which accrue in their personal accounts to be used at a later date for pleasure travel. The fact that the employees' travel could have been made at less cost on another airline is usually irrelevant to them.

Bribes frequently develop between business enterprises and governmental entities. Consider the following example:

PHILADELPHIA—Frank Coccia was an exceptional government employee, or so it seemed. As a top civilian official at a Defense Department procurement agency here, he controlled military clothing and textile purchases of about $1.3 billion annually. He was considered a tough and capable boss and was showered with bonuses and awards for outstanding performance.

But Mr. Coccia stood out in other ways, too. He took big payoffs from clothing contractors and hid most of the booty in his modest suburban home. Federal investigators seized $440,000 in cash, money orders, gold coins and securities from Mr. Coccia as part of a probe that has uncovered one of the most pervasive procurement frauds in recent Pentagon history.[5]

Kickbacks also occur frequently in the business world and are always covert. The following news account illustrates a dollar-significant kickback that has surfaced:

> As a Buyer for J. C. Penney Co., Jimmy Locklear earned $56,000 a year. But he controlled the spending of millions of dollars a year, and in 1988 he started peddling that influence. . . . he admits he sold to some suppliers and manufacturers' representatives crucial information, such as the amounts of their competitors' bids. To others, he flat-out sold the promise of large orders. In exchange, some vendors handed him cash; others wrote checks to front companies he set up. Over four years he supplemented his salary with as much as $1.5 million in bribes and kickbacks. . . . For a retail buyer to be prosecuted is definitely rare, says Assistant U. S. Attorney Michael Uhl. . . . We've had people calling us and telling us that these practices [kickbacks and bribes] are just accepted in the industry, Mr. Uhl says.[6]

SETTING STANDARDS OF CONDUCT

Entities should consider and decide on whether they wish to establish standards of conduct to guide their employees' behavior. Whatever their choice, it should be a carefully considered decision. They may choose not to set any standards, to adopt a zero tolerance for gratuities, or to define specific standards for employees to follow. Where entity management does not initiate an inclination to take action, its auditors should take the responsibility to convince management on the importance of doing so. They also may recommend appropriate standards for management to consider.

The process of setting standards of conduct should begin with the following questions:

- What entity interests would be served if vendors and others that we do business with are allowed to give gifts to our employees?
- In those instances where gratuities are deemed advantageous to the conduct of entity business—such as the provision of a meal as a convenience to a business luncheon—should there be limitations? Should reciprocation be necessary to offset the gratuity? Will reciprocation be an allowable entity expense item? Should value limitations be required? If so, how—per meal? annually?
- What is considered a gift—anything of value? airline frequent flier miles? candy? flowers? expense-paid trips? tickets to sporting events?

- What are the possible consequences of not allowing gifts? Of allowing gifts without limitation? If gifts are to be limited, what type of limitations? Dollar amount?
- What disciplinary actions would be appropriate for violations of standards of conduct?

Although this chapter is concerned primarily with the deleterious effect of unregulated gifts and gratuities to employees, entities may wish to include other employee behavioral standards in their standards of conduct. Any of the entity's policies—regarding lateness, vacations, outside employment, or fraternization between employees, for example—should be expressed in its standards of conduct. The entity's policy on the use of computers and copying equipment by employees also should be clearly stated.

Further, after the standards are decided on by entity management, its auditors should monitor at least once each year to determine whether all entity employees have read them and have signed that they have read and understand them.

In the late 1970s it was discovered that key employees of the U.S. General Services Administration had been accepting lavish gratuities, including large sums of cash, entertainment, vacations, the services of prostitutes, clothing, homes, and the like, from various vendors the agency was doing business with. In one case, a national supplier of millions of dollars in building materials used in the construction of federal buildings was suspected of perpetrating fraud against the government. Using special subpoena authority, all of the firm's records relevant to selected projects were acquired. Among other things, they confirmed the many gratuities the firm had bestowed on GSA employees, all of them dutifully recorded and reimbursed in company expense accounts. The agency considered disciplinary action of the GSA employees involved, including termination of employment and prosecution, in the more outrageous cases, but was hampered by the fact that the GSA had never provided employees with standards of conduct to follow. The agency was counseled that punishment of any kind would likely be protested and be met with defensive claims that acceptance of gifts was a common practice in the private sector. Disciplinary action was declined on the advice of legal counsel. However, GSA's management promptly issued standards of conduct that forbid the acceptance of gifts of any amount: not a cup of coffee; not a lunch; no airline frequent flier miles. Even year-end desk calendars had to be returned. Nothing could be accepted.

Many employers try to be reasonable in allowing some gifts, but place a limit on the amount of gratuities that may be accepted. For example, they may state that a lunch or dinner conducted for business purposes may be accepted provided that it does not exceed a cost of $25, $50, or whatever upper limit they feel appropriate. Alcoholic beverages may or may not be included in the limitations. Some entities limit the cumulative gratuities an employee may accept in a year to a specified amount—such as, perhaps, $300 or $500. Where employees are allowed to accept gratuities, some companies require that they report what was accepted. Regardless, whatever standards are set by an entity, they should be explicit with regard to the sort and value of gifts that may be accepted by employees in the conduct of their employment and, more important, what cannot be accepted.

EXECUTIVE ETHICS

Employers considering the need for standards of conduct for other than executive employees should find the following statistics of interest: A typical executive is in his mid-40s, frequently travels on business, says he values self-respect, and is very likely to commit financial fraud.[7]

Out of a test group of 400 respondents, 47 percent of top executives, 41 percent of controllers, and 76 percent of graduate-level business students surveyed were willing to commit fraud.[8]

RECOMMENDATIONS

Entities considering the adoption of codes of ethics, including standards of conduct, should appoint an ethics officer, whose task it is to oversee the adequacy of entity ethics programs and to monitor compliance with them. Depending on the size of the entity, the ethics officer may be appointed to a full- or a part-time position. The ethics officer and staff should consider formal training in ethics matters and joining professional ethics organizations to share with and benefit from association with ethics officers from other entities. The Center for Business Ethics provides training in ethics; it may be contacted at Web site <bnet.bentley.edu/dept/cbe/>. The Ethics Officer Association, located at 30 Church Street, Suite 331, Belmont, MA 02478, may be contacted at Web site <www.eoa.org/>.

Further, entities considering the adoption or modification of their standards of conduct should begin with a zero tolerance for gratuities. From there, if there are compelling reasons for allowing vendors and contractors to give gifts to employees, the reasons should be evaluated relative to the consequences and gratuities should be allowed as deemed appropriate. In all cases where it is decided to allow gratuities, limits should be imposed.

Whatever the entity's standards of conduct may be, they should be required reading by all employees, executives included. In addition to whatever behavioral standards are required, the statement distributed to employees should make it clear that violations will subject them to disciplinary action, to include termination of employment and possibly prosecution.

The entity's auditors should be instructed to monitor the adequacy of and compliance with the standards of conduct periodically.

NOTES

1. *American Heritage Dictionary,* 2nd college ed. (Boston: Houghton Mifflin Company, 1985); emphasis added.
2. Ed Perkins, "Travel Agents' Games Raise Ethics Issue," *Wall Street Journal,* November 23, 1988, p B1.
3. *American Heritage Dictionary.*
4. Jonathan Kwitny, "The Wrong Stuff—Space Agency Lets Contractors Off Easy If They Overcharge," *Wall Street Journal,* April 6, 1988.
5. Edward T. Pound, "Honored Employee Is a Key in Huge Fraud in Defense Purchasing," *Wall Street Journal,* March 2, 1988.
6. Andrea Gerlin, "How a Penney Buyer Made Up to $1.5 Million on Vendor Kickbacks," *Wall Street Journal,* February 7, 1995, pp. A1, A16.
7. Dawn Blalock, "Many Executives Are Tempted to Commit Fraud, Study Asserts," *Wall Street Journal,* March 26, 1996, pp. C1, C15.
8. Id.

9

EVIDENCE

Evidence is crucial to fraud auditing. The search for it—to prove the crime—is the essence of a fraud-specific audit. For most fraud audits, where fraud is discovered—or at least where fraud is strongly suspected—sufficient evidence to ensure conviction for fraud is usually the deciding factor in any decisions on whether to prosecute. And, aside from prosecution, without sufficient evidence, any remedial action by a victim, including any disciplinary action toward suspected perpetrators, is severely curtailed. Unfortunately, many auditors who are not adequately trained in fraud-specific auditing fail to understand the vital importance of evidence. Prosecution on the cases they develop often is declined, even though they are confident of their findings of fraud and may, in fact, be correct. It is evidence that transcends the gap between the auditor's firsthand knowledge of case circumstances and that which is conveyed to a judge or jury.

Many auditors tend to develop the consequences of fraud, such as the amount of the theft. However, when it comes down to naming the people involved in a manner that is acceptable to the court, they fall short unless they have at least rudimentary training in the nature of evidence. Chapter 1 estimated that group 2 fraud constituted about 40 percent of all fraud. Group 2 fraud constitutes fraud cases which, for the most part, have been discovered or are suspected, but which have been insufficiently documented with the evidence required to ensure successful prosecution. The questions that this condition raises are: Does sufficient additional evidence not exist to be detected? Are auditors not sufficiently proactive or skilled to detect it? Both answers undoubtedly account for the failure of fraud cases discovered to advance beyond group 2. Many perpetrators are very clever and leave few if any clues. In these instances the most skilled and proactive of auditors would be unlikely to detect recognizable evidence of fraud. However, the vast majority of auditors are not skilled in fraud detection and do not have sufficient knowledge of what evidence is required for prosecution purposes. As a result, at least half of the group 2 fraud cases that could have advanced to prosecution do not.

Accordingly, it follows that auditors who are better trained to recognize and gather relevant evidence could have a powerful impact on reducing the proportion of fraud in this category. The aim of this chapter is to sensitize auditors to the absolute necessity to make the discovery and development of evidence a primary audit objective. It provides readers with an awareness of the relevance of evidence in fraud auditing and a rudimentary understanding of the nature and importance of evidence. Only one caveat is offered. The author is an experienced fraud auditor who has worked many times with prosecutors but is not an experienced prosecutor. Important questions involving legal matters with regard to actual audits in progress should be referred to an experienced prosecutor for authoritative answers. For investigative and legal content of a more definitive nature written by subject specialists, readers are referred to the text *Accountant's Guide to Fraud Detection and Control.*[1]

The evidence being collected in fraud-specific auditing falls into one of two groups; indicative evidence and validating evidence. Indicative evidence is always the object of the auditor's search during the proactive stage of fraud-specific auditing.

INDICATIVE EVIDENCE

Indicative evidence tends to indicate that fraud may have occurred, but it does not prove it. During the proactive stage of fraud-specific auditing, auditors are literally fishing for indications that fraud may have occurred without having the benefit of any evidence of any kind that it in fact has. In this stage there is little to guide auditors in the methods to use and few indications to suggest what sort of fraud to look for. Experience and intuition are auditors' only mainstays. In this proactive audit stage auditors' main quest is not necessarily to find fraud, fraud perpetrators, or assemble evidence to prosecute them. That will come later. Rather new auditors merely sift through large amounts of raw data looking for leads or indications that fraud may have occurred. The first sighting of fraud is usually of evidence traces that in themselves do little to suggest fraud. The traces first must be recognized as indicia of fraud and must be seen as a preliminary sign of a fraud determination. Inexperienced auditors often overlook evidence traces and may fail to see their fraud potential.

To illustrate, there was an instance when an auditor who had been examining payments for contract building maintenance services totally missed seeing the fraud potential in indicative evidence he had detected. In the process of examining a payment of about $5,000 for cleaning window blinds in a large building, the auditor noticed that the vendor had failed to deduct a discount of about 25 percent, which had been negotiated as a contract term. The contractor's invoice, when presented, requested payment for $5,000—the open market price advertised for the contractor's services. However, the invoice failed to make any mention of the 25 percent discount or to deduct it from the amount due. The $5,000 amount was approved by the victim's representative and paid in full. Had the 25 percent discount been applied, the amount claimed and paid should have been $3,750. The auditor in this case felt that the overcharge was a simple clerical error. However, experienced fraud-sensitive auditors would have asked themselves if there was any reason to suspect the transaction. That is, they would have considered the questions "Is it reasonable for a competent person not to remember the very significant terms of the contract he or she participated in and/or very likely negotiated?" "Could the failure to deduct the $1,250 discount be more than a mere oversight?" "Was it a simple case of negligence by the contractor and the victim's representative, or was it fraud?" It could have been either. Readers also should ask what they themselves would have done in this case. Those who would suspect the possibility of fraud are entitled to a star.

In the actual case this was drawn from, the auditor was not sensitive to fraud and was not suspicious of the transaction. Acting like most auditors, he proudly reported his finding to operating personnel, who took prompt action to recover the overpayment. Incidentally, it is not unusual for auditors to respond in this "gotcha" manner, and they must be encouraged to act differently. Many are sensitive of a need to justify their existence by reporting opportunities to save their client or employer money.

Experienced fraud-sensitive auditors would suspect that they had discovered indicia of fraud. Naively jumping to the conclusion that his finding was a clerical error, and seeking to recover the overpayment, the auditor should have recognized the possibility that the vendor and the victim's employee who approved the invoice were conspiring to defraud the building operator of $1,250 on the cleaning contract, with the $1,250 overpayment payment subsequently divided between them.

Had he recognized this possibility, he would have quietly noted his observation in his work papers without calling it to anyone's attention or showing any outward indication of his discovery. He then could have chosen to validate his discovery immediately or at a more opportune time. Actually, there would be nothing lost in delaying reporting his discovery of the overcharge and obtaining the $1,250 refund. If the overpayment were later found to be merely an oversight by the contracting officer, it could always have been recovered.

To validate his discovery, the auditor should have assumed the attitude that if his discovery involved fraud, it is likely that it happened before and involved either of or both parties. Accordingly, he should have examined other contracts and/or delivery orders completed by that contractor, and/or other contract transactions involving the same employee. If they were indeed dishonest, it is a good possibility that other similar transactions could be identified. Each additional questionable transaction discovered would irreparably damage any plausibility excuse that the accused might offer and more clearly establish that there was intent to defraud involved.

VALIDATING EVIDENCE

Once auditors have discovered indicative evidence that fraud could have occurred, the object of their search changes to a search for validating evidence. Validating evidence is anything that tends to confirm the indicative evidence. Once this confirmation has been made, the sum of the indicative evidence that the auditors have gathered may be properly described as evidence. Incidentally, the terms "indicative evidence" and "validating evidence" are used here to clarify the progression of a proactive fraud-specific audit from the zero evidence stage through the point where bona-fide evidence is developed and the reactive stage of fraud-specific auditing begins.

The initial search for indicative evidence clearly begins in the proactive audit stage, which involves a search for anything that indicates the possibility of fraud. Technically speaking, indicative evidence is not evidence per se, in that nothing can be concluded from it. Proactive auditing continues until sufficient indications of fraud are detected to conclude that fraud has in fact been detected. Once this point is reached (a personal judgment on the part of the auditor) the audit becomes reactive. In the reactive stage, audit objectives shift to one of searching for validating or corroborating evidence to firm up the proactive audit discovery, or negate it.

Indicative evidence can take any form, and auditors must approach their examination with what might be called a controlled state of paranoia—that is, they must suspect everything.

Often, a fraud victim's losses are noticed before there is any discovery of evidence to conclude whether the losses are due to fraud or waste. In such instances, with no evidence to indicate that fraud was involved, the losses are usually attributed to waste resulting from someone's negligence or incompetence. It is not until sufficient evidence of fraud has been detected, should it be sought, that the losses are attributed to fraud, and most entities experiencing losses rarely look for evidence of fraud, or have the capability to look for fraud. Many would be surprised to find—if they were to employ a fraud competent auditor—that fraud was the real culprit. Experienced fraud auditors usually begin their work with the mind set that experienced employees have the intelligence to not waste assets, and looks for the fraud angle in their actions. Take note that it is evidence that is the determining factor in classifying losses as waste or fraud, and that entities do not find evidence of fraud if they do not look for it.

For the most part, fraud cases considered to be in the group 2 category—fraud that has been discovered but the perpetrators are not being prosecuted—are so classified because the totality of evidence assembled is not sufficient to ensure a conviction if the suspects are prosecuted. To better appreciate this situation, consider that in group 2 fraud cases, victims possess evidence ranging in degree of quantity and quality from cases where the indicative evidence assembled is a bare minimum needed to cause a suspicion of fraud, to cases where considerable evidence has been collected, but there still remains some doubt that a jury might not convict the defendant.

On the bottom end of the range of evidence, victims have a minimum of evidence that leads them to suspect the possibility of fraud. On the other hand, on the substantial end of the group 2 range, victims have accumulated considerable, seemingly irrefutable evidence, clearly establishing—in their opinion—that fraud has occurred. Whether to move the case into the group 1 category by seeking prosecution in court may be a judgment call by a prosecutor. For many prosecutors, there is never too much evidence.

Often deciding to prosecute a case at the top of the group 2 category is difficult for victims. The line between groups 1 and 2 is very indistinct and is often a matter of judgment. Prosecutors may tell victims that a decision to prosecute that does not result in a conviction could be considered a capricious disclosure of defamatory material, which would be triply injurious to victims. In such instances, victims have lost the stolen asset, a court of law has found the perpetrator to be not guilty, and the victim may be sued for defaming the alleged perpetrator.

In cases in which prosecution is declined, what is most frustrating to victims of fraud who feel that the evidence of fraud is clear and a perpetrator's guilt certain is the fact that without a guilty conviction, they may be unable to discipline the suspected perpetrator—at least not for fraud.

Making a case of fraud is surprisingly difficult for most inexperienced fraud auditors. Consider Case 9.1.

CASE 9.1   The Borrowed Assets

John Doe falsified documents on July 1, to obtain $100,000 of his
employer's funds to invest in the stock market. Using the $100,000,
he bought stock on July 6, intending to repay his employer out of his
profits. John was lucky. He sold his stock for $200,000 on July 9 and
promptly replaced the funds he had taken without his employer's
knowledge. However, the falsified documents were discovered on
July 10, and John was accused of defrauding his employer. There is
never any question that John falsified the documents and received
the $100,000. When interrogated, he admitted everything and stated
that he invested the proceeds in the stock market. The employer is
outraged, and wishes to prosecute John for fraud.

Is it likely that John Doe will be prosecuted based on the evidence
given in the illustration? If so, is it likely that he will be found guilty of
fraud? The answers are no, and no. The evidence provided here does not
establish that John intended to steal the $100,000. Nor does it show that
the employer was harmed. At trial, John would be likely to argue that he
only intended to borrow the money for a few days. He is willing to pay the
employer interest. He will say that his investment was based on a dependable tip and will argue that his replacement of the money on July 9, before
it ever was discovered missing, is proof of his claim. John's act was outrageous, and perhaps even illegal, and he may be disciplined by his
employer; but it could be difficult to convict him of fraud.

In a real-life situation, however, involving trained and experienced
fraud auditors, the case would very likely include more evidence than was
presented in the preceding illustration. Trained auditors would recognize
John as a thief and use procedures designed to prove it, if at all possible.
Such auditors would know that if John truly was a thief, he probably
would have borrowed money from his employer on prior occasions, and
they would set out to discover those occasions. They also would assume
that John could not possibly have been lucky in all his prior stock market
investments or other gambling episodes. By documenting the other occasions, some of which John very likely did not repay, auditors would have
shown other instances of John's intention to risk his employer's funds.
Had other examples been provided, John would have been prosecuted and
very likely convicted.

To illustrate the uncertainties in prosecution actions, even when the evidence appears to be compelling, consider Case 9.2. It involved apparent

fraudulent acts by a government contractor in Oklahoma and his subsequent prosecution in a federal district court in the Southern District of Texas. Under the contract, the contractor was responsible for repairing government equipment, such as mobile aircraft electrical generators, shipped to him by military bases in the American Southwest.

CASE 9.2 Equipment Repair Contractor's False Claims

The contract was a time and material (T & M) contract. That is, it provided that the contractor would be reimbursed on the basis of the number of direct labor hours he expended on equipment repaired, at a fixed hourly rate, as specified in the contract. He also would be reimbursed for the actual cost of repair parts purchased. The fixed hourly rate had been bid by the contractor in competition against other contractors and normally would include his average cost of an hour of direct labor, his prorated hourly overhead and administrative costs, and profit applicable to those costs. For example, assuming that the contractor spent 100 direct labor hours to repair an item of equipment at a contract hourly rate of $30, and had purchased $500 of repair parts, he would invoice the government $3,500 (100 hours $\times$ $30 + $500 = $3,500).

The contract also required that the contractor make his records available for audit, should it be requested. It was. The audit disclosed that he had falsely inflated the labor hours he claimed to have expended and had falsely claimed the purchase of repair parts that had not been purchased. The fraud was so blatant, for example, that addresses given for many of the parts suppliers were vacant lots.

Also, as the auditors clearly proved in an audit of payroll records, the hours charged to the contract by the employees alleged to have worked on the job orders audited had far exceeded the total weekly hours that the employees named had worked and been paid for.

Armed with seemingly indisputable evidence of fraud, the contractor was indicted, prosecuted, and convicted of fraud in a federal court in Texas. What is particularly noteworthy in this illustration, however, were the somewhat angry after trial comments of the assistant U.S. attorney who prosecuted the case. He complained to the auditors that he had difficulty convincing the jury of the contractor's guilt and came close to failing. Next time, he advised them,". . . give me stronger evidence of the contractor's 'intent' to defraud the government." What he was looking for, if it were possible, was evidence that the contractor had committed fraud on more than this one contract, thereby making it clear that he had fraudulent intent and that he was, in fact, a criminal.

In this case, the auditors believed that there was compelling evidence of the contractor's guilt. However, the contractor's defense attorney raised a question as to whether the contractor was in fact a criminal, pleading that one apparent crime does not a criminal make. If there was no other evidence of criminal conduct, perhaps this was just a careless bookkeeping error.

This contractor's guilt later appeared to be certain when viewed in the context of a corollary case that involved a U.S. Air Force sergeant who was allegedly in collusion with the contractor. The sergeant was to be tried separately by a military court for sending perfectly serviceable generators, not in need of repair, to the contractor, who merely stored them for a short time before returning them and billing the government for work not done. The contractor allegedly split the proceeds with the sergeant.

Evidence is literally the heart of a fraud-specific audit.

NOTES

1. Howard R. Davia, Patrick C. Coggins, John C. Wideman, and Joseph T. Kastantin, *Accountant's Guide to Fraud Detection and Control* (New York: John Wiley & Sons, 2000).

10

SYMPTOMATIC FRAUD AUDITING

One of the most difficult things about proactive fraud-specific auditing is that it requires auditors to institute search procedures to detect fraud in circumstances where there is no evidence per se to indicate that fraud may exist. Performing proactive fraud-specific auditing is much more difficult than performing reactive fraud-specific auditing, which begins with solid leads. One problem is that indicia of fraud committed by cautious and expert perpetrators is rarely found without initiating relatively blind search procedures. And without that initial finding of indicia of fraud, reactive fraud-specific auditing never occurs. The best perpetrators tend to be cautious and conservative in their criminal endeavors, leaving little if anything to be detected. Luckily for victims, not all fraud perpetrators are ultra cautious and/or conservative, and their crimes do leave faint traces that can be detected by enlightened searches.

In many cases those traces are bona-fide evidence that directly indicates that fraud may have occurred, and those traces can eventually be used as evidentiary material. However, in many other cases the traces—which cannot be characterized as evidence—can be better described as the symptoms or effects of the crime. Rather than having to resort to random or intuitive searches in the hope of detecting scant bits of evidence upon which to build more substantive examinations, auditors are advised first to search for these effects or symptoms to enhance further efforts. This practice is called symptomatic fraud auditing. For the record, a "symptom" is defined as a circumstance or phenomenon regarded as an indication or characteristic of a condition or event.[1] Accordingly, when practicing symptomatic fraud auditing, auditors take note of circumstances or events that could be attributed to fraud and initiate audit procedures as if the circumstances were indicia of fraud. Note that the circumstances or events referred to are not evidence of fraud but may be symptoms of fraud.

Most observers, will not regard these symptoms as suspicious. Nor are they necessarily. In most instances they are merely the result of innocent natural events. However, not infrequently, the symptoms—when properly interpreted—are indications of fraud. Interpreters' mind-sets affect how these symptoms are interpreted. Those people who have confidence in their fellow humans not to steal from them will view the symptoms with concern rather than suspicion. However, good fraud auditors must cultivate an attitude of controlled paranoia, recognizing fraud possibilities in what others may regard as regrettable but normal events. For example, consider a leaking warehouse roof that had been replaced within the last two or three years. How should the leak be regarded? Was the contractor who replaced the roof (1) innocent of any liability? (2) negligent? (3) guilty of fraud? or (4) none of the above? Conceivably, the correct answer could be any one or more of the four given. If the contractor replaced the roof in full accord with the contract's specifications, neither choice (2), (3), or (4) would be appropriate. If the new roof was damaged after the contractor finished the job, and water was able to penetrate the damaged surface, choice (1) is correct, all but ruling out choices (2) through (4). However, if the contractor deviated from contract specifications for the job, perhaps substituting cheaper materials or cutting corners to save costs, then choice (3) is correct. Hence, the symptom of a leaking roof can lead to the discovery of fraud—in this case, defective delivery fraud.

Accordingly, auditors seeking to detect fraud are well advised to look to events and circumstances that may exhibit the effects of fraud. These might be gleaned from an entity's formal as well as informal complaints system. The minutes or memoranda of all meetings should be carefully monitored to detect complaints, performance deviations, and the like. Nonroutine and all emergency spending outlays may harbor fraud possibilities. Auditors should bear in mind that asset theft fraud involves a loss of assets that should leave discernable traces.

SYMPTOMS OF FRAUD

Defective deliveries of goods or services is perhaps one of the foremost fraud symptom generators. Recipients of goods or services that are defective tend to complain. Accordingly, before auditors elect to search for defective delivery fraud (Chapter 6) and begin their examination by selecting random payment transactions involving the acquisition of goods or services, they may choose to begin by determining whether there are any complaints, formal or informal, regarding inferior quality of products or workmanship that has been delivered.

A fraud that once occurred in a Michigan city was discovered somewhat by chance, by auditors searching for defective delivery fraud. However, it is quite likely that it could have been discovered more surely by symptomatic auditing. In a random selection of payment transactions, the auditors chose to examine a payment for about $5,000 made to recondition a water storage tank (see Case 5.1, page 73) located on the roof of a high-rise office building. Upon inspecting the supposedly reconditioned tank, they discovered a shell fraud—that is, no work had been done. The walls of the water-filled tank were encrusted with extensive rust and scale.

The point of this illustration is that since the water tank was badly corroded, as reported by the inspecting engineer hired by the auditors, it is quite likely that the water quality was also bad. And it is likely that users had complained of polluted water. If they had—and it is not known that they did not—auditors reviewing the complaints could have examined the tank's maintenance history and found that the tank supposedly had been reconditioned recently. With that information in mind, they would have had good reason to question if the tank had, in fact, been reconditioned. An inspection similar to the one made by chance would have revealed the fraud.

In an actual illustration of a fraud discovered from symptoms, an Indianapolis office suite complained of persistent water leaks originating from their ceiling. A parking area was located over the office suite, and eventually the leaks were traced to water that had somehow penetrated from the parking area. This was not an unusual event, given the circumstances, except for the fact that the parking area recently had been extensively resurfaced, and the resurfacing contractor had been required to install an extremely durable and dependably waterproof rubberlike membrane. There appeared to be only three possibilities to explain the leaks. The rubberlike material installed itself may have been defective, the membrane was applied improperly, or the contractor did not install the membrane as was required by the contract.

Here is what was interesting. Normally, when a situation such as this occurs, the contracting entity complains to the installing contractor (who may be a fraud perpetrator) and requires that the leak be fixed. In many cases, the leak would never be fixed adequately, and the problem would never be resolved satisfactorily. However, if paranoid fraud auditors were made aware of the leak, they would have suspected faulty performance by the contractor and arranged to test the parking lot surface to determine if the resurfacing job was performed in accordance with contract specifications before the contractor was called in. This is what actually happened, and the auditor discovered that the contractor had failed to install the rubberlike membrane that was specified by the contract, installing a cheaper substitute instead.

VARIATIONS IN ACTUAL VERSUS PLANNED COST

Variations in actual versus planned cost sometimes reveal symptoms of fraud—that is, unexplained differences between planned versus actual costs. An automobile rental entity became concerned when its automobile capital costs had risen significantly over expected costs but was at a loss to explain the increases other than to speculate that the vehicles were receiving hard usage. The auditor who was assigned to investigate the anomaly discovered that fraud may have been the underlying reason when she discovered the following events.

To maintain its automotive fleet properly, the entity involved had contracted with an automotive service company to perform its vehicular maintenance needs as they arose. The contract called for the repair and replacement of necessary parts and components. However, the contractor was also instructed to limit repairs to those vehicles that were economically repairable, factoring in the age of each vehicle involved and the estimated cost of repair. He was instructed to identify those vehicles that were not economically reparable for subsequent sale at the periodic auctions conducted by the entity. So far so good. The auditor, however, was one of those paranoid types that are not easily fooled. She discovered that the service contractor was designating easily reparable vehicles as not economically reparable. Then, when the vehicles were sold at auction, the service contractor's agents knew which vehicles were in excellent condition and were able to acquire them at prices only slightly above those of vehicles in poor condition.

It is important to mention here that comparisons of financial plans with actual costs incurred is not always worthwhile. It makes a difference, for example, whether the entity involved has a suitably fine-tuned accounting system, and whether the system is on the accrual basis or the cash basis of accounting. Cash basis accounting systems, as are typically used in city/county/state/federal governmental organizations, institutions, universities, and many businesses, are of little, if any, value in detecting fraud. In fact, they tend to facilitate fraud.

Unfortunately, the primary financial management objectives of entities with cash-based accounting systems tend to be on spending in accordance with cash availability rather than to spending to meet operating needs. Accordingly, rarely are there notable differences between financial plans and actual expenditures in year-end operating reports. For example, if budget account #12345 plans for the expenditure of $12,568, it is extremely likely that actual costs will be within 1 percent of that amount. In fact, cash basis managers quickly learn to spend everything they are given to spend, or be censured for not meeting their spending goals. And it is not unusual for managers in cash basis environments not to seek the best prices when forced to use up their year-end surpluses. Likewise, clever fraud perpetrators in these cash basis environments are aware of the spending goals and frequently "help" embattled managers by stealing a portion of their year-end surpluses.

CASE 10.1 The Surplus Funds Account

A 33-year-old Virginia woman was sentenced on May 15, 2000 to 18 months in prison for embezzling $395,991 from a branch of the Interior Department where she worked. She was also ordered to pay full restitution. The embezzlement occurred on 46 occasions from January 1997 to June 1999. It was not explained how the discovery occurred.

This case is particularly relevant in discussing symptomatic auditing in that the vagaries of the fiscal systems in use suggest a viable avenue for proactive fraud auditing. It was explained that the woman embezzled the funds from what are known in government as expiring fiscal year appropriations. Any entity operating under the cash basis of accounting is vulnerable to the same fraud. This includes government entities at all levels, most colleges and universities, not-for-profit entities, and the like. They receive their annual operating funds from a funding agency, such as the U.S. Congress, or a state legislature, and their use of the funds is limited to a specific fiscal year. Funds not used at the end of the year may not legally be used in subsequent years.

The perpetrator in this case observed that the federal agency involved ended their fiscal years with large unspent appropriation balances, and she took note of the fact that the status of those unspent funds was never reviewed. Accordingly, she saw the opportunity to embezzle portions of the unspent balances each year, unnoticed, without generating any complaints from the departments involved. The point of this case is that unspent balances remaining unspent at the end of fiscal periods, in agencies operating with annual appropriations, is a symptom of the opportunity for fraud.[2]

Fraud auditors working in organizations employing cash basis accounting systems, however, can be as clever as are the perpetrators by focusing examinations on transactions occurring near but before the close of fiscal periods. The symptoms to look for are surges in spending in the last two months of the fiscal year. This extraordinary spending activity in May of a fiscal year ending in June can easily mask the work of a fraud perpetrator seeking to tap the entity's unspent money. The irony of this situation is that entities on the cash basis of accounting are notorious for bad financial management—truly effective financial management is extremely difficult in a cash-based accounting environment. As a result, managers tend to defer discretionary spending until the end of their fiscal year, at which time they can be confident of how much cash remains available to be spent. Accordingly, the fraud perpetrator who acts just before the start of an entity's "Christmas Eve" shopping spree at the end of a fiscal year often has a wide choice of available fund pools to locate his or her fraud scheme.

There are many illustrations of bad financial management in cash-based organizations. Consider the case of the University of Maryland employee (see Case 1.3, page 11) who was discovered to have created $149,190 in payroll checks for nonexistent employees, over a six-year period, cashed the checks, and pocketed the money. Despite the loss of significant sums to fraud, the university obviously had no suspicions that she was a thief when it awarded her the President's Award in 1996 as the university's most valued employee. There is good reason to wonder what sort of financial management system could they have had to have lost such a significant sum to fraud without suspecting something was amiss. She became a suspect only after her husband was suspected in an unrelated stolen check crime, and U.S. Postal Inspectors searching their home found University of Maryland payroll stubs under different names and became suspicious. In another instance a federal government employee, using a government credit card, was accidentally discovered to have purchased several hundred thousand dollars' worth of Polaroid film, over a period of a year or so, which he resold for cash to finance a drug habit. His crime was discovered when the seller of the film became suspicious of the large purchases and alerted the buyer's employer. Ordinarily any entity employing an accrual basis accounting system would have noticed the large extraordinary expenditures immediately. However, the cash basis federal agency involved had no prior suspicions that its employee was engaged in a theft of such significance.

"SHOULD COST" APPROACH

From time to time fraud auditors speak of a "should cost" approach to fraud auditing. Basically this means that auditors examining a service or product that has been delivered make an attempt to determine whether the price paid is reasonable. That is, what should it cost? The unit price charged for the product or service delivered is, in effect, the symptom of a possible fraud. If the price paid seems to be too high, auditors initiate procedures to determine how the price was established and to verify whether it really was too high. If it indeed was too high, auditors must initiate a fraud-specific examination to determine if someone was culpable, and who.

Auditors are aware that many frauds are enabled by conspiracies that exist between contractors or vendors and key entity employees, wherein the employee—in return for a kickback or other profit-sharing arrangement—takes the necessary steps to direct the contract to his or her conspirator, aware that the price is higher than the best prevailing market price. The contractor or vendor charges more for the product or service to be delivered to pay for the employee's kickback. The excessive price paid is the cost of the fraud to the victim employer.

Some auditors who specialize in should cost auditing are very good at sensing whether their employers paid too much for a product or service. In an actual case that occurred in New York City, an auditor was examining purchases of office equipment when he came across a large order for hand-held printing calculators. The unit price charged his employer troubled him, for it appeared about $100 too high. During his lunch hour he decided to check out the market rate for the calculators and visited an office supply store a few blocks away from his audit site. After inquiring about the sales price for an identical calculator, his suspicions were proven. The merchant would have sold him one of the same calculators for about $100 less than his employer was paying for several dozens of them. The auditor's examination from that point on became a fraud-specific audit designed to prove fraud.

EMPLOYEE LIFESTYLE CHANGES

Invariably, when employees profit from fraud, their lifestyles improve dramatically. Although many auditors find it objectionable to target individuals for fraud-specific fraud audits when there is no evidence that they committed fraud, doing so can be a very productive in disclosing fraud. Of course, any reviews of this nature must be conducted with the utmost discretion, and any information disclosed must be kept very confidential.

However, many thieves steal to enhance their lifestyles, and often they spend their ill-gotten gains openly.

A perpetrator (see Case 3.3, page 45) in Chicago—an accounting clerk—began to spend money far beyond his salary. A kindly man, he periodically took several of his office worker friends out to lunch at fashionable restaurants. He volunteered that a rich aunt had died recently and that he had inherited her fortune. No one questioned his story, until one day the inevitable occurred. Totally by accident it was discovered that he had been submitting false invoices for building maintenance projects and collecting the payments. His total theft exceeded $900,000. It is quite likely that a lifestyle review would have disclosed his fraud much earlier.

In another instance reported in 1997 (see Case 1.1, page 7), a Maryland couple who earned $36,000 and $33,000 a year each were enjoying a lifestyle that was far beyond what those salary amounts would pay for. Federal prosecutors reported that the couple: owned a home with a pool, a hot tub, and a four-car garage; a second home with eight bedrooms and a six-car garage on the waterfront worth $800,000; a cottage on an island; had purchased eight cars and trucks, two boats, three Jet Skis; had a doll collection worth $170,000; had bought $85,000 in U.S. savings bonds for themselves, a son, and a granddaughter; had paid private college tuition for two sons; and gave "substantial sums" to family members. The couple pleaded guilty to embezzling $3.28 million from a union. In the scheme, the wife—the perpetrator—inflated and diverted automatic payroll deductions destined for a credit union to her own account. The amount diverted was reported as $1.03 million in 1995. The fraud had lasted for nine years without detection because the perpetrator was also responsible for reconciling the union's accounts. When asked how the losses could have continued for nine years, a spokesman for the union said, "I'm not sure I could give you an answer to that." The fraud was discovered accidentally when the credit union became suspicious of large sums of money moving into and out of union accounts. One can only wonder how it was that no one observed or questioned the lifestyle of the $33,000-a-year clerk.

NOTES

1. *American Heritage Dictionary,* 2nd college ed. (Boston: Houghton Mifflin Company, 1985).
2. Column compiled from reports by various staff writers and the Associated Press. "Crime and Justice/Virginia," *Washington Post,* May 16, 2000, B2.

11

FRAUD AUDITING ALTERNATIVES

Because detecting fraud is so difficult, fraud auditors must utilize every opportunity to maximize fraud detection/prevention. They must be resourceful and innovative at all times. To that end, certain alternatives to the direct proactive fraud-specific auditing discussed throughout this text can be used to combat fraud. Surprisingly, in some instances that alternative is to do nothing.

MONITORING KNOWN OR SUSPECTED FRAUD

From time to time fraud auditors detect fraud that they have reason to suspect may exist to an extent far beyond that which they have discovered. When it is detected, four hard questions that have to be answered:

1. Do we keep auditing until we have found it all, or most of it?
2. Do we recommend internal controls designed to limit further occurrences of it?
3. Is a processing system change justified?
4. Do we do nothing?

In question 1, if the fraud may be difficult to detect and may require an inordinate amount of audit effort, further auditing may not be a viable option. For example, if the expenditure of audit resources is in excess of the cost of the fraud being detected by the additional audit effort, controlling the fraud by unlimited auditing may not be a prudent decision. It could easily not be a very profitable one. Option 2 is sometimes a viable alternative, provided that suitable internal controls can be devised that are

effective as well as cost beneficial and that do not unduly suppress productivity. Accordingly, internal controls may or may not be a viable alternative. Cost/benefit studies are required to answer option 3. Changes,
particularly in large automated systems, usually are not accomplished easily or cheaply. What about option 4? Are there circumstances where it
would be prudent to do nothing to suppress or disclose fraud that it is
believed will be continuing? The answer is yes.

The merits of doing nothing is best illustrated by an example recalled
from personal experience. A number of years ago the IRS—in a period of
time before its automated surveillance systems were enhanced to provide
the necessary control—discovered that perpetrators were engaging in tax
frauds that were resulting in the payment of illegitimate refunds for
allegedly overpaid taxes. Their audits of relatively small numbers of the
over 100 million individual tax returns filed disclosed what the IRS
believed to be several fraud schemes. One involved a practice wherein tax
filers transposed the amounts withheld from wages when entering the
amounts on their tax returns, the IRS believed many of these transpositions were intentional. The filer might transpose, for example, a $3,600
actual amount withheld as $6,300. Then, after computing a tax liability of,
let's say, $3,500, the tax filer would claim a refund of $2,800 instead if the
$100 amount actually due. For the perpetrators the fraud—if it was
fraud—was an ideal opportunity, for if no one detected the intentional
transposition, they got to keep the ill-gotten gains. If the fraud was
detected, they could always claim that the transposition was accidental.
The IRS estimated that approximately $19 million of the total taxes were
lost annually as a result of the suspected fraud. After considering the various options available to it, the IRS—very logically and justifiably—
decided to do nothing to stop the $19 million annual loss. Its very
appropriate reasons for this course of action are the point of this lesson.

Among the possible alternatives available to the IRS were:

1. Audit all 100 million plus tax returns to detect all instances of
   transpositions.
2. Install the internal controls to prevent and/or significantly reduce
   the losses discovered.
3. Redesign the automated data processing system to capture the
   amounts reported by employers as withheld as well as the amounts
   reported by tax return filers as withheld, and compare them.
4. Do nothing but periodically conduct audit samples of tax returns for
   the purpose of estimating each year's loss to this particular fraud.

The first option—auditing all 100 million plus individual tax returns—was never considered seriously. The enormous cost involved could never be justified to recover $19 million from a cost/benefit standpoint. The internal control that was considered and rejected involved requiring a simple manual comparison of the amount reported as withheld by employers as indicated on each taxpayer's W-2 form submitted with each tax return to the amount recorded by the taxpayer on the tax return as having been withheld. Under the processing system that was in operation at the time, no such automated comparison was ever made because the information necessary to allow the comparison was not being captured in machine-readable form. Any comparisons would have to be done manually by clerks processing the tax returns. The idea, however, was quickly rejected when it was estimated that manual comparisons would involve a cost of approximately $1 per tax return—an aggregate cost of over $100 million a year—to save the $19 million a year estimated as being lost. Not a good idea. The third option—upgrading the automated system to capture the data and automate the comparison function—would have cost several hundred million dollars. The cost/benefit ratio was way out of line. The fourth option, to do nothing—except to audit sample tax returns submitted to estimate the amount of the fraud—was elected. It produced a favorable cost/benefit ratio and under the circumstances was appropriate. If the fraud ever increased to the point where more aggressive action was required, it could be considered.

Many people find the awareness that a fraud may be occurring and inability to stop it disturbing. However vexing as it may be, doing nothing is often a most prudent decision. Nevertheless, the fraud should never be simply forgotten. It should be monitored regularly through statistical sampling and the cost/benefit aspects of controlling it regularly recalculated. Many banks and retail stores have similar situations. Their audits of daily cash shortages occurring at teller windows and cash registers are sometimes so consistent that they are positive that cashiers are stealing petty amounts. Nevertheless, often they have no practical alternative other than to do nothing but monitor the shortages to ensure that they do not exceed tolerable limits.

As a postscript to the IRS example, although the IRS is to be commended for its prudent action, its decision was helped by the fact that the apparent transpositions detected were obviously not all fraud and did not always result in a loss of tax revenues. In many cases the transpositions were bona fide and in the government's favor. For every $19 million in transpositions resulting in losses to the government, there were also $14 million in estimated losses to taxpayers who erred by making transpositions in the

government's favor. Effective measures to stop the frauds that were occurring would also have resulted in the detection of honest taxpayer errors and
the obligation to refund any amounts determined as owed to them.

MONITORING OPERATIONAL AREAS AT RISK OF FRAUD

Besides searching for evidence of fraud, fraud auditors find it worthwhile
to evaluate periodically operational systems that may be at risk of fraud.
In their examinations they, in effect, place themselves in the role of a fraud
perpetrator and attempt to devise schemes to evade internal controls and
perpetrate fraud. In some instances, when they believe that a system can
be penetrated, they actually test their theories by attempting to perpetrate
the fraud envisioned, lacking only the intent to defraud the entities
involved. Note: Any auditors who may be considering doing this are
advised to take care to notify appropriate trustworthy individuals that a
simulated fraud will be attempted.

In one government example, U.S. General Accounting Office (GAO)
auditors examining an automated payroll system felt that a system weakness would allow payroll checks to be issued to nonexistent employees.
To test their theory and to vividly demonstrate the impersonal aspect of
computer-generated payroll checks, they successfully caused the system
to issue phony checks to Disney cartoon characters such as Mickey Mouse
and Donald Duck.

To correct such a situation, auditors normally first consider measures
designed to close the weakness discovered, if that is feasible and cost beneficial. If not, then auditors are obliged to continue to perform test audits
perpetually to ascertain the degree to which the payroll weakness is being
exploited.

In another government example, internal auditors examining a large
supply control system detected what they considered to be a weakness that
would allow fraud to occur. Anticipating that the mere reporting of the
weakness would be contested by the organizational subentity responsible,
they decided to test their theory. Using an unsecured computer terminal,
an auditor entered a purchase order into the supply control system, which
in effect notified the automated supply system that a purchase order for
about $96,000 had been issued for tool kits and was due in. The auditor
assigned a fictitious stock number. Several weeks later the auditor, using
the same unsecured computer, created a false receiving report notice that
caused the supply system to record the receipt of the merchandise ordered
and to update its inventories. The supplies ordered, of course, were never

received. A few days later, the auditor mailed an invoice to the entity involved, requesting payment for the merchandise. The automated system, noting that it had all the required documentary evidence to make payment—a valid order, a notice of receipt of the merchandise, and an invoice requesting payment—caused a check to be issued to the fictitious vendor. A short time later another fictitious order was placed, and another check was issued.

Here the auditor was never able to determine that an actual fraud using the system weakness discovered had been exploited. Although it was suspected as a contributing cause of past inventory shortages, no proof was found. Nevertheless, something had to be done about the newly discovered weakness. The first recommendations involved improving internal controls, such as securing unattended computer terminals and tightening password control. These controls, however, were considered insufficient to fully close the fraud opportunities noted, in that over 200 authorized users had to retain access to the automated system and hence would continue to have the opportunity to conduct the fraud described. The solution elected was to test supply acquisition transactions periodically to determine whether the system weaknesses had been exploited as well as to establish an audit presence that would introduce a risk factor, even though minimal, into any fraud perpetration attempts.

FRAUD AUDITING AND INTERNAL CONTROL

Aside from those internal controls that are designed primarily to ensure the integrity of an entity's accounting system, some internal controls are designed to be fraud specific. The objective of fraud-specific internal controls is to prevent or deter fraud. Internal auditors may recommend the imposition of fraud-specific internal controls as well as suggest design features.

The design and installation of internal control systems is rarely, if ever, a prime responsibility of an entity's internal auditors. This is appropriate, for the most part, for internal auditing tends to be a more or less adversarial activity. An entity's internal auditors, although not usually directly responsible for internal controls, are nevertheless responsible for periodically testing the suitability and efficacy of internal controls in operation. Independent auditors, during their periodic annual audits, are clearly charged with the responsibility of determining that a client's internal control system does, in fact, assure that the client's accounting system does fully and accurately collect and report all financially relevant data.

Some auditors attempt to distance themselves from the design of internal controls, citing a need to maintain objectivity in their review and evaluation of those controls. And there is considerable support in favor of maintaining their objectivity. However, there are also valid arguments for involving internal auditors in the internal control evaluation and design process. Many internal auditors consider reliance on fraud-specific internal controls indispensable, due to the enormity of the fraud universe and the disadvantageous position they occupy in their battle with fraud perpetrators. In most organizations, and particularly in large and complex entities, fraud perpetrators have a clear advantage over fraud auditors in being able to select where and when to commit fraud. Unless they are totally inept—which few are—they can select target areas for fraud in which their advantage is maximized. Conversely, fraud auditors must endure the unenviable position of not knowing where or when fraud perpetrators are likely to strike, and having too few resources to do justice to them all, or even a significant portion of them. The alternative is to resort to internal controls, which increase the risk of detection for fraud perpetrators and in so doing deter them. Arguments for including fraud auditors in the internal control design and evaluation process are likewise strong. They generally have a more comprehensive knowledge of an entity's management process than do accountants—who customarily act as internal control system custodians—and, given their experience in fraud and error detection, they are well prepared to participate in the creation of internal controls. Accordingly, it is highly recommended that internal control system custodians encourage entity internal auditors to participate in the process of evaluating and designing internal controls. In fact, some entities require that newly designed internal controls be submitted to audit staff specialists for comment and approval before those controls are implemented. For example, the U.S. Veterans Administration—which operates massive data processing systems—requires that data processing system changes be reviewed and approved by data processing auditor specialists before any alterations to their massive data processing systems are allowed. The proposed changes are thoroughly reviewed and tested using simulated proofing routines to ensure that any programming changes are sound.

Internal control custodians are charged with comprehensively evaluating the various fraud risks that threaten their employers and assessing what internal controls are needed. In instances where they feel that active fraud-specific internal controls are justified, they proceed to design and install them. And, in most instances, these active fraud-specific controls are independent of any auditor participation. However, in many instances internal control custodians may well decide that the most effective and cost-beneficial internal controls are focused audits. Once determined—preferably with auditor participation—the specifics of what will be required of the auditors, including the frequency of the examinations, are compulsory and leave no audit discretion to them. It cannot be overemphasized that, in these instances, the primary objective is not to detect fraud. Rather, periodic audits are meant to inject an element of risk into perpetrating fraud in the areas targeted. If fraud is detected, all the better. But the measure of the efficacy of these fraud-specific internal control audits should never involve whether or not actual fraud is detected.

Perhaps the simplest and most effective fraud-specific internal control that can be employed is the actual visible presence of the auditor. Some auditors call this practice "showing the flag." The practice involves siting an audit examination in an area that has not seen an auditor for a period of time, in such a manner that would-be perpetrators will be sure to notice. Many fraud perpetrators will be deterred by the auditor's presence. Although some auditors are very discerning in selecting these audit areas, others merely rotate audits in such a manner as to cover all operational areas on a regular basis. The interesting thing about these fraud-specific audits is that auditors need not be doing anything truly productive in terms of detecting fraud. Their mere presence in a certain area warns a would-be perpetrator that his or her perpetration is not without risk.

Appendix A

PROACTIVE FRAUD AUDIT CASE STUDY

The fraud auditor in this simple illustration of proactive fraud-specific auditing procedure is Sandra Clark. Sandra is a certified proactive fraud auditor in the internal audit department of Alpha, Inc., a leading tool manufacturer and distributor. She is one of two Alpha internal auditors who are dedicated to full-time proactive fraud-specific auditing. She has just returned from a 10-day vacation over the Thanksgiving holiday. It is Monday morning, and she has just been introduced to a new auditor, Robert Clark, who has recently graduated from the University of Wisconsin. Sandra is assigned to supervise Robert, who is to become the third member of the Alpha fraud auditing team.

Sandra chooses to begin Robert's on-the-job proactive fraud audit training with a number of simple audits involving elementary frauds. She explains the nature of the three elementary frauds—duplicate payments, multiple payments, and shell fraud—and suggests that they begin by searching for shell fraud, normally one of the easiest to detect. Usually it involves little more than selecting a payment for a service or product and then inspecting the service or product that was paid for to determine whether it was actually delivered. Sandra begins Robert's training by showing him a listing of the cost accounting codes used by Alpha. She explains the codes (a B prefix indicates a building-related cost, followed by an R for a recurring expense or an N indicating a nonrecurring expense) and shows him how to display the Alpha payments register and the "BN" coded payment transactions on his computer. She then instructs him to select three payments between $25,000 and $75,000 bearing the BN prefix, representing building renovation projects delivered during the past 12 months. She also tells him not to expect to find fraud; he may examine hundreds of transactions without ever detecting evidence of fraud.

Robert selects a January 23 payment of $25,700 made to the ABC Company for work completed on January 16, a March 15 payment of $75,000 to the GHI Company for work completed on March 9, and a September 27 payment of $39,000 to the XYZ Builders for work completed on September 20.

Audit Scenario 1

Robert has obtained the underlying document file for the $25,700 payment to the ABC Company and is examining it when Sandra returns and asks about his progress. He explains that he has not completed his review of the many documents in the file. Sandra tells him he doesn't have to review all the documents because he is only searching for shell fraud. To do that, and to save time, he must make his individual examinations as efficient as possible. Accordingly, she instructs him, he need note only two things from the files he obtained: the vendor or contractor's name and whatever was required from the vendor or contractor to earn the payment that was made. Robert already has the contractor's name—the ABC Company. From the Alpha requisition and the contract, he finds that the ABC Company was required to construct a movable walnut-paneled partition to divide Building M conference room 4 and to apply walnut paneling to the remaining walls. With that information, Sandra tells him, "Now go to Building M and inspect the work done."

Robert visits Building M and conference room 4. He finds that there is no conference room 4, but finds instead conference rooms 4A and 4B. The rooms are unused at the time of his visit. He enters and observes that there is a movable wall, which is folded against one wall and which could be used to divide the larger room. He notes that all of the walls are covered with walnut paneling. The rooms are very attractively decorated, but he observes that they must be heavily used in that the relatively new paneling is showing many signs of wear and tear. He returns to his office and reports his observations to Sandra.

Has Robert satisfactorily accomplished his audit objective? Has he eliminated the possibility of fraud in this transaction? What additional procedures should he perform? See Comments/Audit Scenario 1 at the end of this case study.

Audit Scenario 2

Upon returning to report his findings and observations to Sandra, Robert mentions in passing that he was surprised at the condition of the paneling only 10 months after it had been installed. To Sandra, his observation had significance. She explains to Robert that his observation suggests the possibility that the paneling had been in use for a much longer period of time than 10 months and that the $25,700 payment may have involved a multiple-payment fraud. As a continuing training exercise for Robert, she directs him to extend his review of the ABC payment to prove or disprove this suspicion. Given his inexperience, she provides a number of explicit audit procedures for him to follow.

What audit procedures did Sandra prepare for Robert? Bear in mind that the audit procedures Sandra prepared have only a single audit objective, that of determining if multiple-payment fraud occurred. In this instance, searching for multiple-payment fraud simply means that Robert is seeking to determine if the ABC Company got paid $25,700 for installing the partition and paneling in conference room 4, but some other contractor actually did the work. See Comments/Audit Scenario 2 at the end of this case study.

Audit Scenario 3

Robert is progressing so well that, for his next assignment, Sandra suggests that he do something a bit more difficult with the $75,000 payment to the GHI Company. Rather than pursue an elementary fraud examination, she suggests he perform a defective delivery examination. She tells him that this basically involves his making a determination that Alpha received exactly what it had ordered and paid for.

Robert begins with a review of the files. He notes that the contract for the carpeting was advertised. The Alpha request for proposal (RFP) sent to 12 interested carpet companies essentially stated:

> Supply and install DuPont grade AAAA carpeting, pattern 4695, including the best padding, on 800 square yards of designated corridor and office space of Alpha, Inc. executive floors 4 and 5. Contract will require removal and disposition of existing carpeting. To maintain desired privacy of the executive suites, interested bidders will not be allowed access to the areas to be carpeted prior to the award of the contract. However, any relevant questions regarding the installation environment may be directed to Marian Rogers, Assistant Building Manager, at Alpha telephone extension 583.

Robert noted in his review of the bid abstract that five carpet installation companies responded with the following offers.

GHI Company	$75,000
Carpets Inc	77,500
Rugs Company	79,300
Floor Covering Company	79,500
Uptown Carpets Company	78,650

The GHI Company, the low bidder with an offer of $75,000, was awarded the contract. GHI had been notified that Alpha wanted the installation completed by the end of February. The installation was to occur in accordance with a schedule to be arranged with Ms. Rogers. The installation was completed on February 25. Ms. Rogers signed the receiving report on February 27, indicating that the installation was highly satisfactory.

Robert recalled from his prior visits to conference room 4A and 4B that the carpeting was new and very attractive. He did not anticipate finding any defective delivery fraud in the GHI contract. Nevertheless, he visited the area where the carpeting had been installed. During his inspection tour he too was impressed with the fine job that had been done. He also noticed that one of the secretaries was using a small piece of the same carpeting under a piece of office equipment. He asked her if there were any more scraps around. She found several that the workmen had left to be discarded and gave him a piece about a foot square. Pleased with his review, Robert took the carpet sample back to his office and told Sandra what he had done. They discussed what additional work was needed, if any.

What additional work, if any, did Sandra and Robert decide on to complete his proactive examination for defective delivery fraud? See Comments/Audit Scenario 3, below.

Comments

Audit Scenario 1. Yes, Robert has successfully completed his audit objective. In seeking to determine if shell fraud occurred, it was only necessary for him to determine that a new movable partition had been installed and that the room had been paneled. This he has done. Has he completely eliminated the possibility of fraud in this transaction? No! However, it was not his audit objective to exhaust all the possibilities for fraud in the transaction selected. His review was done quickly and efficiently and will allow him time to examine additional transactions. What additional procedures should he perform to complete audit scenario 1? Normally none. However, remember that the detection of fraud often begins with the auditor's discovery of faint clues that in themselves are not evidence of fraud, but indicate the possibility of fraud. In this instance, Robert's observation that the paneling was showing premature signs of wear and tear suggests the possibility that the paneling that was supposedly recently installed by the ABC Company had in fact been installed at some earlier date, possibly by someone else. This could indicate that shell fraud has not been ruled out by his observation, that some other fraud may be present, or that there is no fraud.

Audit Scenario 2A. The first audit task that Robert was given to accomplish was to revisit the area of conference room 4A and 4B and attempt to discover who actually did the work. If he can find any clue, or anyone to suggest that another company may have installed the paneling and the movable partition, he can search for any payments made to that company and possibly prove that it did the work in conference room 4. Since he has been given only a few hours to perform this task, he cannot afford to blindly search among the many contractors who have worked for Alpha.

Robert revisits the area of conference room 4A and 4B, and discusses the paneling job with secretaries and others in the area, but no one remembers the name of the performing contractor. However, in discussing the partitioning job with the secretary in charge of scheduling appointments for conference rooms 4A and 4B, he asked if she was aware of why the partition was necessary. She replied that it was very badly needed. She said that back about 18 months ago, before the partition was installed to allow two meetings to use the room, there was a long wait for conference room 4. However, since then, they have more than enough capacity to meet their needs.

Robert returned to his office, a bit depressed, and told Sandra everything he had learned. He was unable to determine who had done the work. He recommended against any further review of the ABC Company payment. Sandra disagreed. Question: Why did Sandra disagree, and what did she direct him to do next? See Comments for Audit Scenario 2B that follows.

Audit Scenario 2B. When Robert told her what had transpired, and suggested quitting the review of the ABC Company, Sandra broke out in a broad smile. She asked, "How many months ago was it that the ABC Company finished the paneling job?" Robert said, "About 12 months." She then asked, "How many months ago did the scheduling secretary say that conference rooms 4A and 4B came on line?" He replied "Eighteen months ago. I missed that completely."

In a seemingly innocent remark the scheduling secretary had provided the fraud indicia Sandra and Robert were looking for, what was needed to initiate additional work, and the clue needed to know where to look for it—in the period 18 months ago. With the information gained, it was now feasible for Sandra and Robert to attempt to find who the actual performing contractor was. Using the amount of the payment to the ABC Company for the paneling/partition job as an approximate search parameter, they decided to print out a listing of all amounts paid in the period 16 to 20 months ago, which were prefixed with cost accounting code BN, for amounts ranging from $24,000 through $27,000. Their search yielded five payments. They examined each of them, and the fifth one was the one they were looking for. On June 17, 17 months ago, an amount of $27,500 was paid to the Wahl Company. An examination of the document file for the payment revealed that it was for the installation of a movable partition and walnut paneling for conference room 4.

In reviewing the files, Robert found that the partition and paneling job had been an advertised acquisition. The ABC Company had been the second low bidder. The receiving report acknowledging that the ABC work had been delivered in a satisfactory manner was signed by Bill Jackson, the building manager. Robert found Mr. Jackson in his office and asked about the partition and paneling job. Mr. Jackson remembered it well. When shown the receiving report and asked if it was his signature, he said it was but hesitated as he looked the paper over. Then he said, "I don't understand this. It indicates the job was done by the ABC Company and I'm sure it was the Wahl Company that did the work."

Later, Sandra and Robert conferred on what to do next. They had examined the canceled check. It appeared to have been cashed by the ABC Company for deposit to its account. However, they were unsure of Mr. Jackson's involvement and had no clear leads as to whom the inside conspirator might have been. They discussed their discovery and suspicions with the Alpha treasurer—their designated contact for findings of this nature. It was decided to engage a private investigator with fraud investigative experience. Among the things that an investigator was likely to do, more effectively than Sandra and Robert, would be to comprehensively interview people like Mr.

Jackson, who might have pertinent knowledge of the particulars of the case, and to take sworn statements.

Audit Scenario 3A. In defective delivery frauds, the vendor or contractor frequently substitutes inferior materials in place of the higher-quality material ordered and paid for. Accordingly, Sandra and Robert asked an independent carpet shop to identify the sample Robert had taken from the secretary. The shop owner identified the sample as DuPont grade AAAA, in pattern 4695. He commented that it was top-quality carpeting. With the shop owner's verification of the quality of the carpeting, Sandra and Robert considered closing their examination but Sandra decided to keep it open to give Robert the opportunity for a comprehensive defective delivery fraud examination. Question: What additional step(s) did she have in mind? See Audit Scenario 3B below.

Audit Scenario 3B. Sandra asks Robert how much GHI Company was paid. He replies that it was $75,000. She then asks: "How many square yards of carpeting were required by the contract?" He replies that 800 yards were required. She asks, "How much is that a square yard?" He replies that it come to $93.75 a square yard. She then asks, "What if the GHI Company installed only 700 yards?" Robert replies, "I'm on my way!" Robert decides to compute the actual amount of carpeting installed and obtains a copy of the floor plan for the building's fourth and fifth floors. He then tours those floors, using a red pencil on the plans to indicate the floor areas that were carpeted. Once back in his office, he computes the square footage of floor space that is carpeted. He determines that 17,000 square feet, or 630 square yards, were carpeted. Returning to consult with Sandra, they decide to ask Ms. Rogers to help them account for the difference. She is very pleasant, and explains that there is probably 20 percent waste when the roll carpeting is cut to fit the various odd room and corridor spaces. On a scratch pad she writes down 800, the number of square yards of carpeting that was included in the bid advertisement, and multiplied it by 80 percent, to arrive at 640 yards. "Isn't that the figure you arrived at, or close to it?" she asks. She states that every carpet contractor has some waste and that the waste factor is built into bid offers. Sandra and Robert thank Ms. Rogers and leave. Upon returning to their offices, they discuss their findings to date.

Should they accept Ms. Roger's explanation of the 800 versus 640 square yards? If not, why not? What should they do next? See Audit Scenario 3C that follows.

Audit Scenario 3C. Sandra asks Robert for his opinion. Robert replies that Marian Rogers is trying to con them. He states that the RFP that Alpha sent out to interested contractors specifically stated that 800 square yards of room and corridor space was to be carpeted. Any waste that a contractor would incur would have to be figured in excess of the 800-yard figure. Sandra agrees. They agree that Marian Rogers is probably a conspirator in fraud, and they discuss what to do next. Sandra tells Robert that, ordinarily, she would recommend keeping their finding confidential and focusing a further examination on the contracting actions that Marian Rogers was involved in during the past year or two. If she was dishonest, Sandra explains, they will find additional examples in her work. With the additional examples they will have a much better case against Ms. Rogers. However, they feel that they may have already alerted Ms. Rogers to their finding and decide to refer the case to an investigator for continuing investigation. They discuss their finding and conclusions with the Alpha treasurer, who concurs with them. An investigator is engaged and will begin her examination on Monday.

Appendix B

SYMPTOMATIC FRAUD AUDIT CASE STUDY

James Jensen, CPA, known as JJ to his friends, is the third member of the Alpha proactive fraud-specific audit team. JJ is experienced in and tends to favor symptomatic fraud audits. In symptomatic auditing, the auditor, rather than selecting audit subjects randomly, instead relies on adverse symptoms that may have been disclosed in ordinary business operations and pursues them if they were indicia of fraud.

JJ begins his current examination with a matter that he knows has been particularly disturbing to Alpha management. Among its several business pursuits, Alpha acquires and distributes a high-quality line of hand and power tools. Its last three physical inventory counts of its tool inventory have revealed disturbing inventory shortages. For an inventory with a normal value of about $50 million, the physical inventory counts for the last three years—the last of which was completed only recently—have revealed shortages of 4 percent, 6 percent, and 8 percent respectively.

After the 4 percent shortage was disclosed, Alpha management was understandably concerned but was willing to accept various rationalizations offered for it. When the shortage increased to 6 percent a year later, Alpha became convinced that it was experiencing a serious theft problem but was baffled as to how the tools were getting out of the warehouses. All security was reviewed, and merchandise ready to be shipped was double-checked and periodically spot-checked before being loaded by the motor carriers. Also, internal security was reviewed and strengthened in several ways. Video cameras were installed at entrance and exit points, merchandise shipping controls were strengthened, and warehouse security reevaluated. When the third physical inventory count revealed an 8 percent disparity between the count and the book inventory, Alpha management went ballistic.

JJ decided to examine the inventory shortages disclosed to determine if he could detect any indication of fraud. He began by reviewing the procedures for each of the three physical inventory counts and found no significant reason to take exception to them. He reviewed the security measures taken by Alpha subsequent to the initial disclosures of inventory shortages and found them more than adequate. In fact, he believed them to be excessive in that the checking and rechecking of outgoing shipments often delayed the shipments with the result that motor carriers were complaining of the long waits, and the measures were very labor intensive and costly. The videotapes he reviewed often showed the dock areas to be crowded with competing incoming and outgoing shipments. However, after a careful review of all new control measures taken, including hours of reviewing the videotapes, he could see no reason for taking exception to the procedures followed. All shipments appeared to be diligently checked and double-checked as required. He reviewed the entire inventory control system, including the processing of incoming orders by the Sales Department, the preparation of sales/shipping documents, the distribution of the documents to the warehouse authorizing the removal of stock from warehouse inventories, and the Accounting Department's inventory control section accountable for processing changes in inventory balances and posting sales to accounts receivable. He could find no deviant procedures that might explain the inventory shortages.

Troubled by the crowded shipping docks, JJ went back to the videotapes and watched them for many hours, hoping to find a lapse in control. He saw nothing. However, while watching the tapes of the shipping docks, he inadvertently inserted a tape of the receiving docks, and watched it for an hour or so. What he saw tended to prove a concern that he had with regard to the labor-intensive procedures used to control shipments. So much labor was required for the extra controls being exercised over merchandise being shipped out to customers that dock personnel were being drawn from the receiving dock area to the shipping dock. The result, as clearly evident in the videotapes, was that dock workers were not thoroughly checking incoming receipts. JJ observed several pallets of tools that were off-loaded from trucks that dock workers had given only a cursory review, rather than conscientiously counting the actual quantities that were received.

At this point in JJ's examination, based on the information just provided, what is he likely to do next? What could possibly explain the growing inventory shortages? At this point readers should envision a scenario of what may be occurring to account for the inventory shortages and design audit procedures to test the theories.

Comments

Usually when physical inventory counts disclose significant discrepancies between book inventories and the actual counts, it is presumed that the inventory has shrunk as the result of one or more factors, the foremost of which is theft. The only question is how the goods were stolen. Was someone adding extra items to outgoing shipments (defective shipment fraud), or were fictitious sales orders being generated? In this case study, Alpha's efforts were directed to improving control over shipping procedures, security, and fictitious sales orders, but all measures failed to cure the shrinkage. It should be noted that many entities expect and allow for a shrinkage factor where they are warehousing fragile or highly desirable merchandise. And most tolerate a predetermined level of shrinkage as being inevitable. One automobile manufacturer, for example, routinely prepositioned a quantity of parts and tools on assembly lines, in excess of the quantities needed for a given day's production of automobiles, to allow for the shrinkage factor. It expected a certain number of parts, accessories, and tools simply to disappear. However, when the shrinkage extends beyond what has been determined to be "tolerable"—the level at which it would not be cost beneficial to stop the shrinkage—the underlying causes must be determined. In Alpha's case, the inventory shrinkage was considered excessive. Something had to be done.

JJ's examination of Alpha's sales and shipping procedures and warehouse and shipping security disclosed no faults. Desperate for a solution, he reviewed everything he had learned to date and reconsidered his troubling observation of the receiving dock procedure. He speculated on the possibility that if inbound shipments were less than the quantities indicated on the bills of lading and receiving documents, and if receiving dock personnel did not catch the shortages, this could account for a disparity between book inventories and physical counts. In other words, if a quantity of 1,000 of Item X was indicated on the receiving documents, and if only 900 actually were received, and if the Alpha person checking the item in did not detect the short receipt, a shortage would appear at inventory time. That is, the inventory control section would record 1,000 as received, but only 900 would be warehoused. JJ was prone to reject this supposition as unlikely to occur, in that it would require repeated fraud on the part of Alpha's suppliers, so as to account for an 8 percent inventory shrinkage. Out of options, he decided to pursue it anyway. He began by preparing a flow chart that depicted the procedure for controlling and recording incoming shipments of warehouse merchandise. Exhibit B.1

Exhibit B.1   Document Flow—Receiving Procedure

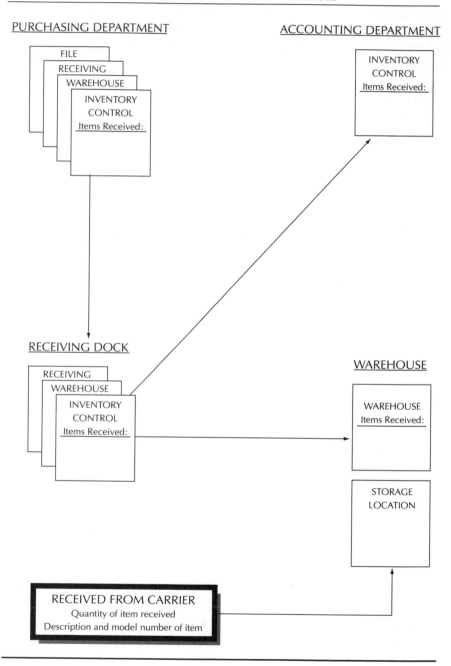

DOCUMENT FLOW - RECEIVING PROCEDURE

PURCHASING DEPARTMENT

FILE
RECEIVING
WAREHOUSE
INVENTORY
CONTROL
Items Received:

ACCOUNTING DEPARTMENT

INVENTORY
CONTROL
Items Received:

RECEIVING DOCK

RECEIVING
WAREHOUSE
INVENTORY
CONTROL
Items Received:

WAREHOUSE

WAREHOUSE
Items Received:

STORAGE
LOCATION

RECEIVED FROM CARRIER
Quantity of item received
Description and model number of item

presents his flow chart. From the graphic, he saw at once how a theft of goods received could go undetected. Study the exhibit to see what he saw.

For his test, he selected a number of recent receiving reports retrieved from the warehouse files, noted the storage locations indicated on the receiving reports, and went into the warehouse to verify the quantities. Verification was not a problem. The receiving pallets were still intact since the warehouse drew stock to be shipped on a FIFO (first in first out) basis. He was able to trace the specific incoming shipments he was interested in to specific warehouse locations—which were indicated on the receiving reports—and to make his counts. He found no exceptions in the counts. However, he discovered that for 5 percent of the receiving reports checked, the receiving dock personnel had indicated that a partial shipment had been received. That is, they discovered that the shipper had delivered fewer items than were expected from the supply source. JJ carefully examined all receiving reports he had selected where Alpha had received less than the complete order. In every case the shipping source was either highly reputable or the receipts were coming from Alpha's own manufacturing facilities. What interested him most, however, was that all of the partial shipments were delivered by the same freight carrier. When he questioned the warehouse manager about the partial orders, he explained that the practice of making partial shipments was not all that unusual. Sometimes it occurs because two or more trucks are required, or at times when Alpha indicates an urgent need for the items, the shipper may send out available inventory of the items ordered, planning to ship the balance later. Where less than the complete order is received, the receiving dock marks the quantity that was received.

JJ was curious as to how, and possibly if, the partial shipments could somehow explain the inventory shortages disclosed. He tested his theory by inserting into his flow chart of receiving procedure a hypothetical instance where 1,000 items were ordered but only 900 were received. Exhibit B.2 presents his chart. How could this procedure result in the disclosure of a subsequent inventory shortage? JJ was convinced that any fraud was occurring on the receiving docks. And he surmised that the shortages were occurring somewhere between the shipper's facilities and the Alpha warehouses. In other words, the freight companies carrying the shipments had to be siphoning off portions of shipments. JJ also concluded that receiving personnel were very likely involved in a conspiracy to defraud Alpha.

After reviewing Exhibits B.1 and B.2 speculate on why JJ came to these conclusions. Why do you think JJ decided that receiving dock personnel were conspiring in the fraud? After all, they were counting the quantities received correctly, indicating their counts on the receiving reports.

Exhibit B.2   Document Flow—Receiving Report

DOCUMENT FLOW - RECEIVING REPORT

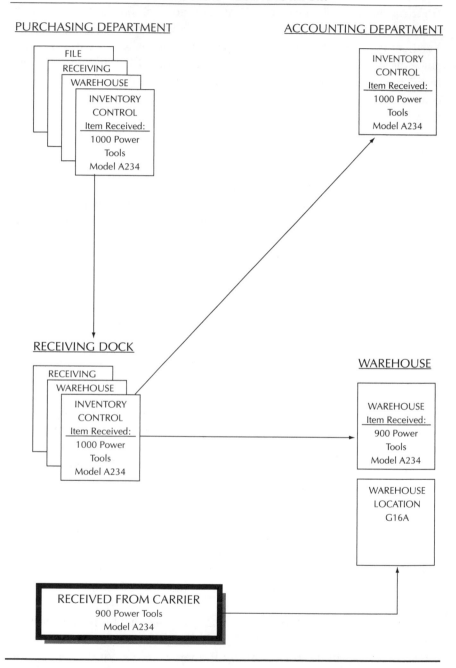

Before discussing his findings and conclusions with the Alpha treasurer to disclose his findings and reveal his suspicions, JJ decided to make a number of additional tests. What additional tests was he likely to make?

Most of JJ's suspicions thus far were speculation. He could not be sure that receiving dock personnel were possible conspirators in fraud until he examined the copies of the receiving reports on partial shipments that had been forwarded to the Accounting Department. Logically, he reasoned, if the receiving dock personnel were conspirators, they could not notify the Accounting Department of the partial shipments. Otherwise, Accounting would not approve a full payment to the shipper until the balance of the shipment was received. The only way to avoid this was to notify Accounting that the full shipment had been received. Exhibit B.2 shows the procedure they would have to follow. That is they would have to indicate on the warehouse copy of the receiving report that 900 units were being forwarded to storage—so that the warehouse would not detect a discrepancy and indicate to the Accounting Department that 1000 units had been received so that Accounting would pay the shipper. He now had to prove that.

Proving it was easy for JJ. Using the partial shipment receiving reports he had selected from the warehouse files, he compared them to the copies that had been forwarded to Accounting. He found the disparity he expected. Next, he searched the inventory control records to determine if the balance of the partial shipments had been received—it is possible that the receiving dock personnel erred in not indicating the partial shipments on the accounting copies—but they had not been. He was now convinced that there was fraud and that the receiving dock personnel were most likely involved.

JJ met with the treasurer to disclose his findings. The treasurer agreed with JJ's conclusions, was ecstatic that the inventory shortage problem seemed to have been solved, and praised JJ's perceptive discovery. He authorized an immediate criminal investigation. A private investigative firm was engaged, confirmed JJ's findings, and prepared the case for prosecution. It confirmed that John Doe, a driver for Road Warrior Freight Lines, had conspired with three Alpha receiving dock employees to withhold a portion of selected shipments of goods being delivered. The withheld goods were later sold to various outlets. All conspirators were prosecuted successfully.

Internal Controls

JJ continued his examination of Alpha's internal control procedures and recommended a change in the flow of Alpha's receiving documents.

Can you anticipate the change that JJ recommended?

Exhibit B.3   Document Flow—Receiving Report (Revised)

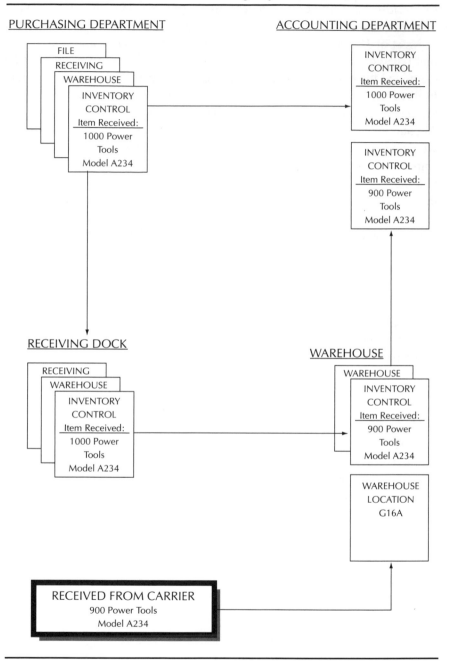

Comments

JJ was concerned that receiving dock personnel could steal incoming goods so easily without the loss being detected. He attributed the problem to the fact that the receiving section controlled the flow of receiving documents to the warehouse and to the Accounting Department. As illustrated in Exhibit B.2, after they diverted 100 Model A234 power tools, they were able to indicate to the warehouse that only 900 were received, thereby precluding the warehouse from discovering the discrepancy if the shipment was recounted. And they were able to signal to the Accounting Department that 1,000 had been received, thereby deflecting any likelihood that the discrepancy would be discovered at that point. JJ recommended a simple change in the flow of documents that would ordinarily preclude the undetected theft of goods prior to the time the goods were received at Alpha's warehouses. He recommended that after goods were received and counted by the Receiving Department, both the warehouse copy and the Accounting Department's copy of the receiving report be forwarded to the warehouse. The warehouse would be responsible for forwarding the Accounting Department's copy to the Accounting Department. If less than the requested quantity of an item was received, as indicated in Exhibit B.2, the Accounting Department would be informed of that fact. See Exhibit B.3 for the change in procedure.

JJ had one additional change in mind. Alpha's past desperate attempts to cure the inventory shrinkage problem had resulted in the imposition of costly internal controls that did not produce a favorable benefit in terms of control achieved versus cost of controls and the adverse effect on Alpha's productivity. He recommended that those controls be deactivated.

Appendix C

FRAUD-SPECIFIC CONTRACT REVIEW CASE STUDY

Sandra, the fraud auditor at Alpha, Inc., is reviewing the latest fraud hotline calls, when one attracts her attention. It is a simple anonymous recorded message, received from an obviously distraught female, who insists that Alpha should take a close look at the fire sprinkler contract given to Murphy Brothers Contractors. She states that it involves the warehouse renovation that was recently completed. She adds that she cannot be more specific for fear that the details may reveal her identity, but she sounds very sincere. Without any further hints as to what the reported fraud may entail, Sandra decides to investigate with a wide-scope examination, which she begins on March 13.

Sandra obtains the Murphy Brothers contract. The contract requires the Murphy Brothers to "Replace existing sprinkler heads throughout the warehouse area, and install new 25 year life sprinkler heads rated at 165°F. $38,100." Sandra notes that the contract had been awarded to Murphy Brothers on January 3. Murphy Brothers was the low bidder in a fierce competition that involved a total of eight bidders. The second lowest bid for the installation of the fire sprinklers was $39,900.

Upon investigating further, Sandra learns that 165°F is the normal temperature at which fire protection sprinkler heads are calibrated to open, so as to quickly extinguish small fires. She also learns that the renovated warehouse building will be used as an archive to store Alpha computer backup records and a variety of administrative records.

During her examination of the contract, Sandra notes that contract specifications were changed on February 1 to provide for the removal of any 165°F sprinkler heads that were already installed and to install 286°F sprinkler heads throughout the new archive. The cost of the change—as estimated by Murphy Brothers—was $40,000. Murphy Brothers claimed that all of the sprinkler heads required by the original contract had been installed, and hence all would have to be removed and scrapped. New 286°F heads would have to be purchased and installed.

Sandra is skeptical of the justification for this change and seeks independent professional advice. She learns that the use of the higher-temperature sprinkler heads in a records storage facility is appropriate. The use of 286°F sprinkler heads for archival purposes is a national standard. Experience has shown that where records are being stored, the fire damage resulting from a small fire ranging up to 286°F would be less devastating than the water damage that would result from sprinkler heads activated at 165°F.

Sandra reviews the receiving report, dated February 21, prepared when Murphy Brothers completed their work. John Green, the Alpha contract manager, signed the report. Sandra then visited the newly renovated warehouse site to inspect the installation. Inspecting the work that had been done is a relatively easy task. No records have yet been moved into the storage area and all the ceiling sprinklers are readily accessible. Sandra obtains the assistance of Robert Clark, and together they find a tall stepladder and begin to inspect the actual sprinkler heads that Murphy Brothers installed. They spend all day Monday inspecting 50 sprinkler heads selected at random throughout the renovated warehouse and make an interesting finding. Thirty of the heads bear the imprint 286°F/2000, the year they were manufactured. Twenty of the sprinkler heads bear the imprint 165°F/1980.

Based on the information provided:

a. Comment on whether Sandra should continue her fraud-specific review of the Murphy Brothers contract.

b. If you think Sandra has not discovered any indicia of fraud, comment on the discoveries she has made and speculate on why you believe they are not indicia of fraud.

c. If you believe Sandra has discovered one or more indicia of fraud, comment on what the fraud types are that you suspect, and why. Feel free to speculate.

d. If you have listed fraud types in the foregoing comment, suggest what additional work you think Sandra should do either to validate or to corroborate the indicia you noted, and/or what other action you think she should take.

Comments

The foregoing case study was adapted from an actual much larger and more complicated case. The circumstances described are fictional but are not exaggerated. They are based on actual events.

The first clue that aroused Sandra's attention that something was wrong was the contract change order issued on February 1. The contract was originally written to provide for the installation of 165°F sprinkler heads, which were later discovered to not be appropriate for an archive. Was this merely a costly error, or was it something else? Sandra suspects that it may have been something else. She suspects contract rigging. She asks herself: What if Murphy Brothers Contractors were in collusion with someone like Mr. John Green, and the mistake was intentional? They would be assured that the contract subsequently would be changed to provide for 286°F sprinkler heads, which would be correct for an archive. Accordingly, they could bid a low price for the contract—one that would very likely result in a loss—knowing that they could recoup all losses when the contract was changed.

After her inspection of the actual installed sprinkler head, Sandra is convinced that she has found strong evidence of fraud. Her inspection has disclosed that 30 of the sprinkler heads comply with the contract change order. That is, they were manufactured in 2000 and have the specified fire temperature rating. However, 20 of the sprinkler heads were imprinted with a temperature rating of only 165°F and are not in compliance with the contract change order. It is readily apparent that Alpha's John Green, who inspected the Murphy Brothers work, was either negligent or a conspirator in fraud against his employer.

It is Sandra's judgment that Mr. Green is involved in a criminal conspiracy, and she discusses her findings with the Alpha treasurer. She recommends that a criminal investigator be engaged to complete the case. The treasurer is not sure that a criminal investigation is indicated at this stage of her examination and asks Sandra to explain further. She explains that, ordinarily, she too would have doubts. However, her physical inspection of the sprinklers convinced her. She pointed out that 40 percent of the sprinkler heads were not replaced after the change order was issued. Further, she emphasized, the same 40 percent had not been replaced under the provisions of the original contract. All displayed a manufacturing date of 1980 and were near the end of their rated life. Had Murphy Brothers installed all of the 165°F sprinkler heads required by the original contract, as they claimed to have done, the 40 percent of the heads discovered with 165°F ratings would have had 1999 or 2000 dates of manufacture imprinted on them rather than the 1980 dates. Murphy Brothers had clearly lied about having installed all the original heads at the time of the contract change order. This strongly suggests the possibility that they were aware that contract specifications would be changed to provide for the 286°F heads at the time the contract was originally bid. This knowledge would allow them to underprice the competition in the initial bidding, in the expectation that they would not have to install the 165°F heads at all but could claim that they did and claim the maximum costs incidental to the contract change order.

The treasurer agreed with Sandra and ordered that a criminal investigator be engaged.

Sandra, however, continued to audit other circumstances of her finding. For example, she began to look for other associations that involved Mr. Green and the Murphy Brothers. Six months prior to the fire sprinkler contract, Sandra found that Mr. Green and the Murphy Brothers firm were involved in what turned out to be a shell fraud. Although the finding involved only a $25,000 job, it nevertheless provided corroborating evidence of a criminal conspiracy between Mr. Green and the Murphy Brothers and an additional example of their fraud.

Appendix D

WORLD TOP CORPORATION CASE STUDY

Serious fraud is very difficult—if not impossible—to detect in its early stages. This case study attempts to demonstrate this fact. After reading it, readers should speculate on the nature of the fraud that may be contemplated. However, readers do no more than speculate because little or no evidence of fraud is provided—just the possibilities of it. Nevertheless, fraud-specific auditors—if to be successful in their searches for serious fraud—always must begin by considering the possibilities and specifics of fraud that may be present before they can begin looking for it. Only once the type of fraud is hypothesized—given the facts at hand and regardless of the evidence in support of the hypothesis—can auditors design their search programs in an attempt to detect it. For the following case study, assuming that auditors entered on the scene in the contract's early stages, their subsequent tactics probably would involve a watchful waiting game to see what contract changes were to occur.

Situation

The World Top Corporation is a leading and highly reputable manufacturer of high-tech satellite launch and tracking systems. It designs, produces, and launches communication and special-purpose satellites. Their products include ground control facilities, antennas, and related equipment to serve a worldwide clientele. The company's primary role is one of conceptual design, engineering, and final assembly of parts and modules that are manufactured by other contractors to World Top specifications.

The World Top satellite launch vehicle is basically composed of an airframe, a propulsion system, and various guidance and control modules, each of which is the responsibility of a separate World Top division.

Payloads are also custom-designed and built to best serve the needs of each customer.

The high reputation that World Top enjoys is well deserved. Its launches and orbital accuracy is unparalleled in the industry. This reputation, however, is not achieved easily or economically. World Top's improvement of its launch vehicles is a continuing and costly obsession that requires careful management of its acquisition of parts and subassemblies and its evolving designs for launch vehicle components.

Because of the wide diversity of launch vehicle components, World Top finds it advantageous to contract out part and subassembly manufacturing to various speciality contractors, usually restricting its own manufacturing to the fabrication of prototype equipment and final assembly. Substantially all of its manufacturing and inventory responsibilities are passed along to supporting contractors. World Top normally requisitions only enough inventory from its suppliers to meet assembly and launch needs for 30 days. This practice has worked well for World Top in the past and allows the firm to concentrate on engineering, design, final assembly, and successful launches. To ensure launch schedules, while recognizing the production needs of contractors, World Top estimates what its parts and subassembly needs will be for the ensuing 90-day period each month during contract periods. Contractors are advised that World Top will not be obligated to purchase more than 90 days' requirements for any one item.

The contracts with supplying contractors are advertised. The invitations for bids (IFB) provide interested contractors with the estimated parts and subassemblies to be manufactured during the contract period and their specifications. The contracts are usually written for a one-year period, and low bidders are selected on the basis of the lowest aggregate bid for the World Top estimated requirements for the contract year. The contractors selected are guaranteed minimum revenue under the contracts equal to their total dollar amount bid and are required to supply up to 150 percent in additional parts and subassemblies—if World Top production needs exceed the estimates provided—at the same unit prices bid.

Because of the high degree of technical obsolescence of parts and subassemblies due to the evolving design of launch vehicle and ground control components, World Top reserves the right to modify its technical specifications at any time. The contracts provide that when a contractor's inventory of parts, subassemblies, and related tooling becomes obsolete because of World Top engineering design changes, World Top will purchase any obsolete inventories of in-process and finished goods up to the 90-day inventory level required. Also, the unamortized cost of any tooling that becomes obsolete as a result of World Top engineering changes also will be reimbursed to the contractor.

In a recent advertised award of the airframe manufacturing contract, which included 1,300 line items, four contractors expressed interest in the World Top contracts. The bidders and the total amounts of their bids were:

True Blue Aerospace, Inc.	$ 12,600,000
The High Company	13,500,000
The Boing Company	11,700,000
Weiss-Kragen-Verbrechen Fabrik (WKV)	11,300,000

Based on its low bid of $11,300,000, WKF was awarded the manufacturing contract. Page 15 of the WKV bid is provided to illustrate the unit cost detail.

Page 15	Item	*	Item No.	Price each
345.	Forward stabilizing control-left	(1)	#135987	$ 231
346	Forward stabilizing control-right	(1)	#135932	231
347.	Aft stabilizing control—left	(1)	#135322	495
348.	Aft stabilizing control—right	(1)	#135324	495
349.	Gyro control	(1)	#786113	456
350.	Jet thruster—maneuvering	(1)	#994566	11,295
351.	Jet thruster—maneuvering	(1)	#994569	11,295
352.	Jet thruster—maneuvering	(1)	#994570	11,295
353.	Jet thruster—maneuvering	(1)	#994573	11,295
354.	Jet nozzles	(8)	#993436	441
355.	Forward Array Panel	(1)	#456112	3,899
356.	Rear UHF Receiver Bracket	(1)	#511987	855
357.	Rear UHF Receiver Antenna Array	(1)	#115891	13,567

* Quantity required for each launch vehicle.

World Top management was particularly happy with the WKV source for jet thrusters. Last year these thrusters were priced at $12,563, although the higher prices offered on other items dampened their enthusiasm somewhat.

Required

There may be no fraud involved in this case study. Nevertheless, assume that you are about to initiate a proactive fraud-specific audit of the case. Accordingly, given the circumstances described, speculate on the nature of any fraud that may have occurred or is likely to occur. Adopt the mental attitude of a perpetrating contractor, and consider how you would profit from fraud in these circumstances. You may assume, if it suits your hypothesis, that you have an inside information source. If so, indicate what sort of inside information might serve your criminal purposes.

Additional Information

While the auditor was gathering information on the case at the World Top plant, she overheard a discussion between several engineers who appeared to be excited about a new design for jet thrusters that was expected to maneuver the launch vehicle into a precision orbit more reliably. Apparently they were arguing over alternative designs and were unaware they were being overheard. The new design would make obsolete a considerable number of subassemblies, including item numbers #994566, #994569, #994570, and #994573. The auditor knew the engineers worked in a secure area of the World Top plant by the red identification badges that they wore. And, from the nature of their conversation, she concluded that they must have been engaged in designing special tooling for the in-house manufacture of prototype parts and subassemblies. This was consistent with her knowledge of World Top's financial plans, which called for a major in-house production effort scheduled to begin sometime within the next 12 months. She knew the project had the highest World Top priority, and all details of it were strictly classified. However, the engineers had been very careless in discussing their project.

Solution

There are various possibilities for fraud in the World Top illustration. However, the most likely possibility is that unbalanced bidding is involved. Although there is no clear indication that this is so, consider that the price offered for the jet thrusters was considered low by World Top managers and that other items were priced a bit higher than they had hoped for or expected. These two facts alone could cause a skilled fraud-specific auditor to theorize—remember, good fraud auditors must be a bit paranoid—that the WKV Company may have had prior knowledge that the jet thrusters (as well as other items) would soon be technically obsolete and canceled from the production contract. If they were, consider the cost effect. Cancellation of the jet thrusters would eliminate underpriced items from the contract and leave the higher-priced items on the production schedule. Further, in the likely event that the successful manufacturing contractor would also be awarded the production of required replacements for the obsoleted jet thrusters, unit prices claimed and allowed would provide an opportunity for high profits not influenced by competitive bidding.

What led WKV to believe that certain specific parts or subassemblies would be obsoleted by newly designed replacements? Surely the company's speculation had to be based on some intelligence source. Perhaps management also overheard conversations by the engineers. Or, more likely, perhaps there was a conspirator working for World Top who provided WKV with information on the design changes. If so, 'who could it have been?'

At this point the auditor can do little to advance his or her speculation other than to wait for the inevitable: contract change(s) that would formally notify WKV of the obsolete parts and subassemblies, advising the company to cease production of the identified items and to scrap the in-process and finished inventories. WKV also would be allowed to claim all costs in connection with the scrapped items, up to the contract limitations imposed, and any unamortized special tooling used to produce the items. If this truly were a fraud conspiracy, WKV would be initially planning to minimize its production of obsoleted parts and related tooling but claiming the maximum for scrap allowance purposes.

Once the contract changes are issued, the auditor would have reason to reexamine the circumstances. Fraud would be very difficult to prove, but every attempt should be made to determine the specifics of the crime suspected and who the perpetrators are. For those readers who may be disappointed in this solution, be advised that fraud auditing is often a most frustrating enterprise. Many times auditors are absolutely certain of the circumstances of a crime and the individuals involved, but are unable to take any appropriate lawful action, which includes any publication of suspicions.

Appendix E

COMMERCIAL LEASING CASE STUDY

Commercial leases are believed to be one of the most fruitful areas for the perpetration of fraud and one of the most difficult to audit to a satisfactory conclusion. Consider, for example, that no two locations are sufficiently comparable to establish what the rental costs should be with reasonable certainty and to determine whether a given rental payment may include a fraud component. Even competitive bidding does not protect the renting entity. The primary factors that must be considered when a rental contract is evaluated, to mention only a few, are

1. Location of the space
2. Size of the space
3. Configuration of the space
4. Condition of the space and building services included

Since many commercial leases involve large blocks of space—100,000 or more square feet—and usually are evaluated on the basis of square-foot rental costs, the addition of, say, $1 a square foot to an annual rental bill can add $100,000 a year, every year of the lease period, to a perpetrator's pockets, and still not appear to be out of line. And the low bidder is not necessarily the honest bidder. For example, in a given city market, where square-foot rental costs for class A rental space may range from $20 to $30 a square foot, who is going to notice that Lessor A has added $1 to the price bid of $24 for a 100,000-square-foot layout, particularly where other bidders have bid in a range of $25 to $30 a square foot. The extra $1—in this case $100,000 a year—would be given to the victim's employee who steered the lease to Lessor A. In examples such as this the leasing entity is usually granted some discretion to select from among the bidders. That is, in evaluating bid proposals, it is difficult to rule out the personal judgment factor. The view may be better from a slightly higher-priced property, or the location may be more favorable. The lower-priced property—in cost per square foot—may have more square feet that have to be taken, thereby raising the gross cost above the next-higher unit cost bidder; and, of course, all properties will not be configured alike, which alters their utility. Any or all of these issues could legitimately influence the selection of the successful bidder. During the time the author served as the federal government's chief executive in a major U.S. city, he could have easily elicited $1 million or more from many lessors offering office space for lease with minimal or no risk of detection. It is almost certainly happening today. What, if anything, should a fraud auditor do when faced with evaluating a commercial lease for evidence of fraud?

Comments

To be perfectly honest, there is little, if anything, that a fraud auditor can do to determine the presence of fraud in most commercial leasing situations, if an entity's leasing agents or other key employees are clever. There are too little criteria for determining what constitutes honest and conscientious performance and usually few, if any, witnesses other than the primary participants in a commercial leasing fraud—only the giver and the receiver of the kickbacks of rental revenues received. Most fraud auditors have many recollections of apparent leasing frauds, some of very significant dollar amounts, wherein they were certain that fraud was involved, but the cases were never prosecuted for lack of reasonable proof that the suspects had acted with criminal intent to defraud the victims.

However, there is no need for entities to despair completely. Where commercial leasing fraud is a possibility—and it is always a possibility—the old saying that an ounce of prevention is worth a pound of cure is applicable. And particularly where commercial leasing activity is significant, fraud auditors should make recommendations to prevent or make it more difficult to commit the crime. In other words, auditors should recommend fraud-specific improvements in the internal control system to make fraud more difficult.

In the case of leasing, the first thing that should be done is to attempt to eliminate as much personal judgment as possible in the selection of an offer to lease from offers received. To do this, it is often advisable to structure a two-step advertising process.

In the first step, all lessors who have space to lease and/or realtors who represent clients with space to lease should be contacted with a notice of the entity's intent to lease space and provided with the particulars of the space that is desired. Particulars should include the exact geographical area in which space is desired, the minimum footage required, as well as any other features that the entity wishes to include. Recipients who have space that meets the entity's specifics should be asked to express their interest in leasing the space to the entity. No price is bid at this point. The entity's representatives should then review the lessor responses received and determine which properties meet the entity's criteria and which don't. If the property is deficient in any significant regard, the property is eliminated from participating in the competitive phase of the acquisition.

In the second step of the space acquisition process, only those lessors of properties that have been approved as meeting the entity's criteria should be invited to submit offers to lease their space. Prospective lessors should be advised that the lessor submitting the lowest annual price for the total space provided will be selected. Any deviations from these requirements by the entity's leasing officer should have to be explained.

Fraud Auditing Hints Fraud auditors planning to audit commercial leases for the first time, should begin by acquiring the specialized training they will need to evaluate them. As an absolute minimum, they should attend a three-day course in commercial leasing such as those offered by many universities. The courses provide invaluable training in the art, law, and practices of commercial leasing. As it is with auditing many operational areas, audit accomplishment is directly relative to the auditor's area-specific expertise.

Appendix F

CONTRACT RIGGING CASE STUDY FROM U.S. CONGRESS COMMITTEE PRINT

Case Prologue

Although all case studies included in the preceding portion of this text are adapted from actual cases or portions thereof, they are hypothetical, and any identities given for individuals and entities involved are fictional. This is done to allow the simplification of illustrations for improved efficiency and perception of relevant subject matter. The actual names of those who may have been involved in the cases are irrelevant. More important, many of the cases were never prosecuted, for various reasons, and the actual facts and circumstances must remain confidential.

However, in an attempt to give the reader a sense of realism, this and the next two case studies present a rare insight into real-world events revealed in sworn testimony offered by various witnesses who were compelled to testify by a committee of the U.S. Congress pursuing fraud in government. Only a portion of the full testimony has been excerpted to convey the gist of the committee's suspicions of fraud involving private sector entities and the government.

After considering the excerpted testimony, readers are urged to speculate on the nature of the alleged fraudulent acts that may be involved and to attempt to link them to the fraud types discussed in Chapters 5 to 7.

The source of the excerpts are public documents commonly referred to as committee prints. A committee print is a U.S. Congress official printed transcript of everything that has occurred during congressional subcommittee hearings—in this case in the U.S. Senate—in which all people quoted are offering sworn testimony. The events described occurred in the late 1970s, and the hearing dates were 1978 and 1979. All dollar figures are relative to that period. To fully appreciate their significance in terms of current money value, the money amounts stated should be approximately doubled. The use of material from this period was necessary because there are no known similarly revealing, comprehensive, or more recent examples available. The apparent fraudulent practices revealed in the testimony are timeless and equally threatening to private entities. They are a valuable learning experience, regardless of the period from which they are taken. A massive investigative effort was necessary—enabled by congressional sub- poena power—to develop the testimony presented by the witnesses.

Case Study

The title of the committee print from which the excerpts selected for this case study were taken is:

Hearings before the Subcommittee on Federal Spending

Practices and Open Government of the Committee on Governmental Affairs

United States Senate

GSA Contract Fraud Investigation

June 22 and 23, 1978

Participants:

Senator Lawton Chiles, Florida

Robert A. Lowry, President, Wibco, Inc., a painting contractor

Senator Chiles: (p. 2) Since we are holding investigative hearings, I believe it would be appropriate to require sworn testimony for all witnesses. Our first witness this morning will be Mr. Robert Lowry, the president of Wibco, Inc., a Washington area painting firm. Mr. Lowry, would you step forward, please, to be sworn? Do you swear that the testimony you are about to give will be the truth, the whole truth, and nothing but the truth, so help you God?

Mr. Robert Lowry: I do. I am a painter by trade, and have engaged in the painting-contracting field for most of my adult life. . . . By 1971, I ceased participating in illicit activities. By 1974, I could no longer bid competitively on GSA contracts simply because I would not par- ticipate in the fraud. In 1975 my company was, as a result, out of business and for the first time in 25 years in the trade, I was unem- ployed. So that the record may be clear, I can sit here today and describe my course of conduct which regularly included the performance of numerous illicit activities in as great detail as you would like. As you probably are aware, my attorneys have obtained for me immunity from prosecution in the current investigation being conducted by the federal government. . . . I have chosen to highlight a few examples of illicit conduct which have regularly gone on over the years to substantiate my claims of gross criminal activity. Moreover, since many of the schemes used to defraud the taxpayer are very sophisticated . . . I have chosen to bring before you the most elementary types of fraud which have been practiced.

From 1968 until 1971, most GSA maintenance work had been performed through informal contracts. Informal contracts are contracts of a face value of $2000 or less. These would be awarded by the building managers under an informal bid system. In practice two or three contractors would decide among themselves who would get a contract on a given day, and each contractor would bid up to the $2000 limit, their bids separated only by several dollars. Until late 1970, in order to get work under such informal contracts, the contractors made a practice of paying off GSA building managers by taking them to lavish lunches, sponsoring parties, paying cash, picking up the bills for their vacation, and in may cases, providing them with prostitutes. By mid-1974, it was impossible to submit a successful bid without first having knowledge of what the involved building manager wished to take by way of cash, gifts, favors, trips and female companionship. Therefore, an arrangement would have to be made with the building manager before an actual bid was submitted.

In 1974, another new element was introduced into the bidding of these contracts, which provided a new scheme. At this time, unbalanced bids came into vogue in the area of term contracting. By their very nature, unbalanced bids are not responsive to the bid invitations. This kind of unbalanced bidding appears to yield the lowest bid, if one focuses only on the bottom line of the bid sheet.

In actuality, these contractors, acting in consort with the building managers, used this system to defraud the Government of millions and millions of dollars. This increased the fraud because the favored contractors were advised by the building managers in advance of bid day as to which items on a bid sheet would, in reality, be used and which would not be. Thus if you knew a building manager would never request you to perform a certain type of work, you could assign an unreasonably low unit price to that element, thereby lowering your aggregate bid price.

In addition, the unsavory relationship between the favored contractors and the building managers had by this time become so entrenched that it had become a widespread practice for building managers to authorize, allegedly inspect, and certify for payment literally millions of dollars of work which was never performed. An example of the misuse of unbalanced bidding to which I refer no doubt will help you to understand this practice.

If by collusion a building manager knows that a contractor will not request one-coat painting, even though the invitation to bid specifies that 1 million square feet of one-coat work will be done, it will permit the contractor to place on the bid sheet an unreasonably low unit price for one-coat work, thereby getting the low bottom line and assuring the contract award. Once the contract has been awarded, the building manager will then authorize only two-coat work which in the bid solicitation was specified as 100,000 square feet, but which, in reality will be written to 1 million or 2 million square feet. Naturally, this will increase the contractor's receipts dramatically if, as was normal practice, he bids two-coat work at excessively high prices. (p. 5)

Furthermore, I wish to stress that by the mid-1970's, it was common practice for crooked building managers to issue procurement requests which inflated by three, four, or five times the actual work which would be performed pursuant to the term maintenance contract. In many cases, the procurement requests were issued, certified as being completed and forwarded for payment when, in fact, no work whatsoever had been performed, provided the building managers were paid off. For example, in 1973, I painted the third floor corridor of the Pentagon Building, which at the time contained 500,000 square feet of paintable surface. A year later, in 1974, the very same third floor corridor was painted by a contracting establishment owned by Charles Bainbridge. The procurement forms, which your staff has in its possession, indicate that 70 percent, I say again 70 percent, of the same third floor corridor was painted. However, the forms reveal an astonishing fact: in 1974, 70 percent of this corridor contained 1,063,000 square feet. In March of 1973, while performing work at the Pentagon, I was told by Robert Jackson, a GSA employee, that if I wanted to get along, I would have to play ball. At that time I responded that I would not, and after that contract was completed, I did no more general contracting work with GSA because I simply could not tolerate the graft.

In summary, I think it is quite fair to say the kind of fraud which I have highlighted for you this morning is now the rule, not the exception. In 1970 I would estimate that fraud and fraudulent practices accounted for approximately 10 percent of the cost of a maintenance contract. Today that figure has escalated to a level of 60 to 70 percent of the actual cost of any maintenance contract, based on the work actually performed at the specified unit prices. For example, the minimum cost, including labor and materials, and not including overhead, of painting one square foot of wall space in an occupied area can be no less than 10 cents per square foot. Nonetheless, an examination of the bid documents under which work is being performed as we sit here today will reveal that all contractors performing such work are receiving, on paper, less than 5 cents a square foot. It is obvious that without fraud and collusion, no contract can be performed. There is no question in my mind that if this committee checked into the performance of contracts and determined what work was actually performed, as opposed to the work actually paid for, it would find that the contractor involved was being paid 20 to 25 cents per square foot, four to five times the bid price.

Senator Chiles: You told my investigators a story about 40 miles of pipe you couldn't find. Would you tell that to this committee? (p. 9)

Mr. Robert Lowry: Well, there are 40 miles of pipe in the Veterans Building on Vermont Avenue that according to form 147's were painted. However, in order to find them, you have to take the plaster walls down, so I don't know how these pipes got painted as it is not physically possible for a building of that size to contain anywhere near that much pipe, either exposed or embedded in the walls.

Senator Chiles: But it is in the contract to paint, to paint this pipe?

Mr. Robert Lowry: It was in the 147 form, the request form, and payment for that much pipe was made. The same exact circumstance has happened no less than seven or eight times.

Senator Chiles: I understand that contracts have been commingled so that GSA would end up paying many times over for a single job. How did that work?

Mr. Robert Lowry: Well, under the term contracts, for instance, you have a partition contract, a ceiling contract, an electrical contract, a painting contract, a flooring contract, a roofing contract, and a mechanical contract. If you have a building manager on your payroll, or if you have him in your pocket, it would be very simple to be the low bidder on all seven to eight contracts within the same group. Each of these contracts has provisions to allow for items which are in the others to be performed, so that it is very simple to cheat: the building manager just writes the same items under all seven contracts, then the contractor is paid seven times for the identical amount of work. And then they quadruple the square footage; meaning, naturally, that in these cases they are being paid 20 to 30 times for work actually performed.

Senator Chiles: I understand that there is supposed to be, by the sort of contracts that have been let, nine coats of paint on the walls of the GSA headquarters building. How many coats do you estimate that are on those walls?

Mr. Robert Lowry: I know for a fact that the walls have one in most places and a second coat on about 30 percent of the area.

Senator Chiles: And yet they are supposed to have nine coats?

Mr. Robert Lowry: According to the documents, yes, sir.

Senator Chiles: Mr. Lowry, we are aware that you have considerable documentation to support your statements. We would be happy to hold the record open and let you submit that information to us as you would like to submit it.

Appendix G

QUALITY CONTROL CASE STUDY, PART I

FROM U.S. CONGRESS COMMITTEE PRINT

(Note: See prologue to Appendix F)
The committee print from which the excerpts selected for this case study were taken is:

Hearings before the Subcommittee on Federal Spending
Practices and Open Government of the Committee on Governmental
  Affairs
United States Senate
GSA Contract Fraud Investigation
June 22 and 23, 1978
Participants (in order of appearance):
Senator Lawton Chiles, Florida
Elmer B. Mr. Staats, Comptroller General of the United States
Howard R. Davia, Chief of the Division of Audits
Senator Sam Nunn, Georgia
Vincent Alto, Special Counsel to the Administrator
William Clinkscales, Chief of the Office of Investigations
Senator H. John Heinz III, Pennsylvania

Opening remarks of Senator Chiles (p. 179)

Senator Chiles: Our session today will go well beyond the hearings that
  this subcommittee held in June into emerging scandals at the GSA.
  At that time we heard case after case of fraud and corruption which
  was seemingly rampant at the General Services Administration.

Mr. Staats: (p. 206) No one knows the magnitude of fraud against the Government. Hidden within apparently legitimate undertakings, it usually is unreported and/or undetected. However, all indications are that fraud is a problem of critical proportion. Department of Justice believe that the incidence of fraud in Federal programs ranges anywhere from 1 to 10 percent of the programs' expenditures.

Senator Chiles: When you say 1 to 10 percent, you are talking about 1 to 10 percent of $250 billion.

Mr. Staats: That is correct. We have no estimates with respect to the remainder of the budget.

Senator Chiles: We are talking about a range of $2.5 to $25 billion annually?

Mr. Staats: That is correct.

Senator Chiles: (p. 234) Let's begin with the case of Art Metal, since it seems to be the subject of a great deal of controversy. Mr. Davia, who is Art Metal, and how long has the government been dealing with them?

Mr. Davia: Art Metal is an office metal furniture manufacturer located in Newark, N.J. It's been in business something like 20 years. The Government has done some $360 million worth of business with them over the last 10 years.

Senator Chiles: I have an audit report that indicates that in 1975, GSA bought 33,000 supply cabinets from Art Metal. That audit report indicates that we ended up not using those supply cabinets. Why didn't GSA end up using them?

Mr. Davia: They required so much maintenance to repair the defects that it was decided that repair was not economically feasible. Later we decided to sell those cabinets at half price, and eventually, as I recall, the decision was made to give them away to any Government agency who could use them, at no cost.

Senator Chiles: But we paid $1.5 million for them?

Mr. Davia: Yes sir.

Senator Chiles: Did we get our money back?

Mr. Davia: No we did not.

Senator Chiles: We turned around and ordered some more cabinets from Art Metal. How much did we buy the second time?

Mr. Davia: 120,000. That's about a five year supply.

Senator Nunn: Have the people in charge of the General Services Administration been notified of this particular case?

Mr. Alto: I think they have been aware of this particular case since the time it occurred, from its inception.

Senator Chiles: My understanding is that after the contract is let then the negotiations really start as to whether there are going to be changes. Every time there is a change, there is a cost added to the contract. Would there have to be all these changes?

Mr. Davia: I would think that unless a change was absolutely essential that we avoid changes, because what it serves to do is open up the cost of the product to negotiation.

Senator Chiles: Well now, Art Metal always got these contracts by being the low bidder, did they not?

Mr. Clinkscales: Yes sir.

Senator Chiles: Well, that is the best way. That is the American way, to have the low bid situation. Why isn't it working?

Mr. Clinkscales: Well, it is possible that something called buying in is in effect there: you get the award by low bid with a possibility of some help from insiders that change orders are going to be effected which will insure you of making a profit.

Senator Nunn: Doesn't that require, in effect, fraud on the part of some Government employees?

Mr. Clinkscales: Yes sir.

Senator Nunn: In other words you are not going to buy into a contract unless you have some pretty good reason to believe there are going to be change orders?

Mr. Clinkscales: I don't see how you could do anything else and make a profit.

Senator Chiles: Well, you said that part of this material has been delivered in bad quality. Is that correct?

Mr. Clinkscales: Yes sir.

Senator Chiles: We have quality assurance people who are supposed to reject furniture or materials that are not up to standards. Did they reject this material?

Mr. Clinkscales: No sir. There seem to be many instances where they pass the materials; then when the recipient or customer received it in bad condition, and they said, "We can't use the product," the defense was, your quality assurance people approved this, therefore, we will not make any settlement of the claim.

Senator Chiles: That sounds like a pretty good defense to me.

Mr. Clinkscales: Excellent.

Senator Chiles: Why did the quality assurance people approve it?

Mr. Clinkscales: We don't have the answer, but we are looking for it, sir.

Senator Chiles: You have explained the term "buying in" and how it would occur. Doesn't GSA have some way to protect itself when there is a change order: isn't there an audit made of that change order to determine if it was valid and if the cost incurred in the change order are all valid and what was done in these cases?

Mr. Davia: What normally happens when a contract is changed is that the contractor, whoever he might be, incurs additional costs which he subsequently presents as a claim. His claim is always audited if the amount is significant.

Senator Chiles: In those audits, they have to prove that the workers worked in addition and additional costs that they had?

Mr. Davia: Oh yes. His claim is normally detailed in such a manner that contract and audit shows that he incurred so many hours of labor at whatever costs.

Mr. Clinkscales: Some of this proof is in the form of time cards for individual workers and would indicate how much time they spent on making a product, and in at least one instance these records were accidentally destroyed. We're talking about 350,000 records.

Mr. Davia: Mr. Clinkscales is describing a change order which subsequently involved a $10 million claim by Art Metal.

Senator Chiles: And the time cards were destroyed? How were they destroyed?

Mr. Davia: I'm not sure.

Senator Chiles: But those are Art Metal's time cards?

Mr. Davia: Yes sir. The time cards that we would normally use in an audit to document that labor had been incurred as claimed.

Senator Chiles: Did GSA pay the claim?

Mr. Davia: What actually happened was this: When we could not look at the actual documentation, we contracted with Booz Allen. The firm's engineers and technicians went into the Art Metal plant and observed certain manufacturing processes; they came up with an estimate of what they thought an appropriate claim should be. They recommend something like $2.5 million as appropriate.

Senator Chiles: Art Metal claimed $10 million and you all got Booz Allen and went in even though their records were destroyed—and that wasn't the government's fault that their records were destroyed?

Mr. Davia: No sir.

Senator Chiles: But you went in and did a time study and came up with $2.5 million. Did you settle the claim on that basis?

Mr. Davia: We had another technical opinion from a statistics expert who concurred that the Booz Allen statistical projections were proper. The claim was subsequently allowed for $5.5 million, or $3 million more than the Booz Allen recommendation.

Senator Chiles: Why?

Mr. Davia: There was very little basis, if any, that I would accept as justifying that action.

Senator Chiles: I understand that you have another change order in which Art Metal had signed a contract change that specifically prohibited them from asking for a profit margin on a change order. Tell me how that came about?

Mr. Davia: They were not really prohibited from asking for profit. They agreed to forgo profit in the production they were about to be given. They went into production, and then in presenting their claim, asked for $1 million profit. There was no documentation in the government files, the contract files, which would indicate that there had been mutual agreement between the government and Art Metal to waive profit. By sheer chance, we had a copy [of the agreement] in our audit files which showed very clearly that both parties to that agreement had signed.

Senator Chiles: Did someone say then "Remember, you agreed to forgo profit?" Someone surely would remember that on an item like that.

Mr. Davia: At the time the claim was presented, even we in audits were not aware that such an agreement had been signed. There were no other protests at the meeting. I wasn't there, but I'm told by our representatives who were there. We subsequently scanned our audit files and found the document I described.

Senator Chiles: So you didn't pay that $1 million because you found a copy of an order that had been signed?

Mr. Davia: Yes, sir.

Senator Heinz: (p. 252) Perhaps you can tell the committee one additional piece of information, if you can, regarding the dispute over the amount of money owed Art Metal on the change order on the rollers that were an issue of contention around 1975. Now, my understanding is that when this was discussed earlier today, nobody quite knew why $5 million settlement was approved but Booz Allen, Hamilton, of course, had recommended a $2.5 million price. Art Metal had said that you owe us $10 million and $5 million was decided upon. My question is, what did the records show as to who approved that?

Mr. Davia: The contractor at the time who made the judgment was a Mr. Carl Davis, who subsequently retired.

[Author's note: Shortly after Mr. Davis allowed the $5 million settlement of the Art Metal claim, which was $3 million in excess of the amount approved by the auditors and the engineering consultant firm Booz Allen, the director of auditing requested that Mr. Davis submit a statement explaining his basis for allowing the large amount in excess of the amount determined by audit. This is required by government regulations. Shortly after this request was made, Mr. Davis retired from government service. Subsequently, Mr. Davis was subpoenaed to appear before the subcommittee to provide his reasons for the large amount awarded. However, he was never called to testify. Mr. Davis, however, was questioned prior to the hearings by Senate investigators as to his justification for the $5 million allowance. He explained that he did not remember, further explaining that he had been "stung by a bee" and had lost his memory.]

Appendix H*

QUALITY CONTROL CASE STUDY, PART 2

FROM U.S. CONGRESS COMMITTEE PRINT

(Note: See case study prologue to Appendix F)

The committee print title from which the excerpts selected for this case study were taken is:

> Hearings before the Subcommittee on Federal Spending
>
> Practices and Open Government of the Committee on Governmental Affairs
>
> United States Senate
>
> Ninety-Sixth Congress
>
> Continued Investigation Into Fraud And Mismanagement In The General Services Administration
>
> June 18, 19, and 20, 1979

The full committee print included 694 pages of text and exhibits. In excerpting material, every attempt has been made to provide the gist of what occurred for maximal understanding without the tedium and obscuring nature of excessive or extraneous material. The excerpts are keyed periodically with the page numbers of the actual subject committee print. The excerpts are in the language of the witnesses, as their words were transcribed, and have not been edited for grammatical correctness or punctuation.

---

*The illustrations in Appendix H are adapted from actual illustrations provided for the Hearings before the Subcommittee on Federal Spending Practices and Open Government of the Committee on Government Affairs, United States Senate.

Part I

Participants:

The Honorable Lawton Chiles, U.S. Senator, Florida

Mr. Joseph Colletti,* Branch Chief, Quality Control Division, GSA, Chicago, IL

Mr. John Costello,* GSA Quality Assurance Specialist

Mr. Peter Boulay, GSA Commissioner, Federal Supply Service, GSA Region III (New York Region)

The Honorable David Pryor, U.S. Senator, Arkansas

Mr. Paul Granetto, Certified Public Accountant, detailed to the Subcommittee from the U.S. General Accounting Office

Mr. Marvin Doyal, Certified Public Accountant, detailed to the Subcommittee from the U.S. General Accounting Office

Mr. Jerry Maloney, Partner, Touche Ross & Co.

The Honorable John C. Danforth, U.S. Senator, Missouri

Mr. Raymond Dearie, former Assistant U.S. Attorney, Southern District of New York

Mr. Louis Arnold, former employee of Art Metal

Mr. Paul Freedman, former quality assurance specialist, General Services Administration, New York Region

Mr. Joseph Markowitz, Comptroller, Art Metal

Mr. Harold Phipps, Art Metal Co.

Mr. Joel Nagel, Traffic Manager, Art Metal Co.

Senator Chiles: (p. 1) The Senate Subcommittee on Federal Spending Practices and Open Government today opens 3 days of hearings into the relationship between the General Services Administration and one of its biggest furniture producers, Art Metal, U.S.A. The relationship between the Nation's office supplier and Art Metal began more than a decade ago and in the last 10 years more than $200 million tax dollars have been paid this firm.

---

*These two gentlemen had been assigned from GSA's Region 5, Chicago, to the Senate Subcommittee's investigative team, for the purpose performing an independent evaluation of the quality of Art Metal products, which is under the supervisory jurisdiction of GSA's Region 2, New York.

[Author's note: Subsequent pages present an abundance of testimony, letters of complaint from customers, and various exhibits that allege that Art Metal manufactured a generally defective product. Only a representative portion of what was included is reprinted here.]

Mr. Colletti: On the afternoon of November 1, a quantity of 23 lateral files were presented to Region 2 Quality Control Division for inspection. Art Metal's Quality Control Division had just completed their 100-percent inspection of these units and had determined them to be acceptable. Mr. Costello and I assisted region 2 personnel in this inspection and asked them to remove several drawers from the files for the purpose of inspecting the interior surfaces of the cabinets. As a result of this routine inspection four major and four minor defects were found in the following areas: [Six defects are listed].

This lot was subsequently rejected based on GSA's rejection criteria. Within an hour the second quantity of lateral files of the same type, size, and color with simulated wood tops was also rejected under the same GSA rejection criteria.

Mr. Costello: On the morning of November 2 an unscheduled meeting was held. The reason for the meeting was a protest by Art Metal to the methods of inspection and judgment employed in rejecting the two lots of lateral files. The meeting was attended by Mr. Kurens, the president of Art Metal, and three of his staff, and by Region 2 Quality Control Division personnel and members of the subcommittee staff. During the 1-hour meeting, under the vociferous domination of Mr. Kurens, Mr. Kurens challenged the judgment and competence of the GSA Quality Control Division personnel attached to the subcommittee, meaning myself and Mr. Colletti, and inferred that the intimidating tactics employed made any impartial inspection evaluation impossible for Region 2 Quality Control Division personnel. Using a variety of vulgar terms he described the criticism of interior spotweld flash and improper location of weld as tactics intended to crucify Art Metal and to shut them down.

Senator Chiles: What else did you observe during your visit to Art Metal?

Mr. Colletti: On the manufacture of the desk, we observed that Art Metal was assembling desks with noticeable defects, such as paint runs, unpainted areas, nicks on laminated plastic tops, and were packing desks with wet paint. Examination of the packing revealed incomplete closure of container flaps, and strapping, which distorted shipping containers, by using an improperly fitted carton. (p. 4)

Senator Chiles: Mr. Costello, tell me something about the items you inspected at the depots (Fort Worth, Texas and Stockton, California)?

Mr. Costello: Mr. Chairman, during our inspection of metal furniture for all the depots visited, we inspected a total of 603 units manufactured by the companies which included Art Metal. For the 17 companies combined, we found 278 units out of the 603 inspected, or 46 percent, to be suitable for issue; 121 units or 20 percent were unsuitable for issue; and 204 units or 34 percent were undesirable but issuable. Of the 603 units inspected, we found 777 total defects. Now, pertaining to Art Metal, for all the depots visited we inspected 303 units manufactured by Art Metal. Only 49 of the 303, or 16 percent, were suitable for issue as found; 107, or 35 percent, were unsuitable for issue; and 147 units, or 49 percent, were undesirable but issuable. Of the 303 Art Metal units inspected, we found 654 defects. This is 84 percent of total of 777 defects for the total of the 17 companies. Of all the items inspected, Art Metal supplied 50.2 percent. Of those units deemed undesirable, Art Metal is responsible for 107 of the 121 units, or 88 percent of the total.

Senator Chiles: You are saying that the furniture manufactured by Art Metal contained far more defects than their 16 competitors and that Art Metal's defects occurred with more frequency and severity than the other 16 companies?

Mr. Costello: That's correct.

Senator Chiles: What kind of defects did you find in Art Metal's furniture that you didn't find in the other companies?

Mr. Colletti: We consistently found the following defects in Art Metal's furniture: Under the category of paint and finish, we found bare or dead paint areas, poor paint touchups, metal painted over foreign matter. We also found a high percentage of filing cabinets, case interiors, already rusted for lack of adequate paint coverage.

Under the spot welding category we found excessive spot weld flash and spatters that weren't removed. Some weld spatters had edges sharp enough to cause injury. Under the cabinet case we found interior and exterior members of the cabinet case containing exposed, sharp, raw, unfinished edges with heavy burrs which also can cause injury. Under construction we found bubble tops, loose binding strips on desks, locks broken, keys missing, inadequate fit of the cabinet top to the body on filing cabinets. Where the chairs had adjustable means, some chairs would not elevate, and loose upholstery and buckles which should have been drawn tighter; filing cabinets with drawers out of alignment. Drawers were binding, not tracking properly. Keys were inoperative. On the typewriter desks some of the drawers were distorted and sprung. Vertical cabinets with lancets not securing drawers in position. Missing rubber bumpers. Under the category of plating we found interior hardware with rusted screw heads, lock levers, chrome plated suspensions were coated with rust. We also found shelves not properly patched, loose drawer dividers, and chair seat cushions badly indented by the edge of corrugated packing material.

Senator Chiles: Is there anything equivalent in commercial situations— in other words, could Art Metal be a supplier to a Sears, Roebuck, or Montgomery Ward with that kind of defect level?

Mr. Colletti: In my determination, Mr. Chairman, in a commercial activity, their quality control people would not accept the quality level of merchandise that is offered by Art Metal to the General Services Administration.

Testimony of Mr. Peter Boulay, Commissioner, Region III, Federal Supply Service (p. 134)

Mr. Boulay: The Federal Supply Service items are routinely put in a hold status in order to protect customer agencies from receiving faulty merchandise. The current situation involving the articles of furniture on quality hold at the Middle River began November 3, 1978. At that time three items were placed in hold status as a result of customer complaints received in this region and other regions.

Senator Chiles: What were the approximate totals of items and dollar values involved here?

Mr. Boulay: Well, between November 3, 1978, and January 18, 1979, a total of approximately 5,000 pieces of furniture from Art Metal were placed on hold in my region, which encompasses three depots. The principal one is at Middle River, outside Baltimore, which is primarily a furniture stocking depot. Of this total of 5,000 pieces, 4,350 pieces are located at Middle River, and 650 pieces at Norfolk, Va. These 5,000 pieces include 23 stock numbers, principally vertical and lateral filing cabinets, desks, with a total dollar value above $800,000.

Senator Chiles: To try to put this in a little better perspective for us, approximately what percentage of defects did you find in the items inspected at Middle River?

Mr. Boulay: Well, again, by the end of June, we had inspected eight different types of cabinets, mostly vertical and lateral filing cabinets. As of July 16, 1979, we have now completed 16 of the 23 and the defective rejection rate is holding at 87 percent.

Senator Chiles: And, did you inspect each cabinet, or is that just by lot?

Mr. Boulay: No, this is a cabinet by cabinet inspection with us documenting the defects we find, the Art Metal repair team in most cases initialing our findings and then setting to work to correct the defects, and then we retain the complete documentation so that we can trace this back to such things as the incoming invoice, the lot number, the inspection by the Art Metal plant.

Senator Pryor: Is the U.S. Government still purchasing equipment from Art Metal today?

Mr. Boulay: Yes, sir.

Senator Pryor: That is incredible. Why are we?

Mr. Boulay: I honestly don't know. I recommended to the central office in recent months that we cease doing that.

Testimony of Mr. Paul Granetto, CPA (p. 139).

Mr. Granetto: A tactic of the company concerning a complaint was to blame all defective merchandise on damage in transit. Other ploys used by the company was to pick obvious errors in the complaint, such as faulty contract numbers, purchase order numbers, even though they knew it was their product, they would deny all knowledge of it, or to state that they never shipped to that location even though they ship to the GSA depot in that region. All else failing, the company simply delayed action on the complaint as long as possible.

Senator Chiles: You stated that the complaint list of the General Services Administration did not include a significant number of complaints for thousands of items. How did you determine this?

Mr. Granetto: Senator, I determined this by comparing Art Metal's files of complaints with complaints listed published by the General Services Administration. A great number of complaints held in Art Metal's files were not shown on the GSA list. As an example, Art Metal's files contained a complaint from GSA, Chicago, IL, dated April 1975, concerning 500 flat top desks. Another example, an August 1978 complaint from GSA concerning 710 defective cabinets, Stockton, CA. These two complaints, and a significant number of others, were omitted from the GSA complaints list. From my review of Art Metal files I would say that the larger the number of items involved in the complaint, the less probability of it appearing in the complaints list.

Senator Chiles: You stated that Art Metal's policy was one of denying all responsibility for damaged or defective merchandise received by the Federal Government. What is the basis for your statement?

Mr. Granetto: My basis is "blind footnotes," which are internal memos written on incoming and outgoing correspondence, which comment on the subject of the correspondence. I refer to correspondence from GSA Quality Control Division, dated December 4, 1975, in which GSA states complaints concerning five office tables received by the U.S. Department of Labor in Chicago. The blind footnote handwritten on the correspondence circulated stated:

When this letter from GSA, QCD, is returned, we can either state DIT (damaged in transit) or never shipped to consigned or shipment made to Bengies, MD, and not to Chicago, IL over one year ago.

Senator Chiles: In another instance, Art Metal received a complaint from Lewis Air Force Base in Arizona, concerning six wardrobe lockers. The complaint that the latching mechanisms were inoperative. Art Metal responded:

With reference to the subject matter, from the contents of your letter it appears that the wardrobes were damaged in transit. These cabinets were dropped on their corners, causing the bent corners and distorting of the cabinet, et cetera. Please request them to send a copy showing exceptions taken to the merchandise at the time of delivery (to the GSA depot) or an exception report made by the delivering carrier after the damage in transit was discovered on the premises.

However, the blind footnote states:

Spiegel (a company associated with Art Metal) delivered the goods and according to the notation we made in our Region Book no exceptions were taken to the delivery bill of lading on 4-9-75.

So they already knew the goods were not damaged in transit, that there was no exception taken, and yet they send a letter saying it had to be damaged in transit, so do this.

Senator Chiles: I see that on January 7 GSA complained of 74 filing cabinets being received with defective locking mechanisms and drawers hard to open and close. GSA specifically stated the filing cabinets were received on order form FW20576-2. I note the last digits are 6-2. On January 13, 1975, Art Metal responded and said:

With reference to the subject matter, please be advised we checked all of our purchase orders against filing cabinet annual contract and do not find any record of shipping against a purchase order FW20576-1 or 7110-551-5489 file cabinets. Will you therefore kindly cancel this complaint and confirm this cancellation in writing.

A blind footnote states, "We actually shipped 84-5489's against FOPOFW20570 on June 11, 1974 and June 19, 1974." GSA then responded to the letter citing the correct number, and Art Metal's response to this on March 3, 1975, was as follows:

With reference to the subject matter, from the contents of your letter it appears that the file cabinets were damaged in transit. These files were dropped on their corners causing the case of the file to twist and distort out of shape. This distorted case would prevent the locking mechanism from opening properly. Please request a damage-in-transit claim be filed promptly by the consignee.

Excerpts—Letters of Complaint

(p. 172)
June 11, 1976
From: General Services Administration
To: Art Metal, U.S.A., Incorporated
This office has been notified of 714 Wardrobe and Storage Cabinets, received by the Naval Construction Battalion, Gulfport, Missouri, An inspection of 103 cabinets revealed that 46 contained two left side panels instead of one right and one left.

(p. 173)
July 18, 1978
From: General Services Administration
To: Art Metal, U.S.A., Incorporated

We have been advised that 34 Wardrobes were received by Folk Polk, LA and found to be defective.

The wardrobes were received with the following defects:

1. Missing bolts and washers.
2. Two wardrobes were received with two bottoms and no tops.
3. Drawer assembly could not be attached to the back of the lockers due to the pre-drilled holes being on the wrong side of the back.
4. Twenty of 34 partitions which attach to the drawer assembly and to the top full-shelf would not attach due to mis-drilled holes.
5. Nylon skids were provided to attach to the bottom for floor protection. In 25 of 34 no holes were provided for attachment.
6. Shelves could not be leveled horizontally due to mis-location of shelving brackets on four of 34 units.
7. Mirrors are missing on 30 of 34 lockers.
8. Assembly instructions does not include the amount, size, or place of installation for screws, nuts, and lock washers.

(p. 178)

December 4, 1975

From: General Services Administration

To: Art Metal, U.S.A., Incorporated

This office has been notified of defective material received by the Department of Labor/RAMO.

The defective material involved is five office tables.

The corners and edge moldings are loose causing exposed sharp edges. The plastic tops are not bonded to the table and the front panel is dented.

(p. 180)

December 11, 1975

From: General Services Administration

To: Art Metal, U.S.A., Incorporated

This office has been notified of defective material received by Luke Air Force Base, Arizona.

The defective material involved is 96 Wardrobe Lockers. The latching mechanisms are inoperative, panel corners are bent, dents in units, bare spots on door frames.

(p. 181)

December 22, 1975

Art Metal, U.S.A., Incorporated reply:

From the contents of your letter it appears these wardrobes were damaged in transit.

(p. 278)

March 20, 1975

From: General Services Administration

To: Art Metal, U.S.A., Incorporated

This office has been notified of a defective steel table received with one leg (3) three inches short, a hole off the center in one leg, and the table top not glued satisfactorily.

(p. 443)

Senator Chiles: We have heard an incredible story here today about the quality of furniture taxpayers shelled out more than $200 million to buy over the past 10 years. I think the testimony today shows conclusively the inferiority of Art Metal furniture, and that it was not a secret to the General Services Administration, and that it was not a secret to Art Metal. The company's own records show us the kind of tricks the company undertook to make sure it didn't have to make good on its contracts, and to attempt to delay and delay until an agency grew tired of the fight and would throw in the towel. Tomorrow's hearings will shed more light on just how that relationship between General Services Administration and Art Metal was nourished and grew over the years. We will hear testimony of amounts of cash at the company's offices and will attempt to trace how that cash came into being and what happened to it. We will also question General Services Administration employees who were responsible for checking some of this Art Metal furniture to make sure of its quality and try to determine their relationship with Art Metal executives.

ILLUSTRATION: CORRESPONDENCE
GSA TO ART METAL (from Art Metals files)

299

UNITED STATES OF AMERICA
GENERAL SERVICES ADMINISTRATION
FEDERAL SUPPLY SERVICE

Region 2
26 Federal Plaza
New York, NY 10007

June, 17, 1975

CERTIFIED MAIL - RETURN RECEIPT REQUESTED
Art Metal - U.S.A. Inc.
300 Passaic St.
Newark, N. J. 07104

Gentlemen:

This office has been notified of 10 defective partitions received
by the Dept. of the Navy, Navy Recruiting Dist., Naval Training
Center, San Diego, Calif., Supply Depot, that was supplied on contract
GS-00S-28920.

The defective partitions involved are Type I, Group 2, Rust colored
Office Partitions, Size 8, NSN 7195-00-118-8967.

An examination of these partitions revealed the following defects:
(1) screws protruding above frame
(2) stains on burlap caused by excessive glue on backing
(3) burlap separating from backing and pulling away from frame, and
(4) color spotted, burlap not properly colored.

Please notify this office when a replacement shipment for the above
material will be available for inspection. In addition, provide
disposition instructions for the defective material located at
complaining agency and Stockton Depot.

Please reply within five days from the date of receipt of this
notification and refer to control number 9QC-399A-75 when
replying to this letter.

Sincerely,

PAUL FREEDMAN
Director, Quality Control Division

ILLUSTRATION: ART METAL RESPONSE
TO GSA CORRESPONDENCE

304

July 14 ,1975

General Services Administration
Federal Supply Service
26 Federal Plaza
New York, New York 10007

Attention: Mr Paul Freedman, Director
            Quality Control Division

Subject: Control #9QC-445-75
          47-7125-00-764-5908
          Storage Cabinets

Gentlemen:

With reference to the subject matter, from the contents of your letter it
appears these storage cabinets were damaged in transit.

These storage cabinets were dropped and mishandled in shipping causing
warped back panels, scratches and dents, misaligned doors, defective
latches and missing springs.

Kindly request the customer, the LAIR Letterman Army Medical Center,
San Francisco, CA, to promptly file a damage in transit claim with the
delivering carrier

Very truly yours,

ART METAL-U.S.A. Inc.

J. Nagel

JN: lf
cc: GSA-FSS QcD, M. Mandel-QAS

bcc: Kurens, Salzman, Ferrone, Assembly (2), JN File

ILLUSTRATION: CORRESPONDENCE
GSA TO ART METAL (from Art Metals files)

305

UNITED STATES OF AMERICA
GENERAL SERVICES ADMINISTRATION
FEDERAL SUPPLY SERVICE

Region 2
26 Federal Plaza
New York, NY 10007

July, 3 ,1975

CERTIFIED MAIL - RETURN RECEIPT REQUESTED
Art Metal - U.S.A Inc.
300 Passaicc St.
Newark, N. J. 07104

Gentlemen:

This office has been notified of 47 defective storage cabinets,
NSN 7125-00-764-5908, received by the LAIR Letterman Army Medical
Center, San Francisco, California, that was supplied on contract
GS-00S-24953.

Eight units were shipped direct on Purchase Order 9XD-S-37215-1 and
39 units were shipped from the Stockton depot on an unknown purchase
order.

An examination of these cabinets revealed the following defects:
(1) all cabinets had defective door latches, some with missing springs or missing keys,
(2) misaligned doors,
(3) warped back panels,
(4) various scratches and dents both inside and outside of the cabinet,
(5) one cabinet door had no hinge pins,
(6) painted over rust spots, and
(7) shelf edges not joined correctly.

Please notify this office when a replacement shipment for the above
material will be available for inspection, and, provide disposition
instructions for the defective cabinets. Ship the replacement cabinets
to the Stockton, Calif., Supply Depot.

Please reply within five days from the date of receipt of this
notification and refer to control number 9QC-445-75 when replying
to this letter.

Sincerely,

PAUL FREEDMAN
Director, Quality Control Division

ILLUSTRATION: CORRESPONDENCE
GSA TO ART METAL (from Art Metals files)

435

UNITED STATES OF AMERICA
GENERAL SERVICE ADMINISTRATION
FEDERAL SUPPLY SERVICE

Region 2
26 Federal Plaza
New York, NY 10007

July 24, 1978

CERTIFIED MAIL - RETURN RECEIPT REQUESTED
Art Metal U.S.A Inc.
300 Passaic St.
Newark, N. J. 07104

Gentlemen:

We have been advised that 710 cabinets, NSN 7125-00-641-5436 were received by the GSA Supply Distribution Facility, Stockton, CA, and found to be defective.

Shipment was made under contract number GS-00S-61189, purchase order SWVE-735-2, 520 each and SWVE-800-1, 190 each.

Examination of a statistical sample reveal longitudinal and end members lumber to be 5/8" to 3/4" instead of required 1" material. Cross members are 3/8" to 7/16" instead of required 1/2". Some individual cabinets have two straps instead of required 3, while others have no straps. Pallets on some are 6" longer than cabinet package. When straps were drawn tight the pallet broke making a loose package.

Staples split wood on several. Some staples missed the second board completely or one leg missed, causing a safety hazard. Pallet straps are loose on several pallets. Side members, end pieces, and cross members are split, (by staples and other means), on several cabinets, causing possible cabinet damage.

Replacement is to be made to the GSA Supply Distribution Facility, Stockton, CA.

It is requested that disposition instructions and a firm replacement date be forwarded to this office within 5 days after receipt of this letter.

All correspondence relating to this complaint must reference control number 2QC-S50-78.

If there are any questions concerning this matter, please contact Mr. Albert Schoenfeld or Mr. Teronia Burks at 212-2640-3573.

Sincerely,

EDWARD H. WYATT, JR.
Director, Quality Control Division

Part II The Investigation (p. 447)

Thursday July 19, 1979

Senator Chiles: Good morning. We will continue our hearings. Our first witness today will tell us what he found in the documents that we subpoenaed from Art Metal and others. Mr. Doyal, would you rise and take the oath? Mr. Doyal, the question that begs to be answered is why the government continued to buy the bulk of its metal furniture from the firm that produced low quality products. Mr. Doyal, how did the investigation proceed, to answer this question?

Mr. Doyal: Sir, we began by examining the books and records of the company looking for things that would cause a presumption of concern or other things known as indicators of corruption.

Senator Chiles: What do you mean when you say, indicators of corruption?

Mr. Doyal: Indicators of corruption, to me, are anything that call the integrity of the company into question. First and foremost among these would be generations of large sums of cash.

Senator Chiles: Why would that be an indicator?

Mr. Doyal: A supply of cash would be an indicator of corruption through payoff. I'd like to add that it's not the only way to corrupt someone but only cash and things of value are traceable and measurable and those are the things we have to stick with.

Senator Chiles: Where else would you go to seek indicators of corruption? How else do you proceed?

Mr. Doyal: We went to the company level, sir, to what we call the inspector level, the next group of people dealing closely with the company. We tested their performance through interviews and other techniques that were designed to determine whether or not they had the requisite independence and objectiveness to perform their functions.

Senator Chiles: Why would you be testing the quality of the company?

Mr. Doyal: These are the Government officials closest to the company. They accept the metal office furniture for the Government accounts and nearly every piece of furniture that Art Metal left either after their inspection or with their blessing.

Senator Chiles: We were told yesterday that in many of the warehouses, where we had defective furniture that the Government had to go in and repair this furniture at the Government's expense and we even found where they had one scheme with which they said they would just send this out and then let the user agencies note the complaints or with furniture that's so bad, GSA would make GSA use it themselves, because, after all, "we are the ones that, I guess, should complain least." All of that would be because that furniture had left the contractor's plant after having been "inspected" and accepted by Government inspectors. Is that correct?

Mr. Doyal: Yes sir. Once the inspector has signed what's known as a 308, the Government has taken title to the product when it leaves the contractor's plant and is responsible for it.

Senator Chiles: So, if you were attempting to put some less than quality furniture on the Government, the weak link or the first link would have that go by those quality inspectors that were at the plant.

Mr. Doyal: Yes sir, that's true.

Senator Chiles: Where else did you look for indicators of corruption?

Mr. Doyal: We sought them at the headquarters level of GSA here in Washington, D.C. because it seemed quite unlikely to us that a problem could continue for as many years as the quality problem of Art Metal has without either passive acceptance or active participation by someone at a higher level.

Senator Chiles: How did you proceed with your examination of Art Metal furniture?

Mr. Doyal: We conducted what we call a cash flow investigation. This type of investigation is designed and concentrates on cash transactions only. It attempts to trace the source of all cash to a company and its ultimate application. There are three steps in a cash flow analysis. The first step is to examine closely all checks. The second is to examine closely all deposits. The third step is to interview the people involved in the transactions.

Senator Chiles: What did the analysis disclose Mr. Doyal?

Mr. Doyal: There were several items that were of interest to us. They were petty cash transactions, payments to related parties, and payments to sales consultants.

Senator Chiles: Tell us about the petty cash transactions.

Mr. Doyal: During the five years we examined their records Art Metal wrote hundreds of checks payable to cash. These checks were endorsed and cashed by various of their employees and the transactions were reported in the petty cash account. During Art Metal's business year ending September 30, 1978, the checks payable to cash totaled about $431,000. The year before the checks payable to cash totaled $203,000. The checks that are drawn payable to cash contain a notation in the upper left hand corner that they were "auction expense." For example, on November 3, 1977, the company drew nine checks on three different banks, each for $1,000, each payable to cash. They were all endorsed and cashed on the same day. For the five year period the company generated through this method a total of $484,000 in cash or currency.

Senator Chiles: Let me ask you, is this (November 3rd) a special day that you picked because there are more checks that day than any other day?

Mr. Doyal: No, sir. That's not one of the largest days at all. There were days when as many as 25 or 30 checks were cashed in this same manner on three or four banks. In examining their books and records we found that, in fact, Art Metal does buy much of its equipment at auction but in the 5-year period of time we are talking about, they never used cash to buy it at auction.

Senator Chiles: But they went to auctions?

Mr. Doyal: Yes, sir, they went to auctions and they bought equipment at auctions but their regular practice was to use certified checks. The general conditions of the auction are 20 percent down at the time of the bid and the remainder prior to delivery. They did participate in auctions. They used certified checks as down payments, regular checks to pay the remainder of the amount, prior to receiving the merchandise that they bought.

Chart D is a chart that will show you how much of petty cash was available and when.

This is the ending balance of auction expense cash on hand at the company for each month during the period of time we were examining the records. The only thing of interest to the pattern is that at the end of September for 2 of the 5 years, there were no balances on hand. We attribute that to the fact that was the month that the CPA's came in, Touche Ross came in to do their annual audit of the firm.

We continued to be interested in this for two reasons. First, it was never used for the purpose they told us it had been generated for. Second, at the time they were generating much of this cash, Art Metal was paying interest at a rate of as much as 18 percent. If you look at 1977, which is one of the bigger years, they have an average of about $73,000 on hand at all times in currency, according to their records.

Senator Chiles: What kind of profit were they generating at this time, to determine whether this looked like it would be a sound business

Subcommittee Chart D

MONTHLY PETTY CASH
AMOUNTS RECORDED BY ART METAL

	1974	1975	1976	1977	1978
JAN	$ 8,500	$ 32,500	$ 27,000	$ 73,500	$ 126,900
FEB	$ 10,500	$ 32,500	$ 11,000	$ 73,500	$ 136,900
MAR	$ 10,500	$ 1,000	$ –0–	$ 83,500	$ 156,900
APRIL	$ 10,500	$ 24,000	$ 3,000	$ 83,500	$ 185,900
MAY	$ 10,500	$ 25,000	$ 3,000	$ 83,500	$ 185,900
JUNE	$ 10,500	$ 20,000	$ 15,000	$ 83,500	$ 192,900
JULY	$ 10,500	$ 20,000	$ 23,500	$ 93,500	$ 227,900
AUG	$ 10,500	$ 25,000	$ 20,500	$ 81,500	$ 258,900
SEPT	$ 10,500	$ –0–	$ –0–	$ 43,000	$ 258,900
OCT	$ 15,500	$ 3,000	$ 35,000	$ 43,000	$ 5,000
NOV	$ 32,500	$ –0–	$ 42,500	$ 60,400	$ 5,000
DEC	$ 32,500	$ –0–	$ 53,500	$ 81,900	$ –0–

practice or not to have this kind of cash laying around when you are borrowing at 18 percent?

Mr. Doyal: In 1974, their annual reports showed that had a loss of a little over $1 million, 1975, 1976, and 1977 show small profits but the amount of cash we are talking about is more than the profits earned in the years 1975, 1976, and 1977.

I have another chart here to show you. It's Chart E.

This is a chart which shows the banks on which these checks were drawn. The cashing follows a little bit of a curious pattern, we thought. On August 15, 1978, 25 checks were cashed. Five for $2,000 cash at one bank and 20 for $1,090 each at another bank. Another example, on August 18, three days later, 15 more checks were cashed, 5 for $1,000 at one bank and 10 for $2,000 at another bank. This same pattern was repeated with regard to deposits. The currency was deposited at three or four different banks on the same day.

Senator Chiles: Did you determine why they were cashing checks in $1,000 amounts at three or four different banks?

Mr. Doyal: We asked several people that question. The answer that we got was "We didn't want banks to know what our business was." That type of answer. There is another chart, chart F, which will show who cashed the checks. The first gentleman is Louis Arnold. He cashed 119 checks during the years 1974, 1975, and 1976 for

Subcommittee Chart E

PETTY CASH–AUCTION EXPENSE
BANKS AND NUMBERS OF CHECKS

YEAR	BANKS				TOTAL
	MIDLANTIC (New Jersey)	FIDELITY UNION (New Jersey)	FIRST NATIONAL (New Jersey)	KEARNY (New Jersey)	
	(Number) Amount	(Number) Amount	(Number) Amount	(Number) Amount	(Number) Amount
1974	(5) $5,000	(10) $10,000	(16) $17,000	(6) $5,500	(37) $37,500
1975	(6) $6,000	(11) $11,000	(13) $13,000	(2) $2,000	(32) $32,000
1976	(13) $13,000	(26) $24,000	(82) $82,000	(1) $1,000	(122) $120,000
1977	(14) $14,000	(40) $41,900	(34) $38,000		(88) $93,900
1978	(5) $5,000	(61) $66,000	(114) $124,000	(5) $6,000	(186) $201,000
TOTAL	(43) $43,000	(148) $152,900	(259) $274,000	(15) $14,000	(465) $484,400

$111,000. Harold Phipps, 323 checks for $342,000. Joe Nagel, 24 checks, $22,500. Mr. Cooperstein cashed six checks. Mr. Slater cashed two checks.

Senator Chiles: Is the denomination of the bills obtained at the bank of any significance?

Mr. Doyal: Yes sir, it is. When Touche, Ross & Co. arrived for their annual audit in September of 1978, they called for account of petty cash. When they did so, they wound up counting 1,399 $100 bills, 940 $50 bills, and 3,600 $20 bills. This money would make a stack about 30 inches high. Chart G would show what the auditor had to see.

Senator Chiles: I think at this time, we'd like to call a representative of the audit firm Touche Ross & Co.

PART III—Touche, Ross & Co., Independent Public Accountants (p. 454)

Senator Chiles: Mr. Maloney, you are a partner of Touche, Ross & Co.; is that correct?

Subcommittee Chart G

ART METAL
PETTY CASH COUNT

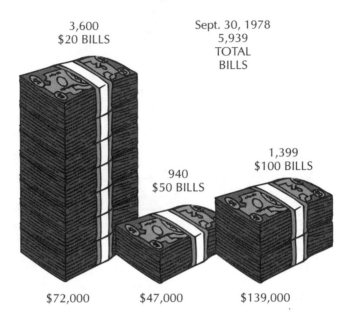

3,600
$20 BILLS

Sept. 30, 1978
5,939
TOTAL
BILLS

1,399
$100 BILLS

940
$50 BILLS

$72,000 $47,000 $139,000

TOTAL VALUE $258,900

Mr. Maloney: That's correct.

Senator Chiles: Were you assigned to the Art Metal account?

Mr. Maloney: Yes; I was assigned to it in September of 1978.

Senator Chiles: Mr. Maloney, in September of 1978, auditors under your direct supervision were at Art Metal in connection with your annual audit of the firm. One of them was assigned to count petty cash when all of this was done, Art Metal had shown your auditor some $258,900 in currency. Describe for us, if you will, the counting procedure?

Mr. Maloney: Basically, when the auditor arrived, Mr. Markowitz, at our request, brought in the petty cash to be counted.

Senator Chiles: How was that brought in?

Mr. Maloney: First, he brought in attaché cases and opened them up on the desk and they were brought full of money. The auditor proceeded to count the cash that was contained in the attaché cases and when he was done with those two, Mr. Markowitz said he had another one. So, the auditor accompanied him back to the safe to get the third case and brought that into the room and he proceeded to count the third case.

Senator Chiles: How many of your clients would have this amount of cash on hand? Is it a normal procedure you would find when you audit a firm, to bring in a couple of suitcases of cash?

Mr. Maloney: For a company of this size, no, this is not a normal amount of petty cash on hand.

Senator Chiles: Art Metal had some $43,000 in cash on hand in their fiscal year 1977. Could you give us the details of that count?

Mr. Maloney: Yes. That count was basically the money brought in by Mr. Markowitz. He put that on the desk, and the count had no bills larger than $20 in it.

Senator Danforth: Now, Mr. Doyal stated with some degree of assurance that the purchase of equipment was not made for cash. It was made instead by cashier's check or certified check?

Mr. Maloney: Certified check.

Senator Danforth: Do you concur in that?

Mr. Maloney: Well, I asked Mr. Kurens who is the president, if he had bought fixed assets at auctions for cash. And he had said he had bought fixed assets for cash. I said, "I know that, But for cash?" and his response was "Are you a detective?" And I said, "No, the account of cash on your end is here. That's all I have to know." I never got an answer as to when he had purchased fixed assets for cash.

Senator Danforth: Do you know how Art Metal paid for the equipment that it bought at the auctions?

Mr. Maloney: The initial down payment was by certified check and the remaining balance due on the purchase was paid by a regular check when the equipment was received.

Senator Danforth: When you make an audit, do you determine the total amount that has been paid for the equipment that's been purchased?

Mr. Maloney: Yes I do.

Senator Danforth: Can you state with confidence how much of the total purchase price was paid by cash during this period of time?

That is, how much cash, how much in greenbacks was paid for equipment during this period of time?

Mr. Maloney: No significant amount that I know of.

Senator Danforth: What would you call a significant amount?

Mr. Maloney: Over $5,000, $10,000.

Senator Danforth: Over $5,000 to $10,000 during a period of 5 years?

Mr. Maloney: Yes. There is no significant acquisition that I know of that was purchased for cash.

Mr. Doyal: We examined each of the vouchers and the method of payment for every item of equipment that they bought over the 5-year period. There was no equipment bought for cash.

Senator Pryor: Who had control over this cash amount?

Mr. Maloney: Mr. Markowitz. As far as we know, he was the custodian of that cash.

Senator Chiles: Mr. Doyal, did you try to determine whether there was any other way of the company putting cash back if they used this cash?

Mr. Doyal: Yes sir, we did. We identified people who cashed the checks. We interviewed them. One of these people gave us what we thought was a clue to it. We were asking him about cash and he volunteered the information and when Art Metal ran short of cash, they called Mr. Spiegel and Mr. Spiegel brought the cash to them. We found out he was referring to Mr. Isadore Spiegel, the owner of the trucking firm that hauls Art Metal products. I'll cite some of the reasons why I call him a related party and while I'm doing so, it might be a good idea to keep in mind that transportation costs by Spiegel are 6 to 10 percent of Art Metal's gross sales. (p. 462) Spiegel carries under an ICC license as a contract carrier for Art Metal, which means that in one of his entities, he hauls only for Art Metal, U.S.A., and the entity is Spiegel Trucking Inc. During 1977 Art Metal wrote some 520 checks to Spiegel. For the most part the checks were written to Spiegel Co., were endorsed by a rubber stamp, and the banking information on the checks showed that the checks were deposited to Spiegel Trucking Company accounts. However, the checks written just to the name I. Spiegel, some of those were not endorsed by rubber stamp. They were either in hand and either cashed or re-endorsed by others. Spiegel, according to state records, was also an incorporate and/or a director of Steel Sales Inc., which, according to the books and records of Art Metal, was a wholly owned subsidiary of Art Metal. On at least seven occasions we identified Steel Sales checks that had been signed by Isadore Spiegel as the maker, that is, he signed the checks as one of the owners of the firm. During the 5 years covered by our investigation, Art Metal made payments to Spiegel totaling some $4.7 million. These payments were made by some 406,000 different checks made out to the various names, Spiegel, Inc., I. Spiegel, I. & L., Inc., Spiegel Distribution Center, and other names. For these checks that we will call questionable or unusual Spiegel checks, there is no indication that they went through Spiegel's account.

Senator Chiles: What would be the value of the checks that were handled questionably?

Mr. Doyal: The ones that we considered questionable, total over $854,000 over a period of 5 years. This is an example of the checks we are talking about from Art Metal made out to I. Spiegel. They were all written on August 17, 1977, and cashed on September 8, 1977. They are $4,000 apiece, totaling $12,000 in cash. They were all cashed not deposited. The next day Art Metal deposited $9,500 in its banking account in cash.

Senator Pryor: Do you consider it to be a little strange that the checks were for an even number? They are rounded off like $4,000.

Mr. Doyal: Yes sir, in this type of investigation, one of the first things anyone looks for is even amount checks.

Senator Pryor: There is one more interesting thing about these checks. They appear to have been folded.

Mr. Doyal: Yes sir. They do appear to have been folded, almost as if they had been carried in a wallet and between the period of time when they were written and actually cashed, which is about a month meaning Mr. Spiegel was walking around or someone was walking around with $12,000 in checks in their pockets.

Senator Chiles: (p. 469) Were there any other matters or violations that your audit disclosed?

Mr. Doyal: Yes sir, Federal procurement regulations prohibit certain types of contract or agent relationships. Our examination disclosed that Art Metal did retain Mr. Arthur Lowell but did not disclose this arrangement on any of its contract bids.

Senator Chiles: Did Mr. Lowell work for other firms?

Mr. Doyal: Yes sir, . . . the president of Atlas Paint and Varnish stated that Lowell was retained by his firm from early 1968 to late 1971. During that period of time he paid Lowell some $228,000.

Part IV—The Assistant U.S. Attorney, Southern District of New York

Senator Chiles: (p. 471) The Government's last line of defense against poor quality is the quality assurance inspector. These are Government employees who work in the contractor's plant. They inspect the items to insure that they meet the Government's qualifications and the Government needs them and has paid for them. Earlier testimony shows us that this last line of defense was not very effective despite their presence and despite inspections that the Government continually got poor quality merchandise. To find out why, of course, you need to look at the inspectors and try to determine who is responsible for this. We found that several years ago an inspector who had worked in a New York region who was not at Art Metal was convicted of distorting money from certain contractors and reviewing testimony from that trial, we found that the convicted inspector had told the company officials that the money he collected was shared with higher-ups in the quality inspection organization.

He also stated that a number of firms were making payoffs. Additionally, the retired Art Metal employee told us that it was common knowledge that inspectors were being paid off and specifically named two inspectors that were taken care of, one of which was the head of the New York region quality control group. We will now go into hearing information on these matters and I will call Mr. Raymond Dearie, a former U.S. attorney from the southern district of New York. Mr. Dearie, you investigated a contract by a General Services Administration employee. Can you give us some of the details of that case please?

Mr. Dearie: Certainly Senator. I guess I should state the point in time when I first became aware of the case. In February 1975, while I was serving as the Chief of the Criminal Division of the U.S. Attorney's Office, I received a telephone call from the Special Division of the FBI to advise me that he had just spoken to a gentleman by the name of Michael Lioi who explained that a representative of the General Services Administration, a gentleman by the name of Harry Iaconetti, had solicited a bribe from Mr. Lioi in connection with a contract that Mr. Lioi's company, Champion Envelope, had successfully bid on with the General Services Administration. Mr. Lioi explained, on the morning of January 10, 1975, to the special agent that this Mr. Iaconetti was returning, as he put it, to discuss the matter further and that Mr. Lioi had inquired whether or not he could tape record the conversation that was going to take place. And so a tape recording of that conversation was made. Mr. Lioi explained that he had done some small Government contract work, Champion Envelope that is, but he had never had any problem at all with the General Services Administration, and had, in fact, had a similar experience with Mr. Iaconetti which was satisfactory. He explained that in January of 1975, he had bid on a contract with the General Services Administration successfully covering a 6-month period and a sum total of approximately $1,250,000. That he received a telephone call shortly thereafter from Mr. Iaconetti who explained that he had been assigned to conduct what is known as a "preaward study" of the contract in question, the idea of which is to determine whether or not the contractor who has become the low bidder is physically and financially capable of performing the contract according to specifications. This preaward study was to be performed by Mr. Iaconetti. (p. 473) As Mr. Lioi explained, as soon as he had heard from Mr. Iaconetti, Mr. Iaconetti explained this was a big one, Mike, a big contract and was going to be very difficult to justify, which in retrospect, as Mr. Lioi told us thereafter, struck him as unusual, but did not alert him as to what was eventually to transpire.

The first day that Mr. Lioi and Mr. Iaconetti met at the facility at Champion Envelope in Brooklyn, N.Y., Mr. Iaconetti came in and told Mr. Lioi and his partner about how this was a big contract and going to be very, very difficult to justify, and explained that he could perhaps justify a portion of the contract, but it was going to be very difficult to justify the entire award. Mr. Lioi and his partner, Mr. Babiuk, pressed Mr. Iaconetti for some details or reasons as to why he doubted Champion's ability to perform the contract.

Later, on February 10, without the benefit of a recording, Mr. Iaconetti was sitting down with Mr. Babiuk and began the process of actually reviewing the contract specifications. At one point he asked Mr. Babiuk whether or not he had a form 123, which as I understood, is nothing more than a standard notice to Government contractor of the packaging, labeling, and shipping specifications applicable to all Government contracts. Mr. Babiuk said that he did. Mr. Iaconetti asked to see the form. Mr. Iaconetti then told Mr. Babiuk that this form had been suspended two months earlier. Mr. Babiuk inquired as to whether there were any substantive changes and Mr. Iaconetti said, "No, but I can disqualify you on the entire contract for this and this alone." Finally, Mr. Iaconetti and Mr. Lioi, president of that company, met in Mr. Lioi's office. Mr. Iaconetti told Mr. Lioi "Mike, this is a big contract. I'd like to see you get it. I'd like you to get even bigger ones."

Senator Chiles: Is this taped now?

Mr. Dearie: This is not. He said "There are hurdles, Mike, upper eschelon hurdles that must be overcome." Lioi asked, "Well what would convince these upper echelon people that we are, in fact, capable of performing this contract?" "Well, we could save you approximately 1 percent, or $12,500." The meeting was adjourned with an agreement to meet the following day. They contacted their attorney. He recommended they contact the New York office of the FBI, which they did the following morning, and as a result, some minutes thereafter, I received the phone call from the FBI.

Mr. Iaconetti arrived on schedule on February 11 at about 11 o'clock at Mr. Lioi's office, this time with the benefit of a tape recording, Mr. Lioi's own voice activated recorder and the conversation that the three of them had turned immediately to question of justifying the contract; Mr. Iaconetti said right off the bat. He said "I'll be able to justify a portion of it, otherwise, instead of all of it." Mr. Lioi said "When you say 'otherwise,' what do you mean?" Mr. Iaconetti said "Well, instead of justifying all of it." Later the subtlety subsided and Mr. Iaconetti said "All right, all right, what it amounts to in the long run, is $1\frac{1}{2}$ percent. Three quarters of it goes to a certain area. A quarter of it goes to another area and possibly," he said, "I'll get a percent." There was some discussion as to the specific price and eventually, the figure of $9,600 was agreed as an advance payment to the upper echelons as Mr. Iaconetti referred to them.

Several days later, plans were made for the meeting between Mr. Lioi and Mr. Iaconetti and after a series of travels to and from diners and selected spots in the Brooklyn area, eventually Mr. Iaconetti's trunk was opened. He instructed Mr. Lioi to put it in there, Mike and when Mr. Lioi put it there Mr. Iaconetti was placed under arrest.

He was charged with five counts of bribery and extortion involving various situations. He was convicted and sentenced to 4 years in prison. It is my personal belief, Senator, that Mr. Iaconetti did not operate alone. First of all, the most telling thing and to really appreciate this you have to hear the transcript of the recordings. The sophistication, the subtleness, the articulateness of Mr. Iaconetti on that tape, convinced me beyond any doubt, when I heard it, that Mr. Iaconetti had done this before. That, in large measure, was why he waited 3 months before proceeding to the grand jury in the hope that was eventually realized that we could come up with another instance as we indeed did. My knowledge, as we began to get into the investigation itself of the inner workings, the procedural workings of the General Services Administration in the quality assurance area, told me, that indeed, if an inspector was going to attempt to solicit payments from contractors who were clearly, particularly in the case of Champion Envelope, capable of performing the contract, he would have to have some kind of support from the supervisory staff of personnel of the General Services Administration to back him up.

There was considerable evidence from the very outset that at least Mr. Iaconetti, and I think, to a certain extent the supervisory staff of the quality assurance branch enjoyed a lifestyle that was not consistent with their personal incomes with the Government. Mr. Iaconetti would repeatedly boast of his killings in the stock market, and of his home in Dix Hills, a kind of wealthy suburban area on Long Island, and of his new Cadillac, and when we looked into that, we saw that indeed Mr. Iaconetti was active in the stock market but Mr. Iaconetti was a loser by far, but nevertheless had available to him significant sums of money.

Senator Chiles: Did you look into the lifestyle of any of these other individuals besides Iaconetti?

Mr. Dearie: We did, Senator, and again the pattern continued. We received information concerning certain investments of Mr. Freedman, of Mr. Ponzio. Certain investments of Mr. Freedman in race horses.

We were advised of repeated and continual trips outside the country to certain Government contractors in Puerto Rico. We received a series of information about loans of money from Mr. Freedman to Mr. Iaconetti.

Senator Chiles: When the trial was over, with the conviction of Mr. Iaconetti, did you consider the case closed concerning the conspiracy theory that you felt existed?

Mr. Dearie: No sir, we did not. We made no secret about the fact and we solicited Mr. Iaconetti's cooperation. We made no secret of that to Judge Weinstein. After Iaconetti was sentenced to 4 years, he nevertheless refused to cooperate.

Senator Chiles: Thank you very much for your appearance here and your testimony in this case. Mr. Doyal, it was mentioned on a number of occasions a retired Art Metal employee concerning the generation of cash. I would call Mr. Arnold, a former employee of Art Metal. Mr. Arnold, how long did you work at Art Metal, and what was your position there?

Part V—Testimony of Art Metal Officers and Others
Louis Arnold, Former Employee of Art Metal

Mr. Arnold: (p. 481) I worked for Art Metal for 22 years, but 7 of the 22 years I worked as an outside salesman, and 15 years I worked inside.

Senator Chiles: When you worked inside, who did you report to and what were your duties?

Mr. Arnold: I worked in the accounting department. I reported to Joe Markowitz who was the treasurer.

Senator Chiles: Did you know Phillip Kurens and Mr. Irving Cooperstein and Mr. Art Lowell?

Mr. Arnold: I knew them very well. Mr. Kurens was the half owner of the corporation. Mr. Cooperstein was half owner of the company. Mr. Lowell was in charge of the sales division of the company.

Senator Chiles: Did you know Isadore Spiegel?

Mr. Arnold: Yes I did. Mr. Spiegel was a very good friend of the corporation. He was in the trucking business and did most of the trucking.

Senator Chiles: Did you ever have occasion to see Mr. Spiegel bring cash to the company?

Mr. Arnold: I didn't see him bring cash in, but I knew that he brought cash in to the company.

Senator Chiles: When would that be?

Mr. Arnold: When we were short of money.

Senator Chiles: When you were short of money, the company could call Mr. Spiegel and he would bring it?

Mr. Arnold: Whatever they asked him. Yes sir.

Senator Chiles: Your job, I think, during part of this time was to go to the bank?

Mr. Arnold: Every day.

Senator Chiles: And you would make cash deposits?

Mr. Arnold: Yes.

Senator Chiles: And you would also cash checks?

Mr. Arnold: That's right sir.

Senator Chiles: Did a number of those checks contain the inscription marked for auction expense?

Mr. Arnold: Auction expense. Yes sir.

Senator Chiles: What would you ask for when getting cash for those auction expense checks.

Mr. Arnold: I'd like to have $20 bills, please.

Senator Chiles: Twenty dollar bills. Did you get any other type of denomination of bills?

Mr. Arnold: No.

Senator Chiles: Why did you get just $20 bills?

Mr. Arnold: I haven't got the slightest idea Senator.

Senator Chiles: And you would go to three banks and get $20 bills?

Mr. Arnold: That's right.

Senator Chiles: And it was Mr. Markowitz that sent you?

Mr. Arnold: Yes; just Mr. Markowitz.

Senator Chiles: Did you know Mr. Joe Nagel?

Mr. Arnold: Very well, sir.

Senator Chiles: What did Mr. Nagel do in the company?

Mr. Arnold: Mr. Nagel worked in the sales department under Arthur Lowell. It was his job to make out the bids for General Services and he would go down there when the bids were opened.

Senator Chiles: Did Mr. Nagel ever take GSA inspectors to lunch?

Mr. Arnold: Everyday.

Senator Chiles: How many inspectors would there normally be?

Mr. Arnold: Three, four or five.

Senator Chiles: Did you ever suspect that the Government inspectors were being paid off?

Mr. Arnold: I never suspected it but it was common knowledge that they were being paid.

Senator Chiles: You say it was common knowledge. How did you know that?

Mr. Arnold: Well, you know, when you work in a company for a long time, conversation is made with most people who you know for a long time would say "Well, he's getting paid and he's getting paid and he's getting paid." And, that's the conversation.

Senator Chiles: Which inspectors would you know about?

Mr. Arnold: I'm sorry, I just forget the name. Give me a minute.

Senator Chiles: We can give you a copy of the statement you gave the subcommittee and see if that would refresh your memory.

Excerpt from Mr. Arnold's sworn statement to the subcommittee (p. 492): "40. It is common knowledge that GSA inspectors are paid off every week and that Mr. Kurens is the person who pays them. I don't know if Mike Mandel or Bill Mucci were paid off. Paul Freedman and one

Mr. Dickstein got paid off very well. These payoffs were in addition to the meals and gifts of turkeys at Christmas time."

"43. I recall that occasionally it was necessary to get Paul Freedman off the golf course to come and sign GSA forms 308's which are shipping documents for the merchandise manufactured by Art Metal for GSA."

Senator Chiles: These are the names that you remembered?

Mr. Arnold: I remember, sir. Yes, now I know.

Senator Chiles: You had occasion to see a number of inspectors there. What would happen if there was a tough inspector assigned?

Mr. Arnold: An honest one?

Senator Chiles: Yes.

Mr. Arnold: He wouldn't last very long, sir. He'd be transferred somewhere else.

Senator Chiles: How would that happen?

Mr. Arnold: Well, you'd make a telephone call and he would be transferred.

Senator Pryor: What would a good inspector require that a dishonest inspector would not require?

Mr. Arnold: Well, we had a large place there and we had one floor where we manufactured and where the merchandise of desks and files would be finished. And, it would be up to the inspector to pass them through or don't pass them through. Now, if they weren't passed through, that would mean we would have to redo them all, complete redoing, whether we would have to redo the top or the base or the whole thing and that would cost us a great deal of money and would slow up line. So, we couldn't afford to have that done. And, when the inspector said we don't like this, it's no good, do it over, that would cost us a lot of money and we couldn't get any production out.

Senator Chiles: I'd like to call Mr. Paul Freedman to testify. Mr. Freedman retired in 1978, after many years of service as a quality assurance specialist in GSA's New York region. During a long part of that time he served as head of the region's Quality Assurance Division, where he exercised supervisory control over Art Metal as well as over many other GSA contractors in that area. Mr. Freedman is here in response to a subpoena from the subcommittee and Mr. Freedman, I'd like to swear you at this time.

Senator Chiles: Mr. Freedman, you have heard statements here this morning, and for the record, I'd like to ask you to state your name and address for us.

Testimony of Paul Freedman, Former Quality Control Assurance Specialist, General Services Administration, New York Region, Accompanied by William I. Rogers, Counsel

Senator Chiles: All right sir, Mr. Freedman, have you at any time received any money or anything of value from anyone connected with Art Metal Company, or any other persons representing that firm or any other persons doing business with the Federal Government?

Mr. Freedman: Senator Chiles, upon advice of counsel, I have determined to invoke my right to remain silent, accorded to me under the 5th amendment of the Constitution of the United States. I therefore respectfully decline to answer your questions.

Senator Chiles: Counselor, are you advising your client to continue to invoke his fifth amendment rights on all questions that we might ask him?

Mr. Rogers: Yes sir, that is correct.

Senator Chiles: Mr Freedman, you are excused.

Mr. Doyal, as a result of our investigation and information you have received, we have, and I think you have with our other investigation been able to develop some information concerning Mr. Freedman's financial activities. Would you outline for us that information and how we obtained it please?

Mr. Doyal: Yes sir. There have been several things developed during the investigation that pointed toward Mr. Paul Freedman. As a result of that, we began a search to determine what his financial resources were.

Senator Chiles: Would you put up Chart I please?

Mr. Doyal: This chart, Mr. Chairman, describes some of Mr. Freedman's banking activities as we have identified them thus far. We have obtained this information through subpoena to the bank as directed by you. We examined the activities in a number of these accounts. There are some that are not on that chart that were identified since the chart was sent to the printer.

Senator Chiles: So you are saying you are not satisfied whether it is all the accounts or not?

Mr. Doyal: I'm not. Nor is our analysis finished. Thus for banks, for example, in New York we have identified in a period 1974 through 1978, some $8,000 in cash deposits. In even amount deposits, that's deposits with two zeros just before the decimal place, we have some $30,000 in deposits to those accounts.

Senator Chiles: Why are even amount deposits significant?

Subcommittee Chart I

BANKING ACTIVITIES
OF PAUL FREEDMAN

BANK	NO. OF ACCTS	LAST ACCT. CLOSED
NEW YORK		
COUNTY FEDERAL	9	3/9/79
BANK OF NEW YORK	1	12/31/72
METROPOLITAN	6	12/12/78
MANUFACTURERS HANOVER	2	*
DIME	3	12/30/77
CHASE MANHATTAN	*	*
FLORIDA		
PENINSULA	*	*
CORAL GABLES	5	Open
ATLANTIC FEDERAL	1	Open
FLORIDA COAST	1	10/16/78
LANDMARK	1	8/22/78

* Data has been requested but not yet available.

Mr. Doyal: Again, your paychecks and other checks seldom come out in double zeros. It's a tip that most examiners, investigators use to identify unusual transactions or transactions they suspect and want to examine further. Other deposits to these accounts total some $150,000 in this period of time.

In the Florida banks, we have identified cash deposits totaling some $45,000 in the period of time those accounts have been open, which is about 2 years. In addition there are other deposits totaling some $144,000 which were made in the form of check or air bank transfers. The total amount of this, cash deposits identified thus far in the period 1974 through 1979, some $54,000 in cash deposits in total of $294,000 in other deposits to these accounts. We have identified some other banks who have stated they have accounts.

Senator Pryor: Could we have Mr. Freedman's salary put into the record at this point? What was his salary at this stage?

Mr. Doyal: We are talking about a gross salary of about $33,000 to $35,000 every year. These are cash deposits, 1979, First National Bank of Broward County: February 1, 1979, $300; February 5, 1979, $1,600; March 15, 1979, $200; March 23, 1979, $300; April 3, 1979, $1,100; April 10, 1979, $1,000; April 16, 1979; $800; and in the Coral Gables Bank, April 24, 1979, $8,000.

Senator Chiles: Now this is in cash?

Mr. Doyal: These are deposits in currency, bills; not checks. Checks were accounted for separately. If we go to the Florida coast, January 11, 1978, $600; February 7, 1978, $500; February 16, 1978, $500; March 7, 1978, $500; March 14, 1978. $350; March 21, 1978, $275; April 11, 1978, $500; April 18, 1978, $350; May 11, 1978, $500; probably enough to show the nature of the deposits and their size.

Senator Chiles: How many total accounts have you found?

Mr. Doyal: I think there are 36 accounts in total.

Senator Chiles: I understand that Mr. Freedman was an advocate of the sport of kings. Was he successful as an owner of his horses?

Mr. Doyal: I have another Chart J here to show you that. Here's a listing of horses we have been able to identify thus far, that Mr. Freedman has purchased. He's owner in, part owner in some association with—again, starting from 1974 going to the present time. The purchases exceed the value of the sales thus far by about $40,000. I think the purchase amounts—you can see there are some horses we still don't know the purchase amounts for, but right now, they are running about $100,000 in sales.

Senator Chiles: Do you know anything about the successes that these horses had in purses or races?

Mr. Doyal: Yes sir. I can tell you in a number of races that all the horses have run in and how they finished in those races. Take Shiaway Rill, for example. In the first period of ownership, the horse entered 27 races. It won twice. The purses were for $1,200 on one occasion, and $3,200 on another occasion. In the second period of ownership, it was entered in 19 races that we have record of. Three wins, the largest purse being $6,500, another $4,500, and another $3,500.

Senator Chiles: What would it cost to keep these horses and did you run any kind of comparison between the purses won and the cost of keeping the horses as to whether he was making any money on the horses or not?

Subcommittee Chart J

PURCHASE and SALES
of HORSES
BY PAUL FREEDMAN

NAME	PURCHASE		SALE	
	DATE	AMOUNT	DATE	AMOUNT
Port Getaha	1/16/74	$5,000	8/17/75	$1,200
Duane's Twist	3/5/75	*	1/12/77	*
Shiaway Rill	5/18/76	$18,000	1/23/77	$15,000
	2/12/77	$15,000	8/23/77	$12,000
Nelson Lo Bell	10/3/76	$5,000	8/23/77	*
Saratoga Ideal	1/2/77	$12,000	2/17/77	$12,500
Duane Brewster	12/23/77	$9,000	4/10/79	*
Beautis Lucky Boy	2/12/78	*	3/31/79	$2,000
Greenwood Muffy	2/17/78	$18,000	9/7/78	$24,000
Kenston Hi	2/27/78	$20,000	*	*
Sir Butler P. J.	5/21/78	*	*	*
Matchman	12/9/78	$3,000	*	*

* Data has been requested but not yet available.

Mr. Doyal: None of us are big horsemen, so we called some people who had that kind of experience and we told them what the horse had been winning and asked them for what it should cost to keep it and they stated first, that it wasn't even paying feed bills and they also gave us an estimate of the cost to keep the horse by day or by month and depending on which track you're dealing with, which expert you happen to be dealing with the price to keep a horse, ranges between $500 or $1,000 a month. These are pacers.

Mr. Doyal: Taking the lower figure, the time he's owned these horses, the cost to maintain them would have been about $100,000; just the maintenance, not the purchase price or anything else.

Senator Chiles: And what were the total purses during that period of of time they were owned?

Mr. Doyal: I don't have a figure on the total purses, sir, but there may be $40,000 or $50,000 at the most during that period of time from the information that we have.

Senator Chiles: Our next witness will be Mr. Joseph Markowitz, the Comptroller of Art Metal.

Testimony of Joseph Markowitz, Comptroller, Art Metal Company, Accompanied by Jacob A. Stein, Counsel

Senator Chiles: (p. 507) Mr. Markowitz, our staff has testified that under your supervision, Art Metal employees, over a $4\frac{1}{2}$ year period of time, created and gave currency in the amount of approximately $484,000 and on September 30, 1978, Touche Ross auditors counted $258,900 in cash which you presented to them in three briefcases. We are still seeking a clear understanding of the reason why these checks were written, the flow of cash that was generated and how the cash was used and who used it. Mr. Nagel and Mr. Phipps and Mr. Arnold told us that they got the cash from you, and delivered the cash that they then negotiated at the banks to you. We'd like to ask you when this cash was returned to you, what you actually did with the money?

Mr. Markowitz: I have fully discussed this matter with my lawyer. He advised me that I have a valid right to assert my right not to answer that question. I have decided to take his advice and I assert my fifth amendment right not to answer.

Senator Chiles: You are excused. And now we will call Mr. Joe Nagel, who is the traffic manager for Art Metal.

Testimony of Joel Nagel, Traffic Manager, Art Metal Company, Accompanied by Jacob A. Stein, Counselor (p. 507)

Mr. Nagel: Sir, I have a valid right under the Constitution of the United States, to refuse to testify any further.

Senator Chiles: Mr. Nagel, you may be excused for right now. And, we would call Mr. Phipps. During the years of 1975, 1976, 1977, and 1978, you cashed some 323 checks issued by Art Metal, labeled auction expenses, which were made to cash and obtained $342,400 in cash. Did you cash those checks and what did you do with the funds that you derived from those checks?

Testimony of Harold Phipps, Accompanied by Jacob A. Stein, Counselor

Mr. Phipps: I believe all my acts have been legal. I, nevertheless, on advice of counsel, choose to assert my rights under the Constitution of the United States and decline to testify further.

Testimony of Arthur Lowell, General Counsel and Commissioned Salesman for Art Metal

Mr. Lowell: With great respect and deference to you, Senator, and even with much great reluctance, I am directed by counsel, and therefore feel compelled to exercise my rights under both the fifth amendment and the sixth amendment.

Senator Chiles: The Subcommittee will now call Mr. Philip J. Kurens, the President of Art Metal.

Testimony of Philip J. Kurens, President, Art Metal Company, Accompanied by Judah Best and Barry Levine, Counsels to Mr. Kuren

Mr. Kurens: My name is Philip J. Kurens, 151 Montrose Avenue, South Orange, N.J.

Senator Chiles: Mr. Kurens, do you know of any kickbacks or favors to GSA employees that have been made by any company, certainly including your own, but any company for a Government contract or for a better treatment of contracts?

Mr. Kurens: Upon the advice of counsel, I have determined to invoke my right to remain silent accorded to me under the fifth amendment of the Constitution of the United States. I therefore respectfully decline to answer your question.

POSTSCRIPT TO APPENDIX H:

August 10, 1984
The New York Times
"Federal Official Accused of Taking $64,000 in Payoffs"

The deputy regional administrator of the United States General Services Administration was arrested on a Manhattan street yesterday after he pocketed a $4,000 bribe from a businessman whose company sold supplies to the government, federal authorities said. The officials charged that the payment was the latest of $64,000 in bribes that the 51-year-old official,

Edward H. Wyatt, Jr., had received from the businessman in a series of 25 payments going back to September 1980. The payments were to "insure a hassle-free environment" between the General Services Administration and the payer's company, according to Raymond J. Dearie, the United States Attorney for the Eastern District of New York, in Brooklyn. The arrest was made by investigators from Mr. Wyatt's agency and agents from the Federal Bureau of Investigation, who said they had videotaped a meeting Mr. Wyatt had just had with the businessman. At the meeting, officials charged, the $4,000 was paid to Mr. Wyatt in $100 bills.

[Note: See letter exhibit of July 24, 1978, Subcommittee print page #435]

March 17, 1987
The Washington Post
"Contractor Pleads Guilty"

Phillip J. Kurens, former president of one of the federal government's largest suppliers of office furniture, pleaded guilty in federal court here yesterday to one count of interstate travel in aid of racketeering. Kurens was arrested last March 19 by the FBI after he paid a General Services Administration quality assurance inspector $5,000 for information about firms competing against his firm, Art Metal-USA Inc., of Newark, for a $15 million contract to supply ergonomic, or adjustable, desk chairs. . . . He could be sentenced to a maximum of five years in prison and fined $250,000.

[Note: See testimony of Art Metal officials]

March 20, 1980
Commentary
Tampa, Florida

U.S. Senator Lawton Chiles found that despite a GSA order (prompted by the subcommittee) to buy no more furniture, $13 million was spent in compliance with a court order forbidding the government to stop buying furniture for which it had contracted with Art Metal-USA, Inc.

Another source of Chile's frustration was the discovery GSA is still doing business with a New Jersey paint manufacturer convicted last year of bribing GSA officials. The Justice Department this week sued 13 contractors, five corporations, and nine former GSA employees seeking to recover more than $11.6 million in connection with rigged contracts.

January 17, 1990

The Washington Star

The former head of quality control for the General Services Administration's supply division has been named in federal testimony as the recipient of at least $12,000 in bribes.

The president of Atlas Paint and Varnish Co. of Irvington, N.J., testified late last year that his firm paid Roger F. Carroll, Jr., $500 a month from 1969 to 1971 in an attempt to win GSA contracts.

In U.S. District court in Newark, N.J., Atlas Paint president Dennis Tepperman said payments to Carroll and two other GSA officials were paid through attorney Arthur Lowell to ensure approval of the $5 million worth of paint the company sold the government each year.

Lowell and a GSA quality control inspector were convicted of conspiracy to defraud the U.S. government through the bribery scheme. A GSA chemist pleaded guilty to the same charge. Tepperman said the money, usually in $20 bills, was passed to Lowell in plain envelopes. Lowell, who is awaiting sentencing, is also under investigation by federal prosecutors for his role as attorney for Art Metal-USA, Inc.

January 17, 1990

UP-127

Roger Carroll was responsible for drawing up strict specifications which GSA-purchased supplies had to meet.

According to the court transcript, Tepperman said, "Arthur Lowell would come in and say, 'I am going to Washington; give me my white envelope.' I would put the money in twenties in a white envelope and give it to him and he would put it in his pocket."

GLOSSARY

accounting, accrual basis: An accounting system based on resources consumed.

accounting, cash basis: An accounting system based on cash consumed.

advertised acquisition: The procurement of property or services based on open competition among bidders.

AICPA: American Institute of Certified Public Accountants.

asset-theft fraud: Fraud that involves the loss of something of value. Generally, fraud other than financial statement balance fraud.

auditing, proactive fraud-specific: Examinations that have the sole objective of searching for indicia of fraud before there is reason to suspect fraud.

auditing, reactive: Fraud examinations conducted based on evidence disclosed.

auditing, traditional: Examinations that seek to verify reported accounting balances or conditions.

bribe: A bilateral gratuity.

Cohen committee: The Commission on Auditors' Responsibilities (Manuel F. Cohen, chairman), 1978. An independent commission established by the American Institute of Certified Public Accountants to develop conclusions and recommendations regarding the appropriate responsibilities of independent auditors.

collusion: Conspiracy.

committee print: The printed official record of a hearing held by a committee of the U.S. Congress.

conspiracy: The participation of two or more people in the commission of a criminal act, which otherwise would be difficult or impossible by either person acting alone.

contract change order: A formal amendment of contract terms or specifications.

contract rigging: A term used to describe the measures taken by a bidding contractor to assure the award of a contract, with the intention of subsequently profiting through contract changes. Usually involves conspiracy with a trusted employee or officer of the contracting entity.

corroborating evidence: Independent evidence that supplements and strengthens evidence already discovered.

covert: Concealed, secret.

criminal investigator: An individual trained in criminology and paralegal essentials for discovering and documenting the evidence needed to prove fraud.

Such investigators often are engaged to react to evidence of fraud detected by auditors.

engineering change orders: See *contract change order*. Usually involves product specification changes.

ethical behavior: Conduct in accordance with right or good principles.

evidence: Something that furnishes or tends to furnish proof.

expectation gap: With regard to the detection of fraud, the difference in understanding that exists between what many internal and external users of audit services believe an independent auditor's responsibility is and what the auditors limit it to.

financial statement balance fraud (FSB): The intentional misstatement of one or more financial statement balances by a reporting entity for the purpose of deceiving one or more external entities as to the reporting entity's net worth, prosperity, or for some other self-serving purpose.

fraud: An intentional perversion of the truth to induce another to part with some valuable thing belonging to him or her.

fraud, defective delivery: The receipt of products or services that are inferior in some manner, without appropriate disclosure or compensation to the recipient.

fraud, defective pricing: Involves charging the victim a price higher than the price that was agreed upon or falsely representing prices so as to deceive the victim.

fraud, defective shipment: Involves the transfer of products or services in excess of those authorized by the delivering entity without appropriate compensation. Invariably involves a conspiring employee.

fraud, duplicate payment: The intentional issuance of two or more identical checks to the same payee. One is used to pay the creditor, while the other(s) are fraudulent, and are recovered and cashed by the perpetrator.

fraud, group 1: All the fraud that has been publically revealed. With few exceptions this includes all the fraud that has been prosecuted.

fraud, group 2: All the fraud that has been detected or suspected by its victims but has never been prosecuted and particulars have not been publicaly revealed.

fraud, group 3: All the fraud that has never been detected or suspected.

fraud, multiple payee: Involves two or more payments to different vendors or contractors for the same debt. One of the payees usually is the one that actually delivered the product or services being paid for. The other(s) are fraudulent.

fraud, off-the-books: The theft of assets not recorded in accounting records.

fraud, rotation: Fraud where two or more contractors conspire to alternately submit the lowest bid of those that may be involved. Normally requires that the contractors dominate an industry in a given region. The practice defeats the theoretical advantages of competitive bidding.

fraud, shell: Involves payments for fictitious projects, material, or services. All underlying documentation is forged. It may or may not involve conspiracy with contractors or suppliers. All of the payment money generated is pocketed by the perpetrator(s).

fraud hotline: A mechanism provided for reporting fraud, usually by telephone.

fraud indicia: Hints or clues, usually not evidence, that suggest the possible existence of fraud.

gratuity: Something of value provided by a contractor or vendor to a customer's employee, usually given in expectation of—or in return for—something of value. Note: Although a gratuity is commonly defined as a gift, in this instance it is more appropriately defined as compensation.

gratuity, bilateral: Something of value given by a contractor or vendor to a customer's employee in return for specific favors. Always involves a quid pro quo agreement.

gratuity, closed: Applies only to a one-time or specific contract or purchase order. Not an open or continuing offer.

gratuity, unilateral: A gift provided by one party to another that does not involve a formal quid pro quo agreement. However, the provider of the gift normally expects—and usually receives—favorable treatment from the recipient.

independent auditors: Certified Public Accountants (CPAs).

indicative evidence: Indicia of fraud. Something that implies fraud may have occurred but does not by itself constitute proof.

indicia of fraud: See *fraud indicia* and *indicative evidence.*

internal auditors: Auditors employed by some entities. Not independent auditors.

internal controls, fraud-specific: Internal controls having the primary objective of preventing or deterring fraud.

internal controls, passive: See *internal controls, risk.*

internal controls, risk: Controls that seek to deter fraud through certain or increased risk of detection rather than prevention.

invitations for bid (IFBs): Formal requests provided to contractors or vendors inviting them to submit price proposals on a proposed contract.

kickback: A share of a contract or purchase order profits returned to a victim's employee in return for conspiratorial assistance.

land flipping: An illegal practice involving the purchase of real estate and subsequent resale of it a number of times between conspiring associates, each time raising the selling price substantially, for the purpose of artificially raising the apparent ultimate value.

McKesson Robbins: A corporation involved in a 1937 financial statement balance fraud that reported $19 million of nonexistent inventories and accounts receivable. The case marked the beginning of required generally accepted auditing standards for independent public auditors.

open gratuity: A standing offer of compensation to any customer's employee who complies with the terms of the offer: for example, a new television set in return for a $25,000 order of merchandise.

pseudoconspiracy: A situation where one or more people who are key participants in a fraud scheme are innocent of any criminal intent to commit fraud. Their de facto participation usually occurs as a result of their negligence in performing a control function, making fraud by another person or persons possible.

reactive auditing: Examinations performed subsequent to, and as a result of, the detection of indicia or evidence of fraud.

recurring expense: An entity's operating expense of a predictably repeating nature: for example, periodic maintenance.

right-brain orientation: Involves inductive creative thought processes rather than deductive reasoning; thought to occur in the brain's right hemisphere.

SAS: AICPA Statements on Auditing Standards.

SEC: Securities and Exchange Commission.

skimming: The practice of stealing a small portion of a commodity that presumably will not be noticed.

standards of conduct: An employer's interpretation of what is considered ethical behavior.

straw borrowers: Conspirators in mortgage fraud who—for a commission—act as the buyers of mortgaged real estate. After receiving the borrowed funds—which they return to the prime perpetrators—they disappear, defaulting on repayment.

sworn statements: Declarations taken under oath.

symptomatic fraud auditing: Examinations inspired by entity operating problems.

unbalanced bidding: Similar to contract rigging. A bidding contractor varies the unit prices bid for contract items in such a manner that he or she submits the lowest aggregate bid, in the expectation that those items for which low unit prices have been offered will be subsequently eliminated from the contract requirements.

world of fraud: All the fraud in existence. The fraud universe.

INDEX